Welfare Ministry

Ellen G. White

1952

LS Company

ISBN:978-1-0879-8073-7

Copyright © 2021

Contents

Foreword vi
Section 1—The Divine Philosophy of Suffering and Poverty ... 9
    Gem Thought 9
    Chapter 1—Why Poverty and Distress? 10
    Chapter 2—Christ's Sympathy for Suffering Humanity 16
Section 2—God's Program for His Church 19
    Gem Thought 19
    Chapter 3—Isaiah 58—A Divine Prescription 20
    Chapter 4—This is Pure Religion 24
    Chapter 5—The Parable of the Good Samaritan 29
Section 3—The New Testament Pattern 35
    Gem Thought 35
    Chapter 6—Our Example in Welfare Ministry 36
    Chapter 7—Visitation—The New Testament Plan 40
    Chapter 8—Dorcas—Her Ministry and its Influence 45
Section 4—Neighborhood Evangelism 47
    Gem Thought 47
    Chapter 9—Types of Work in Neighborhood Evangelism .. 48
    Chapter 10—Kindness the Key to Hearts 56
    Chapter 11—How to Visit and What to Do 61
    Chapter 12—The Effectiveness of Visitation Evangelism .. 68
    Chapter 13—Organizing the Church for Welfare Ministry .. 74
Section 5—Relieving Suffering Humanity 81
    Gem Thought 81
    Chapter 14—In the Footsteps of the Master 82
    Chapter 15—Medical Ministry in the Homes 88
    Chapter 16—Preparing for Last-Day Crises and Disasters .. 95
Section 6—The Dorcas Movement in the Church 101
    Gem Thought 101
    Chapter 17—Women Called to the Work 102
    Chapter 18—Qualifications of Women for Service 107
    Chapter 19—The Influence of Christian Women 113
Section 7—The Poor 121

Gem Thought.. 121
Chapter 20—Ministry to the Poor........................... 122
Chapter 21—The Poor in the Church........................ 128
Chapter 22—The Poor of the World......................... 136
Chapter 23—Helping the Poor to Help Themselves........ 141
Chapter 24—Poor to Exercise Benevolence................. 148
Section 8—The Unfortunate..................................... 151
Gem Thought.. 151
Chapter 25—Our Duty to the Unfortunate.................. 152
Chapter 26—Help and Encouragement for Widows........ 156
Chapter 27—The Care of Orphans........................... 161
Chapter 28—Adopting Children.............................. 170
Chapter 29—The Care of the Aged.......................... 174
Chapter 30—Our Responsibility to the Blind............... 176
Section 9—The Outcasts.. 179
Gem Thought.. 179
Chapter 31—Working for Outcasts.......................... 180
Chapter 32—Cautions Sounded.............................. 186
Chapter 33—The Call for a Balanced Work................. 189
Section 10—Financial Resources for Welfare Work............ 193
Gem Thought.. 193
Chapter 34—Our Individual Responsibility................. 194
Chapter 35—Releasing the Streams of Benevolence...... 198
Chapter 36—Specific Funds for Welfare Work............. 201
Chapter 37—The Wealth of the Gentiles................... 205
Chapter 38—Food Sales...................................... 210
Chapter 39—Forbidden Money-Raising Methods......... 214
Section 11—The Fruitage of Welfare Ministry................. 217
Gem Thought.. 217
Chapter 40—The Influence of Neighborhood Ministry.... 218
Chapter 41—Reflex Blessings................................ 222
Chapter 42—The Present and Eternal Rewards........... 229
Appendix.. 237
Personal Experiences of Ellen G. White as a Welfare
Worker... 237
Ellen G. White in Practical Dorcas Work.................... 239
Welfare Ministry Through the Years........................ 241
Pioneering in Australia...................................... 243

Mrs. White Retained Broad Sympathies Throughout Life 252
A Letter to Fatherless Children 254

Foreword

Welfare Ministry presents spirit of prophecy instruction in the delicate work of reaching hearts and winning souls through neighborly kindness. This is a type of soul-winning ministry with which many Seventh-day Adventists are but casually acquainted—yet a work ordained of God as the most appropriate means of bringing Christ and Christianity to the attention of the peoples of the world. It is a work that promises rich rewards.

Not only by concise, well-worded precept has the author set before us this type of ministry, but through the years, although busy with her home duties and her responsibilities as the messenger of the Lord, she often unwittingly set an example as her heart was drawn out to the needy about her. The autobiographical record of the unselfish ministry of Ellen G. White as a welfare worker, drawn from her diary and letters, as found in the appendix of this volume, will be perused with eager interest and well might be read before the counsels found in the body of the text are studied. Be that as it may, the reader will soon observe that the welfare ministry to which the church is summoned is not merely a community service but a kind of loving ministry and soul-winning endeavor—the highest type of welfare evangelism.

In the assembling of Spirit of Prophecy counsels relating to this important field of endeavor, excerpts have been drawn from the vast reservoir of precious instruction penned through seven decades. They have been gathered not only from currently available published books but also from the thousands of E. G. White articles which were prepared for the journals of the denomination, the special testimonies issued in pamphlet form, and the E. G. White manuscript files. Selected as they are from these various sources written at different times, they inevitably bring the reader over the same path he has traversed before, to emphasize some important point vital to a full development of the subject. Such repetition, though reduced to a minimum, cannot be avoided entirely in such a compilation as this, for the compilers are limited in their work to the selecting of the subject matter and the arranging of it in its logical sequence, supplying only the headings.

It has been difficult and well-nigh impossible to bring within the covers of one book the vast amount of instruction Ellen G. White has given concerning this particular kind of work, and which might rightly appear in a volume bearing the title *Welfare Ministry*. It is not a simple matter to select the material and draw the line between the neighborly visit and the missionary call, nor to separate the work of noble Seventh-day Adventist women in its broader aspects from the more well-defined task undertaken with solely missionary objectives. To the child of God these blend together in the varied activities of daily life.

Attention is here called to certain terms occurring frequently in this volume such as "medical missionary work" and "Christian help work." It should be noted that a careful study of the Ellen G. White writings reveals that the phrase "medical missionary work" is employed by the author to include professional services of consecrated doctors and nurses, and that its significance also reaches far beyond these bounds to include all acts of mercy and disinterested kindness. "Christian help work" is also a term more commonly employed by Seventh-day Adventists in their earlier years than now and refers to the type of work described in this volume. Writing as she did in different continents, the author in her reference to money at times speaks of dollars and at other times of pounds and shillings. [11]

It is urged that the reader study the instruction in its proper setting, to discover the basic principles involved in each case. For instance, a study of the counsels regarding "Church suppers" will reveal that although we are warned against utilizing the appeal to indulged appetite and love of pleasure as a means of raising church funds, yet it is the privilege of Church groups to engage in the preparation and sale of healthful food if the work is properly conducted and done in an appropriate place.

Except in a very few cases where a sentence or two may clearly enunciate a principle, the compilers have endeavored to include sufficient of the context of each excerpt to assure the reader of the proper use of the selected statement. In each case the date of writing or of first publication is indicated in connection with the notation of the source from which the statement is drawn.

This document has been prepared in the office of the Ellen G. White publications by the Trustees, who carry the responsibility of the care and publication of the E. G. White writings. The work has been done in full harmony with Mrs. White's instruction to these Trustees in providing "for the printing of compilations from my manuscripts," for they contain, she said, "instruction that the Lord has given me for his people."

That this volume of instruction addressed to Seventh-day Adventists—laity and ministry alike—may encourage the church to take advantage of the opportunities in neighborhood ministry; that its instruction may guide in intelligent, conscientious, loving service; and that through its guidance there may be an abundant harvest of souls in the kingdom of God.

Section 1—The Divine Philosophy of Suffering and Poverty

Gem Thought

Sin has extinguished the love that God placed in man's heart. The work of the church is to rekindle this love. The church is to cooperate with God by uprooting selfishness from the human heart, placing in its stead the benevolence that was in man's heart in his original state of perfection.—Letter 134, 1902.

For the poor shall never cease out of the land: therefore I command thee, saying, Thou shalt open thine hand wide unto thy brother, to thy poor, and to thy needy in thy land. Deuteronomy 15:11.

Chapter 1—Why Poverty and Distress?

Blessed Are the Merciful—The Lord Jesus said, "Blessed are the merciful: for they shall obtain mercy." There never was a time when there was greater need for the exercise of mercy than today. The poor are all around us, the distressed, the afflicted, the sorrowing, and those who are ready to perish.

Those who have acquired riches have acquired them through the exercise of the talents that were given them of God, but these talents for the acquiring of property were given to them that they might relieve those who are in poverty. These gifts were bestowed upon men by Him who maketh His sun to shine and His rain to fall upon the just and the unjust, that by the fruitfulness of the earth men might have abundant supplies for all their need. The fields have been blessed of God, and "of His goodness He hath prepared for the poor."—The Signs of the Times, June 13, 1892.

Suffering and Misery Not Intended by God—There are many who complain of God because the world is so full of want and suffering, but God never meant that this misery should exist. He never meant that one man should have an abundance of the luxuries of life while the children of others cry for bread. The Lord is a God of benevolence.—Testimonies for the Church 6:273.

[16] God has made men His stewards, and He is not to be charged with the sufferings, the misery, the nakedness, and the want of humanity. The Lord has made ample provision for all. He has given to thousands of men large supplies with which to alleviate the want of their fellows; but those whom God has made stewards have not stood the test, for they have failed to relieve the suffering and the needy.

When men who have been abundantly blessed of Heaven with large wealth fail to carry out God's design, and do not relieve the poor and the oppressed, the Lord is displeased and will surely visit them. They have no excuse for withholding from their neighbors the help that God has put it into their power to provide; and God is dishonored,

His character is misinterpreted by Satan, and He is represented as a stern judge who causes suffering to come upon the creatures He has made. This misrepresentation of God's character is made to appear as truth, and thus through the temptation of the enemy men's hearts are hardened against God. Satan charges upon God the very evil he himself has caused men to commit by withholding their means from the suffering. He attributes to God his own characteristics.—The Review and Herald, June 26, 1894.

There Need Be No Suffering, No Destitution—If men would do their duty as faithful stewards of their Lord's goods, there would be no cry for bread, none suffering in destitution, none naked and in want. It is the unfaithfulness of men that brings about the state of suffering in which humanity is plunged. If those whom God has made stewards would but appropriate their Lord's goods to the object for which He gave to them, this state of suffering would not exist. The Lord tests men by giving them an abundance of good things, just as He tested the rich man of the parable. If we prove ourselves unfaithful in the unrighteous mammon, who shall entrust to us the true riches? It will be those who have stood the test on the earth, who have been found faithful, who have obeyed the words of the Lord in being merciful, in using their means for the advancement of His kingdom, that will hear from the lips of the Master, "Well done, good and faithful servant."—Ibid.

Some Rich—Some Poor—The reason why God has permitted some of the human family to be so rich and some so poor will remain a mystery to men till eternity, unless they enter into right relations with God and carry out His plans instead of acting on their own selfish ideas.—Testimonies to Ministers and Gospel Workers, 280.

To Encourage Love and Mercy—In the providence of God events have been so ordered that the poor are always with us, in order that there may be a constant exercise in the human heart of the attributes of mercy and love. Man is to cultivate the tenderness and compassion of Christ; he is not to separate himself from the sorrowing, the afflicted, the needy, and the distressed.—The Signs of the Times, June 13, 1892.

To Develop a Godlike Character in Man—While the world needs sympathy, while it needs the prayers and assistance of God's people, while it needs to see Christ in the lives of His followers, the people of God are equally in need of opportunities that draw out their sympathies, give efficiency to their prayers, and develop in them a character like that of the divine pattern.

[18] It is to provide these opportunities that God has placed among us the poor, the unfortunate, the sick, and the suffering. They are Christ's legacy to His church, and they are to be cared for as He would care for them. In this way God takes away the dross and purifies the gold, giving us that culture of heart and character which we need.

The Lord could carry forward His work without our cooperation. He is not dependent on us for our money, our time, or our labor. But the church is very precious in His sight. It is the case which contains His jewels, the fold which encloses His flock, and He longs to see it without spot or blemish or any such thing. He yearns after it with unspeakable love. This is why He has given us opportunities to work for Him, and He accepts our labors as tokens of our love and loyalty.—Testimonies for the Church 6:261.

That We May Understand the Mercy of God—The poor man as well as the rich man is the object of God's special care and attention. Take away poverty, and we should have no way of understanding the mercy and love of God, no way of knowing the compassionate and sympathetic heavenly Father.—Letter 83, 1902.

God Gives to Us That We Might Give to Others—God imparts His blessing to us that we may impart to others. When we ask Him for our daily bread He looks into our hearts to see if we will share the same with those more needy than ourselves. When we pray "God be merciful to me a sinner," He watches to see if we will manifest compassion toward those with whom we associate. This is the evidence of our connection with God, that we are merciful even as our Father in heaven is merciful.—Testimonies for the Church 6:283, 284.

[19] **Withholding Dwarfs Spiritual Growth**—Nothing saps spirituality from the soul more quickly than to enclose it in selfishness and self-caring. Those who indulge self and neglect to care for the souls and bodies of those for whom Christ has given His life, are not eating of the bread of life or drinking of the water of the well of salvation. They are dry and sapless, like a tree that bears no fruit. They are spiritual dwarfs, who consume their means on self; but

"whatsoever a man soweth, that shall he also reap."—The Review and Herald, January 15, 1895.

It is because the rich neglect to do the work for the poor that God designed they should do, that they grow more proud, more self-sufficient, more self-indulgent, and hardhearted. They separate the poor from them simply because they are poor, and thus give them occasion to become envious and jealous. Many become bitter, and are imbued with hatred toward those who have everything when they have nothing.

God weighs actions, and everyone who has been unfaithful in his stewardship, who has failed to remedy evils which were in his power to remedy, will be of no esteem in the courts of heaven. Those who are indifferent to the wants of the needy will be counted unfaithful stewards, and will be registered as enemies of God and man. Those who misappropriate the means that God has entrusted to them to help the very ones who need their help, prove that they have no connection with Christ, because they fail to manifest the tenderness of Christ toward those who are less fortunate than themselves.—The Review and Herald, December 10, 1895.

If the Rich Walk in Christ's Footsteps—The rich man is a steward of God, and if he walks in Christ's footsteps, maintaining a humble, godly life, he becomes, through the transformation of character, meek and lowly in heart. He realizes that his possessions are only lent treasures, and he feels that a sacred trust has been committed to him to help the needy and suffering, in Christ's stead. This work will bring its reward in talents and treasures laid up beside the throne of God. Thus the rich man may make a spiritual success of life, as a faithful steward of his Lord's goods.—Manuscript 22, 1898.

Suffering—One Means of Perfecting Character—The Saviour's words have a message of comfort to those also who are suffering affliction or bereavement. Our sorrows do not spring out of the ground. God "doth not afflict willingly nor grieve the children of men." When He permits trials and afflictions, it is "for our profit, that we might be partakers of His holiness." If received in faith, the trial that seems so bitter and hard to bear will prove a blessing. The cruel blow that blights the joys of earth will be the means turning our eyes to Heaven. How many there are who would never have known Jesus had not sorrow led them to seek comfort in Him!

The trials of life are God's workmen, to remove the impurities and roughness from our character. Their hewing, squaring, and chiseling, their burnishing and polishing, is a painful process; it is hard to be pressed down to the grinding wheel. But the stone is brought forth prepared to fill its place in the heavenly temple. Upon no useless material does the Master bestow such careful, thorough work. Only His precious stones are polished after the similitude of a palace.

The Lord will work for all who put their trust in Him. Precious victories will be gained by the faithful. Precious lessons will be learned. Precious experiences will be realized.—Thoughts from the Mount of Blessing, 10, 11.

[21] **Affliction and Calamity No Indication of God's Disfavor—** "As Jesus passed by, He saw a man which was blind from his birth. And His disciples asked Him, saying, Master, who did sin, this man, or his parents, that he was born blind? Jesus answered, Neither hath this man sinned, nor his parents: but that the works of God should be made manifest in him."

It was generally believed by the Jews that sin is punished in this life. Every affliction was regarded as the penalty of some wrongdoing, either of the sufferer himself or of his parents. It is true that all suffering results from the transgression of God's law, but this truth had become perverted. Satan, the author of sin and all its results, had led men to look upon disease and death as proceeding from God—as punishment arbitrarily inflicted on account of sin. Hence one upon whom some great affliction or calamity had fallen, had the additional burden of being regarded as a great sinner....

God had given a lesson designed to prevent this. The history of Job had shown that suffering is inflicted by Satan, and is overruled by God for purposes of mercy. But Israel did not understand the lesson. The same error for which God had reproved the friends of Job was repeated by the Jews in their rejection of Christ.

The belief of the Jews in regard to the relation of sin and suffering was held by Christ's disciples. While Jesus corrected their error. He did not explain the cause of the man's affliction, but told them what would be the result. Because of it the works of God would be made manifest. "As long as I am in the world," He said, "I am the light of the world." Then having anointed the eyes of the blind man, He sent him to wash in the pool of Siloam, and the man's sight was restored. Thus Jesus answered the question of the disciples in a practical way, as He usually answered questions put to Him from curiosity. The disciples were not called upon to discuss the question as to who had sinned or had not sinned, but to understand the power and mercy of God in giving sight to the blind.—The Desire of Ages, 470, 471.

Christ to Be Seen and Heard Through Us—God designs that the sick, the unfortunate, those possessed of evil spirits, shall hear His voice through us. Through His human agents He desires to be a comforter, such as the world has never before seen. His words are to be voiced by His followers: "Let not your heart be troubled: ye believe in God, believe also in Me."

The Lord will work through every soul that will give himself up to be worked, not only to preach but to minister to the despairing and to inspire hope in the hearts of the hopeless. We are to act our part in relieving and softening the miseries of this life. The miseries and mysteries of this life are as dark and cloudy as they were thousands of years ago. There is something for us to do: "Arise, shine; for thy light is come, and the glory of the Lord is risen upon thee." There are needy close by us; the suffering are in our very borders. We must try to help them. By the grace of Christ, the sealed fountains of earnest, Christlike work are to be unsealed. In the strength of Him who has all strength we are to work as we have never worked before.—Manuscript 65b, 1898.

Chapter 2—Christ's Sympathy for Suffering Humanity

Christ Himself Suffers With Suffering Humanity—Christ identifies His interest with that of suffering humanity. He reproved His own nation for their wrong treatment of their fellow men. The neglect or abuse of the weakest, the most erring believers He speaks of as rendered to Himself. The favors shown them are accredited as bestowed upon Himself. He has not left us in darkness concerning our duty, but often repeats the same lessons through different figures and in different lights. He carries the actors forward to the last great day, and declares that the treatment given to the very least of His brethren is commended or condemned as if done to Himself. He says, "Ye did it unto Me," or, "Ye did it not unto Me."

He is our substitute and surety; He stands in the place of humanity, so that He Himself is affected as His weakest follower is affected. Such is the sympathy of Christ, which never allows Him to be an indifferent spectator of any suffering caused to His children. Not the slightest wound can be given by word, spirit, or action, that does not touch the heart of Him who gave His life for fallen humanity. Let us bear in mind that Christ is the great heart from which the lifeblood flows to every organ in the body. He is the head, from which extends every nerve to the minutest and remotest member of the body. When one member of that body with which Christ is so mysteriously connected, suffers, the throb of pain is felt by our Saviour.

Will the church arouse? Will its members come into sympathy with Christ, so they will have His tenderness for all the sheep and lambs of His fold? For their sake the Majesty of heaven made Himself of no reputation; for them He came to a world all seared and marred with the curse, He toiled day and night to instruct, to elevate, and to bring everlasting joy to a thankless, disobedient people. For their sake He became poor, that they through His poverty might be rich. For them He denied Himself; for them He endured privation, scorn, contempt, suffering, and death. For them He took the form of a servant. This is our pattern; will we copy it? Will we have a care for God's heritage? Will we cherish tender compassion for the erring, the tempted, and the tried?—Letter 45, 1894.

Touched With the Feelings of Our Infirmities—Christ, our substitute and surety, was a man of sorrows and acquainted with grief. His human life was one long travail in behalf of the inheritance He was to purchase at such an infinite cost. He was touched with the feelings of our infirmities. In consideration of the value He places upon the purchase of His blood, He adopts them as His children, makes them the objects of His tender care, and in order that they may have their temporal and spiritual necessities supplied, He commits them to His church, saying, "Inasmuch as ye do it unto one of the least of these My brethren, ye do it unto Me."—Manuscript 40, 1899.

Christ Came to Relieve Suffering—This world is a vast lazar house, but Christ came to heal the sick, to proclaim deliverance to the captives of Satan. He was in Himself health and strength. He imparted His life to the sick, the afflicted, those possessed of demons. He turned away none who came to receive His healing power. He knew that those who petitioned Him for help had brought disease upon themselves; yet He did not refuse to heal them. And when virtue from Christ entered into these poor souls, they were convicted of sin, and many were healed of their spiritual disease, as well as of their physical maladies. The gospel still possesses the same power, and why should we not today witness the same results?

Christ feels the woes of every sufferer. When evil spirits rend a human frame, Christ feels the curse. When fever is burning up the life current, He feels the agony. And He is just as willing to heal the sick now as when He was personally on earth. Christ's servants are His representatives, the channels for His working. He desires through them to exercise His healing power.—The Desire of Ages, 823, 824.

Christ alone had experience in all the sorrows and temptations that befall human beings. Never another of woman born was so fiercely beset by temptation; never another bore so heavy a burden of the world's sin and pain. Never was there another whose sympathies were so broad or so tender. A sharer in all the experiences of humanity He could feel not only for, but with, every burdened and tempted and struggling one.—Education, 78.

Christ Reached Rich and Poor Alike—Christ took a position which was on a level with the poor, that through His poverty we might become rich in beauty of character, and be, as He was, a savor of life unto life. By becoming poor He could sympathize with the poor. His humanity could touch their humanity and help them to gain the perfection of right habits and a noble character. He could teach them how to lay up for themselves in heaven imperishable treasures. The commander in the heavenly courts, He became one with humanity, a partaker of their sufferings and afflictions, that through the representation of His character in its unsullied purity they might become partakers of the divine nature, escaping the corruption that is in the world through lust. And Christ was a joy to the rich, for He could teach them how to sacrifice their earthly possessions to help to save the souls perishing in the darkness of error.—Letter 150, 1899.

Cultivate Christlike Compassion and Sympathy—The tender sympathies of our Saviour were aroused for fallen and suffering humanity. If you would be His followers, you must cultivate compassion and sympathy. Indifference to human woes must give place to lively interest in the sufferings of others. The widow, the orphan, the sick, and the dying will always need help. Here is an opportunity to proclaim the gospel—to hold up Jesus, the hope and consolation of all men. When the suffering body has been relieved, and you have shown a lively interest in the afflicted, the heart is opened, and you can pour in the heavenly balm. If you are looking to Jesus, and drawing from Him knowledge and strength and grace, you can impart His consolation to others, because the Comforter is with you.—The Medical Missionary, January, 1891.

Section 2—God's Program for His Church

Gem Thought

Read Isaiah 58, ye who claim to be children of the light. Especially do you read it again and again who have felt so reluctant to inconvenience yourselves by favoring the needy. You whose hearts and houses are too narrow to make a home for the homeless, read it; you who can see orphans and widows oppressed by the iron hand of poverty and bowed down by hardhearted worldlings, read it. Are you afraid that an influence will be introduced into your family that will cost you more labor? Read it. Your fears may be groundless, and a blessing may come, known and realized by you every day. But if otherwise, if extra labor is called for, you can draw upon One who has promised: "Then shall thy light break forth as the morning, and thine health shall spring forth speedily."

The reason why God's people are not more spiritually minded, and have not more faith, I have been shown, is because they are narrowed up with selfishness. The prophet is addressing Sabbathkeepers, not sinners, not unbelievers, but those who make great pretensions to godliness. It is not the abundance of your meetings that God accepts. It is not the numerous prayers, but the rightdoing, doing the right thing and at the right time. It is to be less self-caring and more benevolent. Our souls must expand. Then God will make them like a watered garden, whose waters fail not.—Testimonies for the Church 2:35, 36.

Pure religion and undefiled before God and the Father is this, To visit the fatherless and widows in their affliction, and to keep himself unspotted from the world. James 1:27.

Chapter 3—Isaiah 58—A Divine Prescription

The Chapter That Defines Our Work—The whole of the fifty-eighth chapter of Isaiah is to be regarded as a message for this time, to be given over and over again.—Special Testimonies, Series B 02:5.

What saith the Lord in the fifty-eighth chapter of Isaiah? The whole chapter is of the highest importance.—Testimonies for the Church 8:159.

I have been instructed to refer our people to the fifty-eighth chapter of Isaiah. Read this chapter carefully and understand the kind of ministry that will bring life into the churches. The work of the gospel is to be carried by means of our liberality as well as by our labors. When you meet suffering souls who need help, give it to them. When you find those who are hungry, feed them. In doing this you will be working in lines of Christ's ministry. The Master's holy work was a benevolent work. Let our people everywhere be encouraged to have a part in it.—Manuscript 7, 1908.

The Work Outlined—Please read Isaiah 58: "Is it such a fast that I have chosen? a day for a man to afflict his soul? is it to bow down his head as a bulrush, and to spread sackcloth and ashes under him? wilt thou call this a fast, and an acceptable day to the Lord? Is not this the fast that I have chosen? to loose the bands of wickedness, to undo the heavy burdens, and to let the oppressed go free, and that ye break every yoke? Is it not to deal thy bread to the hungry, and that thou bring the poor that are cast out to thy house? when thou seest the naked, that thou cover him; and that thou hide not thyself from thine own flesh? Then shall thy light break forth as the morning, and thine health shall spring forth speedily: and thy righteousness shall go before thee; the glory of the Lord shall be thy rereward. Then shalt thou call, and the Lord shall answer; thou shalt cry, and He shall say, Here I am. If thou take away from the midst of thee the yoke, the putting forth of the finger, and speaking vanity; and if thou draw out thy soul to the hungry, and satisfy the afflicted soul; then shall thy light rise in obscurity, and thy darkness be as the noonday: and the Lord shall guide thee continually, and satisfy thy soul in drought, and make fat thy bones: and thou shalt be like a watered garden, and like a spring of water, whose waters fail not."

This is the special work now before us. All our praying and abstinence from food will avail nothing unless we resolutely lay hold of this work. Sacred obligations are resting upon us. Our duty is plainly stated. The Lord has spoken to us by His prophet. The thoughts of the Lord and His ways are not what blind, selfish mortals believe they are or wish them to be. The Lord looks on the heart. If selfishness dwells there, He knows it. We may seek to conceal our true character from our brethren and sisters, but God knows. Nothing can be hid from Him.

The fast which God can accept is described. It is to deal thy bread to the hungry and to bring the poor which are cast out to thy house. Wait not for them to come to you. The labor rests not on them to hunt you up and entreat of you a home for themselves. You are to search for them and bring them to your house. You are to draw out your soul after them. You are with one hand to reach up and by faith take hold of the mighty arm which brings salvation, while with the other hand of love you reach the oppressed and relieve them. It is impossible for you to fasten upon the arm of God with one hand while the other is employed in ministering to your own pleasure.

[31]

If you engage in this work of mercy and love, will the work prove too hard for you? Will you fail and be crushed under the burden, and your family be deprived of your assistance and influence? Oh, no; God has carefully removed all doubts upon this question, by a pledge to you on condition of your obedience. This promise covers all that the most exacting, the most hesitating, could crave. "Then shall thy light break forth as the morning, and thine health shall spring forth speedily." Only believe that He is faithful that hath promised. God can renew the physical strength. And more, He says He will do it. And the promise does not end here. "Thy righteousness shall go before thee; the glory of the Lord shall be thy rereward." God will build a fortification around thee. The promise does not stop even here. "Then shalt thou call, and the Lord shall answer; thou shalt cry, and He shall say, Here I am." If ye put down oppression and remove the speaking of vanity, if ye draw out your soul to the hungry, "then shall thy light rise in obscurity, and thy darkness be as the noonday: and the Lord shall guide thee continually, and satisfy thy soul in drought [famine], and make fat thy bones: and thou shalt be like a watered garden, and like a spring of water, whose waters fail not."—Testimonies for the Church 2:33-35.

[32] **The Twofold Reform of Isaiah 58**—The work specified in these words [Isaiah 58] is the work God requires His people to do. It is a work of God's own appointment. With the work of advocating the commandments of God and repairing the breach that has been made in the law of God, we are to mingle compassion for suffering humanity. We are to show supreme love to God; we are to exalt His memorial, which has been trodden down by unholy feet; and with this we are to manifest mercy, benevolence, and the tenderest pity for the fallen race. "Thou shalt love thy neighbour as thyself." As a people we must take hold of this work. Love revealed for suffering humanity gives significance and power to the truth.—Special Testimonies, Series A 10:3, 4.

A True Interpretation of the Gospel—It is only by an unselfish interest in those in need of help that we can give a practical demonstration of the truths of the gospel. "If a brother or sister be naked, and destitute of daily food, and one of you say unto them, Depart in peace, be ye warmed and filled; notwithstanding ye give them not those things which are needful to the body; what doth it profit? Even so faith, if it hath not works, is dead, being alone." "And now abideth faith, hope, charity, these three; but the greatest of these is charity."

Much more than mere sermonizing is included in preaching the gospel. The ignorant are to be enlightened; the discouraged are to be uplifted; the sick are to be healed. The human voice is to act its part in God's work. Words of tenderness, sympathy, and love are to witness to the truth. Earnest, heartfelt prayers are to bring the angels near....

[33] The Lord will give you success in this work; ... it is interwoven with the practical life, when it is lived and practiced. The union of Christlike work for the body and Christlike work for the soul is the true interpretation of the gospel.—The Review and Herald, March 4, 1902.

The Counsel Is Explicit—I have no fears of workers who are engaged in the work represented in the fifty-eighth chapter of Isaiah. This chapter is explicit, and is enough to enlighten anyone who wishes to do the will of God. There is plenty of opportunity for everyone to be a blessing to humanity. The third angel's message is not to be given a second place in this work, but is to be one with it. There may be, and there is, a danger of burying up the great principles of truth when doing the work that is right to do. This work is to be to the message what the hand is to the body. The spiritual necessities of the soul are to be kept prominent.—Letter 24, 1898.

Our God-appointed Work—I cannot too strongly urge all our church members, all who are true missionaries, all who believe the third angel's message, all who turn away their feet from the Sabbath, to consider the message of the fifty-eighth chapter of Isaiah. The work of beneficence enjoined in this chapter is the work that God requires His people to do at this time. It is a work of His own appointment. We are not left in doubt as to where the message applies, and the time of its marked fulfillment, for we read: "They that shall be of thee shall build the old waste places: thou shalt raise up the foundations of many generations; and thou shalt be called, The repairer of the breach, The restorer of paths to dwell in." Verse 12. God's memorial, the seventh-day Sabbath, the sign of His work in creating the world, has been displaced by the man of sin. God's people have a special work to do in repairing the breach that has been made in His law; and the nearer we approach the end, the more urgent this work becomes. All who love God will show that they bear His sign by keeping His commandments....

When the church accepts its God-given work, the promise is: "Then shall thy light break forth as the morning, and thine health shall spring forth speedily: and thy righteousness shall go before thee; the glory of the Lord shall be thy rereward."—Testimonies for the Church 6:265-267.

Chapter 4—This is Pure Religion

Pure Religion Defined—What is pure religion? Christ has told us that pure religion is the exercise of pity, sympathy, and love in the home, in the church, and in the world. This is the kind of religion to teach to the children, and is the genuine article. Teach them that they are not to center their thoughts upon themselves, but that wherever there is human need and suffering, there is a field for missionary work.—The Review and Herald, November 12, 1895.

Pure religion and undefiled before the Father is this: "To visit the fatherless and widows in their affliction, and to keep himself unspotted from the world." Good deeds are the fruit that Christ requires us to bear: kind words, deeds of benevolence, of tender regard for the poor, the needy, the afflicted. When hearts sympathize with hearts burdened with discouragement and grief, when the hand dispenses to the needy, when the naked are clothed, the stranger made welcome to a seat in your parlor and a place in your heart, angels are coming very near, and an answering strain is responded to in heaven.—Testimonies for the Church 2:25.

God's Test of Our Religion—I have been shown some things in reference to our duty to the unfortunate which I feel it my duty to write at this time.

I saw that it is in the providence of God that widows and orphans, the blind, the deaf, the lame, and persons afflicted in a variety of ways have been placed in close Christian relationship to His church; it is to prove His people and develop their true character. Angels of God are watching to see how we treat these persons who need our sympathy, love, and disinterested benevolence. This is God's test of our character. If we have the true religion of the Bible, we shall feel that a debt of love, kindness, and interest is due to Christ in behalf of His brethren; and we can do no less than to show our gratitude for His immeasurable love to us while we were sinners unworthy of His grace, by having a deep interest and unselfish love for those who are our brethren and who are less fortunate than ourselves.—Testimonies for the Church 3:511.

How Does Your Light Shine?—Those who should have been the light of the world have shed forth but feeble and sickly beams. What is light? It is piety, goodness, truth, mercy, love; it is the revealing of the truth in the character and life. The gospel is dependent on the personal piety of its believers for its aggressive power, and God has made provision through the death of His beloved Son, that every soul may be thoroughly furnished unto every good work.—The Review and Herald, March 24, 1891.

The Sign Distinguishing True and False Religion—True sympathy between man and his fellow man is to be the sign distinguishing those who love and fear God from those who are unmindful of His law. How great the sympathy that Christ expressed in coming to this world to give His life a sacrifice for a dying world! His religion led to the doing of genuine medical missionary work. [The reader should bear in mind that the term "medical missionary work" as often employed by Mrs. White stretched far beyond the bounds of professional medical service to embody all acts of mercy and disinterested kindness.—Compilers.] He was a healing power. "I will have mercy, and not sacrifice," He said. This is the test that the great Author of truth used to distinguish between true religion and false.—Manuscript 117, 1903.

Practical Sympathy the Test of Purity—Satan is playing the game of life for every soul. He knows that practical sympathy is a test of the purity and unselfishness of the heart, and he will make every possible effort to close our hearts to the needs of others, that we may finally be unmoved by the sight of suffering. He will bring in many things to prevent the expression of love and sympathy. It is thus that he ruined Judas. Judas was constantly planning to benefit self. In this he represents a large class of professed Christians of today. Therefore we need to study his case. We are as near to Christ as he was. Yet if, as with Judas, association with Christ does not make us one with Him, if it does not cultivate within our hearts a sincere sympathy for those for whom Christ gave His life, we are in the same danger as was Judas of being outside of Christ, the sport of Satan's temptations.

We need to guard against the first deviation from righteousness; for one transgression, one neglect to manifest the spirit of Christ, opens the way for another and still another, until the mind is overmastered by the principles of the enemy. If cultivated, the spirit of selfishness becomes a devouring passion which nothing but the power of Christ can subdue.—Testimonies for the Church 6:264, 265.

Pure Religion Is Doing Deeds of Mercy and Love—True godliness is measured by the work done. Profession is nothing; position is nothing; a character like the character of Christ is the evidence we are to bear that God has sent His Son into the world. Those who profess to be Christians, yet do not act as Christ would were He in their place, greatly injure the cause of God. They misrepresent their Saviour, and are standing under false colors....

Pure and undefiled religion is not a sentiment, but the doing of works of mercy and love. This religion is necessary to health and happiness. It enters the polluted soul temple, and with a scourge drives out the sinful intruders. Taking the throne, it consecrates all by its presence, illuminating the heart with the bright beams of the Sun of Righteousness. It opens the windows of the soul heavenward, letting in the sunshine of God's love. With it comes serenity and composure. Physical, mental, and moral strength increase, because the atmosphere of heaven as a living, active agency fills the soul. Christ is formed within, the hope of glory.—The Review and Herald, October 15, 1901.

To become a toiler, to continue patiently in well-doing which calls for self-denying labor, is a glorious work, which Heaven smiles upon. Faithful work is more acceptable to God than the most zealous and thought-to-be holiest worship. It is working together with Christ that is true worship. Prayers, exhortation, and talk are cheap fruits, which are frequently tied on; but fruits that are manifested in good works, in caring for the needy, the fatherless, and widows, are genuine fruits, and grow naturally upon a good tree.—Testimonies for the Church 2:24.

Are We the Children of God?—It is not fitful service that God accepts; it is not emotional spasms of piety that make us children of God. He calls upon us to work for principles that are true, firm, and abiding. If Christ is formed within, the hope of glory, He will be revealed in the character, it will be Christlike. We are to represent Christ to the world, as Christ represented the Father.—The Review and Herald, January 11, 1898.

We want to show Christian warmth and heartiness, not as though we were doing some wonderful thing, but just what we would expect any real Christian to do in our own case were we placed in like circumstances.—Letter 68, 1898.

Not to Be Weary in Well-doing—Many times our efforts for others may be disregarded and apparently lost. But this should be no excuse for us to become weary in well-doing. How often has Jesus come to find fruit upon the plants of His care, and found nothing but leaves! We may be disappointed as to the result of our best efforts, but this should not lead us to be indifferent to others' woes and to do nothing. "Curse ye Meroz, said the angel of the Lord, curse ye bitterly the inhabitants thereof; because they came not to the help of the Lord, to the help of the Lord against the mighty."—Testimonies for the Church 3:525.

In Doing for Others We Are Doing for Christ—From what has been shown me, Sabbathkeepers are growing more selfish as they increase in riches. Their love for Christ and His people is decreasing. They do not see the wants of the needy, nor feel their sufferings and sorrows. They do not realize that in neglecting the poor and the suffering they neglect Christ, and that in relieving the wants and sufferings of the poor as far as possible, they minister to Jesus....

"Then shall He say also unto them on the left hand, Depart from Me, ye cursed, into everlasting fire, prepared for the devil and his angels: for I was an hungred, and ye gave Me no meat: I was thirsty, and ye gave Me no drink: I was a stranger, and ye took Me not in: naked, and ye clothed Me not: sick, and in prison, and ye visited Me not. Then shall they also answer Him, saying, Lord, when saw we Thee an hungred, or athirst, or a stranger, or naked, or sick, or in prison, and did not minister unto Thee? Then shall He answer them, saying, Verily I say unto you, Inasmuch as ye did it not to one of the least of these, ye did not to Me. And these shall go away into everlasting punishment: but the righteous into life eternal." Matthew 25:41-46.

Jesus here identifies Himself with His suffering people. It was I who was hungry and thirsty. It was I who was a stranger. It was I who was naked. It was I who was sick. It was I who was in prison. When you were enjoying the food from your bountifully spread tables, I was famishing in the hovel or street not far from you. When you closed your doors against Me, while your well-furnished rooms were unoccupied, I had not where to lay My head. Your wardrobes were filled with an abundant supply of changeable suits of apparel, upon which means had been needlessly squandered, which you might have given to the needy. I was destitute of comfortable apparel. When you were enjoying health, I was sick. Misfortune cast Me into prison and bound me with fetters, bowing down My spirit, depriving Me of freedom and hope, while you roamed free. What a oneness Jesus here expresses as existing between Himself and His suffering disciples! He makes their case His own. He identifies Himself as being in person the very sufferer. Mark, selfish Christian: every neglect of the needy poor, the orphan, the fatherless, is a neglect of Jesus in their person.

[41] I am acquainted with persons who make a high profession, whose hearts are so encased in self-love and selfishness that they cannot appreciate what I am writing. They have all their lives thought and lived only for self. To make a sacrifice to do others good, to disadvantage themselves to advantage others, is out of the question with them. They have not the least idea that God requires this of them. Self is their idol. Precious weeks, months, and years pass into eternity, but they have no record in heaven of kindly acts, of sacrificing for others' good, of feeding the hungry, clothing the naked, or taking in the stranger. This entertaining strangers at a venture is not agreeable. If they knew that all who sought to share their bounty were worthy, then they might be induced to do something in this direction. But there is virtue in venturing something. Perchance we may entertain angels.—Testimonies for the Church 2:24.

Chapter 5—The Parable of the Good Samaritan

The Nature of True Religion Illustrated—In the story of the good Samaritan, Christ illustrates the nature of true religion. He shows that it consists not in systems, creeds, or rites, but in the performance of loving deeds, in bringing the greatest good to others, in genuine goodness.... The lesson is no less needed in the world today than when it fell from the lips of Jesus. Selfishness and cold formality have well-nigh extinguished the fire of love and dispelled the graces that should make fragrant the character. Many who profess His name have lost sight of the fact that Christians are to represent Christ. Unless there is practical self-sacrifice for the good of others, in the family circle, in the neighborhood, in the church, and wherever we may be, then whatever our profession we are not Christians.—The Desire of Ages, 497, 504.

Who Is My Neighbor?—Among the Jews the question, "Who is my neighbor?" caused endless dispute. They had no doubt as to the heathen and the Samaritans. These were strangers and enemies. But where should the distinction be made among the people of their own nation, and among the different classes of society? Whom should the priest, the rabbi, and elder, regard as neighbor? They spent their lives in the round of ceremonies to make themselves pure. Contact with the ignorant and careless multitude, they taught, would cause defilement that would require wearisome effort to remove. Were they to regard the "unclean" as neighbors?

This question Christ answered in the parable of the good Samaritan. He showed that our neighbor does not mean merely one of the church or faith to which we belong. It has no reference to race, color, or class distinction. Our neighbor is every person who needs our help. Our neighbor is every soul who is wounded and bruised by the adversary. Our neighbor is everyone who is the property of God.—Christ's Object Lessons, 376.

Illustrated by the Parable—Christ was speaking to a large company. The Pharisees, hoping to catch something from His lips that they could use to condemn Him, sent a lawyer to Him with a question, "What shall I do to inherit eternal life?" Christ read the hearts of the Pharisees as an open book, and His answer to the questioner was, "What is written in the law? how readest thou?" "And he answering said, Thou shalt love the Lord thy God with all thy heart, and with all thy soul, and with all thy strength, and with all thy mind; and thy neighbour as thyself."

"Thou hast answered right," Christ said; "this do, and thou shalt live." The lawyer knew that by his own answer he had condemned himself. He knew that he did not love his neighbor as himself. But willing to justify himself, he asked, "And who is my neighbour?"

Christ answered this question by relating an incident, the memory of which was fresh in the minds of his hearers.—Manuscript 117, 1903.

"A certain man," He said, "went down from Jerusalem to Jericho, and fell among thieves, which stripped him of his raiment, and wounded him, and departed, leaving him half dead."

[44] In journeying from Jerusalem to Jericho, the traveler had to pass through a portion of the wilderness of Judea. The road led down a wild, rocky ravine, which was infested with robbers and was often the scene of violence. It was here that the traveler was attacked, stripped of all that was valuable, and left half dead by the wayside. As he lay thus, a priest came that way; he saw the man lying wounded and bruised, weltering in his own blood; but he left him without rendering any assistance. He "passed by on the other side." Then a Levite appeared. Curious to know what had happened, he stopped and looked at the sufferer. He was convicted of what he ought to do, but it was not an agreeable duty. He wished that he had not come that way, so that he would not have seen the wounded man. He persuaded himself that the case was no concern of his, and he too "passed by on the other side."

But a Samaritan, traveling the same road, saw the sufferer, and he did the work that the others had refused to do. With gentleness and kindness he ministered to the wounded man. "When he saw him, he had compassion on him, and went to him, and bound up his wounds, pouring in oil and wine, and set him on his own beast, and brought him to an inn, and took care of him. And on the morrow when he departed, he took out two pence, and gave them to the host, and said unto him. Take care of him; and whatsoever thou spendest more, when I come again, I will repay thee." The priest and the Levite both professed piety, but the Samaritan showed that he was truly converted. It was no more agreeable for him to do the work than for the priest and the Levite, but in spirit and works he proved himself to be in harmony with God.

In giving this lesson Christ presented the principles of the law in a direct, forcible way, showing His hearers that they had neglected to carry out these principles. His words were so definite and pointed that the listeners could find no opportunity to cavil. The lawyer found in the lesson nothing that he could criticize. His prejudice in regard to Christ was removed. But he had not overcome his national dislike sufficiently to give credit to the Samaritan by name. When Christ asked, "Which now of these three, thinkest thou, was neighbour unto him that fell among the thieves?" he answered, "He that shewed mercy on him."

"Then said Jesus unto him, Go, and do thou likewise." Show the same tender kindness to those in need. Thus you will give evidence that you keep the whole law.—Christ's Object Lessons, 379, 380.

Anyone in Need Is Our Neighbor—Any human being who needs our sympathy and our kind offices is our neighbor. The suffering and destitute of all classes are our neighbors; and when their wants are brought to our knowledge, it is our duty to relieve them as far as possible.—Testimonies for the Church 4:226, 227.

By this parable the duty of man to his fellow man is forever settled. We are to care for every case of suffering and to look upon ourselves as God's agents to relieve the needy to the very uttermost of our ability. We are to be laborers together with God. There are some who manifest great affection for their relatives, for their friends and favorites, who yet fail to be kind and considerate to those who need tender sympathy, who need kindness and love. With earnest hearts let us inquire, Who is my neighbor? Our neighbors are not merely our associates and special friends; they are not simply those who belong to our church, or who think as we do. Our neighbors are the whole human family. We are to do good to all men, and especially to those who are of the household of faith. We are to give to the world an exhibition of what it means to carry out the law of God. We are to love God supremely and our neighbor as ourselves.—The Review and Herald, January 1, 1895.

True Religion Misrepresented—The priest and the Levite had been for worship to the Temple, whose service was appointed by God Himself. To participate in that service was a great and exalted privilege, and the priest and Levite felt that having been thus honored, it was beneath them to minister to an unknown sufferer by the wayside. Thus they neglected the special opportunity which God had offered them as His agents to bless a fellow being.

Many today are making a similar mistake. They separate their duties into two distinct classes. The one class is made up of great things, to be regulated by the law of God; the other class is made up of so-called little things, in which the command, "Thou shalt love thy neighbour as thyself," is ignored. This sphere of work is left to caprice, subject to inclination or impulse. Thus the character is marred, and the religion of Christ misrepresented.

There are those who would think it lowering to their dignity to minister to suffering humanity. Many look with indifference and contempt upon those who have laid the temple of the soul in ruins. Others neglect the poor from a different motive. They are working, as they believe, in the cause of Christ, seeking to build up some worthy enterprise. They feel that they are doing a great work, and they cannot stop to notice the wants of the needy and distressed. In advancing their supposedly great work they may even oppress the poor. They may place them in hard and trying circumstances, deprive them of their rights, or neglect their needs. Yet they feel that all this is justifiable because they are, as they think, advancing the cause of Christ.—Christ's Object Lessons, 382, 383.

Far-reaching Requirements of God's Law—To leave the suffering neighbor unrelieved is a breach of the law of God. God brought the priest along that way in order that with his own eyes he might see a case that needed mercy and help; but the priest, though holding a holy office, whose work it was to bestow mercy and to do good, passed by on the other side. His character was exhibited in its true nature before the angels of God. For a pretense he could make long prayers, but he could not keep the principles of the law in loving God with all his heart and his neighbor as himself. The Levite was of the same tribe as was the wounded, bruised sufferer.

All Heaven watched as the Levite passed down the road, to see if his heart would be touched with human woe. As he beheld the man he was convicted of what he ought to do; but as it was not an agreeable duty, he wished he had not come that way, so that he need not have seen the man who was wounded and bruised, naked and perishing, and in want of help from his fellow men. He passed on his way, persuading himself that it was none of his business, and that he had no need to trouble himself over the case. Claiming to be an expositor of the law, to be a minister in sacred things, he yet passed by on the other side.

Enshrined in the pillar of cloud, the Lord Jesus had given special direction in regard to the performance of acts of mercy toward man and beast. While the law of God requires supreme love to God and impartial love to our neighbors, its far-reaching requirements also take in the dumb creatures that cannot express in words their wants or sufferings. "Thou shalt not see thy brother's ass or his ox fall down by the way, and hide thyself from them: thou shalt surely help him to lift them up again." He who loves God not only will love his fellow men but will regard with tender compassion the creatures which God has made. When the Spirit of God is in man, it leads him to relieve rather than to create suffering.—The Review and Herald, January 1, 1895.

The Principles of God's Law Were Forgotten—The priest and Levite had no excuse for their cold-hearted indifference. The law of mercy and kindness was plainly stated in the Old Testament Scriptures. It was their appointed work to minister to just such cases as the one whom they had coldly passed by. Had they obeyed the law they claimed to respect, they would not have passed this man by without helping him. But they had forgotten the principles of the law that Christ, enshrouded in the pillar of cloud, had given to their fathers as He led them through the wilderness....

Who is my neighbor? This is a question that all our churches need to understand. Had the priest and the Levite read understandingly the Hebrew code, their treatment of the wounded man would have been far different.—Manuscript 117, 1903.

Conditions of Inheriting Eternal Life—The conditions of inheriting eternal life are plainly stated by our Saviour in the most simple manner. The man who was wounded and robbed represents

[49] those who are subjects of our interest, sympathy, and charity. If we neglect the cases of the needy and the unfortunate that are brought under our notice, no matter who they may be, we have no assurance of eternal life; for we do not answer the claims that God has upon us. We are not compassionate and pitiful to humanity, because they may not be kith or kin to us. You have been found transgressors of the second great commandment, upon which the last six commandments depend. Whosoever offendeth in one point is guilty of all. Those who do not open their hearts to the wants and sufferings of humanity will not open their hearts to the claims of God as stated in the first four precepts of the Decalogue. Idols claim the heart and affections, and God is not honored and does not reign supreme.—Testimonies for the Church 3:524.

Your Opportunity and Mine—Today God gives men opportunity to show whether they love their neighbor. He who truly loves God and his fellow man is he who shows mercy to the destitute, the suffering, the wounded, those who are ready to die. God calls upon every man to take up his neglected work, to seek to restore the moral image of the Creator in humanity.—Letter 113, 1901.

How We May Love Our Neighbors as Ourselves—We can love our neighbor as ourselves only as we love God supremely. The love of God will bear fruit in love to our neighbors. Many think that it is impossible to love our neighbor as ourselves, but it is the only genuine fruit of Christianity. Love to others is putting on the Lord Jesus Christ; it is walking and working with the invisible world in view. We are thus to keep looking unto Jesus, the Author and Finisher of our faith.—The Review and Herald, June 26, 1894.

Section 3—The New Testament Pattern

Gem Thought

Christ's followers have been redeemed for service. Our Lord teaches that the true object of life is ministry. Christ Himself was a worker, and to all His followers He gives the law of service—service to God and to their fellow men. Here Christ has presented to the world a higher conception of life than they had ever known. By living to minister for others, man is brought into connection with Christ. The law of service becomes the connecting link which binds us to God and to our fellow men.

To His servants Christ commits "His goods,"—something to be put to use for Him. He gives "to every man his work." Each has his place in the eternal plan of heaven. Each is to work in cooperation with Christ for the salvation of souls. Not more surely is the place prepared for us in the heavenly mansions than is the special place designated on earth where we are to work for God.—Christ's Object Lessons, 326, 327.

Even the Son of man came not to be ministered unto, but to minister. Mark 10:45.

Chapter 6—Our Example in Welfare Ministry

Christ Stands Before Us as the Great Pattern—Make Christ's work your example. Constantly He went about doing good—feeding the hungry and healing the sick. No one who came to Him for sympathy was disappointed. The commander of the heavenly courts, He was made flesh and dwelt among us, and His lifework is an example of the work we are to do. His tender, pitying love rebukes our selfishness and heartlessness.—Manuscript 55, 1901.

Christ stood at the head of humanity in the garb of humanity. So full of sympathy and love was His attitude that the poorest was not afraid to come to Him. He was kind to all, easily approached by the most lowly. He went from house to house, healing the sick, feeding the hungry, comforting the mourners, soothing the afflicted, speaking peace to the distressed.... He was willing to humble Himself, to deny Himself. He did not seek to distinguish Himself. He was the servant of all. It was His meat and drink to be a comfort and a consolation to others, to gladden the sad and heavy-laden one with whom He daily came in contact.

Christ stands before us as a pattern Man, the great Medical Missionary—an example for all who should come after. His love, pure and holy, blessed all who came within the sphere of its influence. His character was absolutely perfect, free from the slightest stain of sin. He came as an expression of the perfect love of God, not to crush, not to judge and condemn, but to heal every weak, defective character, to save men and women from Satan's power. He is the Creator, Redeemer, and Sustainer of the human race. He gives to all the invitation, "Come unto Me, all ye that labour and are heavy laden, and I will give you rest. Take My yoke upon you, and learn of Me; for I am meek and lowly in heart: and ye shall find rest unto your souls. For My yoke is easy, and My burden is light."

What, then, is the example that we are to set to the world? We are to do the same work that the great Medical Missionary undertook in our behalf. We are to follow the path of self-sacrifice trodden by Christ.—Special Testimonies, Series B 8:31, 32.

Christ Moved With Compassion—When Christ saw the multitudes that gathered about Him, "He was moved with compassion on them, because they fainted, and were scattered abroad, as sheep having no shepherd." Christ saw the sickness, the sorrow, the want and degradation of the multitudes that thronged His steps. To Him were presented the needs and woes of humanity throughout the world. Among the high and the low, the most honored and the most degraded, He beheld souls who were longing for the very blessings He had come to bring....

Today the same needs exist. The world is in need of workers who will labor as Christ did for the suffering and the sinful. There is indeed a multitude to be reached. The world is full of sickness, suffering, distress, and sin. It is full of those who need to be ministered unto—the weak, the helpless, the ignorant, the degraded.—Testimonies for the Church 6:254.

The Model We Should Copy—The true missionary spirit is the spirit of Christ. The world's Redeemer was the great model missionary. Many of His followers have labored earnestly and unselfishly in the cause of human salvation; but no man's labor can bear comparison with the self-denial, the sacrifice, the benevolence, of our Exemplar.

The love which Christ has evinced for us is without a parallel. How earnestly He labored! How often was He alone in fervent prayer, on the mountainside or in the retirement of the garden, pouring out His supplications with strong crying and tears. How perseveringly He urged His petitions in behalf of sinners! Even on the cross He forgot His own sufferings in His deep love for those whom He came to save. How cold our love, how feeble our interest, when compared with the love and interest manifested by our Saviour! Jesus gave Himself to redeem our race, and yet how ready are we to excuse ourselves from giving all that we have for Jesus. Our Saviour submitted to wearing labor, ignominy, and suffering. He was repulsed, mocked, derided, while engaged in the great work which He came to earth to do.

Do you, my brethren and sisters, inquire: What model shall we copy? I do not point you to great and good men, but to the world's

Redeemer. If we would have the true missionary spirit, we must be imbued with the love of Christ; we must look to the Author and Finisher of our faith, study His character, cultivate His spirit of meekness and humility, and walk in His footsteps.

[56] Many suppose that the missionary spirit, the qualification for missionary work, is a special gift or endowment bestowed upon the ministers and a few members of the church and that all others are to be mere spectators. Never was there a greater mistake. Every true Christian will possess a missionary spirit, for to be a Christian is to be Christlike. No man liveth to himself, and "if any man have not the Spirit of Christ, he is none of His." Everyone who has tasted of the powers of the world to come, whether he be young or old, learned or unlearned, will be stirred with the spirit which actuated Christ. The very first impulse of the renewed heart is to bring others also to the Saviour. Those who do not possess this desire give evidence that they have lost their first love; they should closely examine their own hearts in the light of God's Word, and earnestly seek a fresh baptism of the Spirit of Christ; they should pray for a deeper comprehension of that wondrous love which Jesus manifested for us in leaving the realms of glory and coming to a fallen world to save the perishing.—Testimonies for the Church 5:385, 386.

Christ's Interpretation of the Gospel—The divine commission needs no reform. Christ's way of presenting truth cannot be improved upon. The Saviour gave the disciples practical lessons, teaching them how to work in such a way as to make souls glad in the truth. He sympathized with the weary, the heavy laden, the oppressed. He fed the hungry and healed the sick. Constantly He went about doing good. By the good He accomplished, by His loving words and kindly deeds, He interpreted the gospel to men.

Brief as was the period of His public ministry, He accomplished the work He came to do. How impressive were the truths He taught! How complete His lifework! What spiritual food He daily imparted as He presented the bread of life to thousands of hungry souls! His life was a living ministry of the word. He promised nothing that He did not perform.

[57] The words of life were presented in such simplicity that a child could understand them. Men, women, and children were so impressed with His manner of explaining the Scriptures that they would

catch the very intonation of His voice, place the same emphasis on their words, and imitate His gestures. Youth caught His spirit of ministry, and sought to pattern after His gracious ways by seeking to assist those whom they saw needing help.

Just as we trace the pathway of a stream of water by the line of living green it produces, so Christ could be seen in the deeds of mercy that marked His pathway at every step. Wherever He went health sprang up, and happiness followed wherever He passed. The blind and deaf rejoiced in His presence. His words to the ignorant opened to them a fountain of life. He dispensed His blessings abundantly and continuously. They were the garnered treasures of eternity, given in Christ, the Lord's rich gift to man.

Christ's work in behalf of man is not finished. It continues today. In like manner His ambassadors are to preach the gospel and to reveal His pitying love for lost and perishing souls. By an unselfish interest in those who need help they are to give a practical demonstration of the truth of the gospel. Much more than mere sermonizing is included in this work. The evangelization of the world is the work God has given to those who go forth in His name. They are to be co-laborers with Christ, revealing to those ready to perish His tender, pitying love. God calls for thousands to work for Him, not by preaching to those who know the truth for this time, but by warning those who have never heard the last message of mercy. Work with a heart filled with an earnest longing for souls. Do medical missionary work. Thus you will gain access to the hearts of people, and the way will be prepared for a more decided proclamation of the truth. [58]

Who are laborers together with Christ in this blessed medical missionary work? Who have learned the lessons of the Master and know how to deal skillfully with souls for whom Christ has died? We need, oh, so much, physicians for the soul who have been educated in the school of Christ and who can work in Christ's lines.—The Review and Herald, December 17, 1914.

Chapter 7—Visitation—The New Testament Plan

Christ's Methods of Labor—From Christ's methods of labor we may learn valuable lessons. He did not follow merely one method; in various ways He sought to gain the attention of the multitude, that He might proclaim to them the truths of the gospel.

Christ's chief work was in ministering to the poor, the needy, and the ignorant. In simplicity He opened before them the blessing they might receive, and thus aroused a soul hunger for the bread of life. Christ's life is an example to all His followers. It is the duty of all who have learned the way of life to teach others what it means to believe in the Word of God. There are many now in the shadow of death who need to be instructed in the truths of the gospel. Nearly the whole world is lying in wickedness. Yet we have words of hope for those who sit in darkness.—The Review and Herald, May 9, 1912.

The Scope of Christ's House-to-House Ministry—Our Saviour went from house to house, healing the sick, comforting the mourners, soothing the afflicted, speaking peace to the disconsolate. He took the little children in His arms and blessed them and spoke words of hope and comfort to the weary mothers. With unfailing tenderness and gentleness He met every form of human woe and affliction. Not for Himself, but for others, did He labor. He was the servant of all. It was His meat and drink to bring hope and strength to all with whom He came in contact.—Gospel Workers, 188.

Christ's Method Brings True Success—Christ's method alone will give true success in reaching the people. The Saviour mingled with men as one who desired their good. He showed His sympathy for them, ministered to their needs, and won their confidence. Then He bade them, "Follow Me."—The Ministry of Healing, 143.

This was the way the Christian Church was established. Christ first selected a few persons and bade them follow Him. They then went in search of their relatives and acquaintances, and brought them to Christ. This is the way we are to labor. A few souls brought out and fully established on the truth will, like the first disciples, be laborers for others.—The Review and Herald, December 8, 1885.

The Divine Example of Personal Evangelism—Jesus came in personal contact with men. He did not stand aloof and apart from those who needed His help. He entered the homes of men, comforted the mourner, healed the sick, aroused the careless, and went about doing good. And if we follow in the footsteps of Jesus, we must do as He did. We must give men the same kind of help that He gave.—The Review and Herald, April 24, 1888.

It is not preaching that is the most important; it is house-to-house work, reasoning from the Word, explaining the Word. It is those workers who follow the methods that Christ followed who will win souls for their hire.—Gospel Workers, 468.

The Lord desires that His word of grace shall be brought home to every soul. To a great degree this must be accomplished by personal labor. This was Christ's method. His work was largely made up of personal interviews. He had a faithful regard for the one-soul audience. Through that one soul the message was often extended to thousands. Christ's Object Lessons, 229.

The Twelve Sent Forth in House-to-House Labor—On this first tour the disciples were to go only where Jesus had been before them and had made friends.... Nothing must be allowed to divert their minds from their great work or in any way excite opposition and close the door for further labor. They were not to adopt the dress of the religious teachers, nor use any guise in apparel to distinguish them from the humble peasants. They were not to enter into the synagogues and call the people together for public service; their efforts were to be put forth in house-to-house labor.... They were to enter the dwelling with the beautiful salutation, "Peace be to this house." That home would be blessed by their prayers, their songs of praise, and the opening of the Scriptures in the family circle.—The Desire of Ages, 351, 352.

The Seventy Likewise—Calling the twelve about Him, Jesus bade them go out two and two through the towns and villages. None were sent forth alone, but brother was associated with brother, friend with friend. Thus they could help and encourage each other, counseling and praying together, each one's strength supplementing the other's weakness. In the same manner He afterward sent forth the seventy. It was the Saviour's purpose that the messengers of the gospel should be associated in this way. In our own time evangelistic work would be far more successful if this example were more closely followed.—The Desire of Ages, 350.

Paul Went From House to House—Paul, as well as laboring publicly, went from house to house preaching repentance toward God and faith toward our Lord Jesus Christ. He met with men at their homes and besought them with tears, declaring unto them the whole counsel of God.—The Review and Herald, April 24, 1888.

The Secret of Paul's Power and Success—On one occasion Paul said: "Ye know, from the first day that I came into Asia, after what manner I have been with you at all seasons, serving the Lord with all humility of mind, and with many tears, and temptations, which befell me by the lying in wait of the Jews: and how I kept back nothing that was profitable unto you, but have shewed you, and have taught you publickly, and from house to house." ...

These words explain the secret of Paul's power and success. He kept back nothing that was profitable for the people. He preached Christ publicly, in the market places and the synagogues. He taught from house to house, availing himself of the familiar intercourse of the home circle. He visited the sick and sorrowing, comforting the afflicted, and lifting up the oppressed. And in all that he said and did he preached a crucified and risen Saviour.—The Youth's Instructor, November 22, 1900.

Paul Also Found Access to Others Through His Trade—During the long period of his ministry in Ephesus, where for three years he carried forward an aggressive evangelistic effort throughout that region, Paul again worked at his trade....

There were some who objected to Paul's toiling with his hands, declaring that it was inconsistent with the work of a gospel minister. Why should Paul, a minister of the highest rank, thus connect mechanical work with the preaching of the Word? Was not the laborer worthy of his hire? Why should he spend in making tents time that to all appearance could be put to better account?

But Paul did not regard as lost the time thus spent. As he worked with Aquila he kept in touch with the Great Teacher, losing no opportunity of witnessing for the Saviour and of helping those who needed help. His mind was ever reaching out for spiritual knowledge. He gave his fellow workers instruction in spiritual things, and he also set an example of industry and thoroughness. He was a quick, skillful worker, diligent in business, "fervent in spirit, serving the Lord." As he worked at his trade, the apostle had access to a class of people that he could not otherwise have reached....

Paul sometimes worked night and day, not only for his own support, but that he might assist his fellow laborers. He shared his earnings with Luke, and he helped Timothy. He even suffered hunger at times, that he might relieve the necessities of others. His was an unselfish life.—The Acts of the Apostles, 351, 352.

Paul's Practical Example to Self-supporting Laymen—Paul set an example against the sentiment, then gaining influence in the church, that the gospel could be proclaimed successfully only by those who were wholly freed from the necessity of physical toil. He illustrated in a practical way what might be done by consecrated laymen in many places where the people were unacquainted with the truths of the gospel. His course inspired many humble toilers with a desire to do what they could to advance the cause of God, while at the same time they supported themselves in daily labor.

Aquila and Priscilla were not called to give their whole time to the ministry of the gospel, yet these humble laborers were used by God to show Apollos the way of truth more perfectly. The Lord employs various instrumentalities for the accomplishment of His purpose; and while some with special talents are chosen to devote all their energies to the work of teaching and preaching the gospel, many others, upon whom human hands have never been laid in ordination, are called to act an important part in soulsaving.

There is a large field open before the self-supporting gospel worker. Many may gain valuable experiences in ministry while toiling a portion of the time at some form of manual labor, and by this method strong workers may be developed for important service in needy fields.—The Acts of the Apostles, 355.

Go in the Spirit That Endued Paul—Go to your neighbors one by one, and come close to them till their hearts are warmed by your unselfish interest and love. Sympathize with them, pray with them, watch for opportunities to do them good, and as you can, gather a few together and open the Word of God to their darkened minds. Keep watching as he who must render an account for the souls of men, and make the most of the privileges that God gives you of laboring with Him in His moral vineyard.

Do not neglect speaking to your neighbors and doing them all the kindness in your power, that you "by all means may save some." We need to seek for the spirit that constrained the apostle Paul to go from house to house, pleading with tears and teaching "repentance toward God, and faith toward our Lord Jesus Christ."—The Review and Herald, March 13, 1888.

The First Works of the New Testament Church—The first works of the church were seen when the believers sought out friends, relatives, and acquaintances, and with hearts overflowing with love, told the story of what Jesus was to them.—Special Testimonies, Series A 02a:17.

Success of the New Testament Plan—The more closely the New Testament plan is followed in missionary labor, the more successful will be the efforts put forth. We should work as did our divine Teacher, sowing the seeds of truth with care, anxiety, and self-denial. We must have the mind of Christ if we would not become weary in well-doing. His was a life of continual sacrifice for others' good. We must follow His example.—Testimonies for the Church 3:210.

Chapter 8—Dorcas—Her Ministry and its Influence [66]

Restored to Life to Continue Her Ministry—In the course of his ministry the apostle Peter visited the believers at Lydda. Here he healed Aeneas, who for eight years had been confined to his bed with palsy. "Aeneas, Jesus Christ maketh thee whole," the apostle said; "arise, and make thy bed." "He arose immediately. And all that dwelt at Lydda and Saron saw him, and turned to the Lord."

At Joppa, which was near Lydda, there lived a woman named Dorcas, whose good deeds had made her greatly beloved. She was a worthy disciple of Jesus, and her life was filled with acts of kindness. She knew who needed comfortable clothing and who needed sympathy, and she freely ministered to the poor and the sorrowful. Her skillful fingers were more active than her tongue.

"And it came to pass in those days, that she was sick, and died." The church in Joppa realized their loss; and hearing that Peter was at Lydda, the believers sent messengers to him, "desiring him that he would not delay to come to them. Then Peter arose and went with them. When he was come, they brought him into the upper chamber: and all the widows stood by him weeping, and shewing the coats and garments which Dorcas made, while she was with them." In view of the life of service that Dorcas had lived, it is little wonder that they mourned, that warm teardrops fell upon the inanimate clay.

The apostle's heart was touched with sympathy as he beheld [67] their sorrow. Then, directing that the weeping friends be sent from the room, he kneeled down and prayed fervently to God to restore Dorcas to life and health. Turning to the body, he said, "Tabitha, arise. And she opened her eyes: and when she saw Peter, she sat up." Dorcas had been of great service to the church, and God saw fit to bring her back from the land of the enemy, that her skill and energy might still be a blessing to others and also that by this manifestation of His power the cause of Christ might be strengthened.—The Acts of the Apostles, 131, 132.

A Worthy Disciple Who Could not Be Spared—She [Dorcas] had been a worthy disciple of Jesus Christ, and her life had been characterized by deeds of charity and kindness to the poor and sorrowful and by zeal in the cause of truth. Her death was a great loss; the infant church could not well spare her noble efforts....

This great work of raising the dead to life was the means of converting many in Joppa to the faith of Jesus.—The Spirit of Prophecy 3:323, 324.

Section 4—Neighborhood Evangelism

Gem Thought

Church members are to do evangelistic work in the homes of their neighbors who have not yet received full evidence of the truth for this time. The presentation of the truth in love and sympathy, from house to house, is in harmony with the instruction that Christ gave to His disciples when He sent them out on their first missionary tour. By songs of praise to God, by humble, heartfelt prayers, by a simple presentation of Bible truth in the family circle, many will be reached. The divine [Worker] will be present to send conviction to hearts. "I am with you alway" is His promise. With the assurance of the abiding presence of such a Helper, we may labor with hope and faith and courage....

My brethren and sisters, give yourselves to the Lord for service. Allow no opportunity to pass unimproved. Visit those who live near you, and by sympathy and kindness try to reach their hearts. Visit the sick and suffering, and show a kindly interest in them. If possible, do something to make them more comfortable. Through this means you can reach their hearts, and speak a word for Christ. Eternity alone will reveal how far reaching such a line of labor can be.—The Review and Herald, November 21, 1907.

Let your light so shine before men, that they may see your good works, and glorify your Father which is in heaven. Matthew 5:16.

Chapter 9—Types of Work in Neighborhood Evangelism

A Large Work Before Our Churches—There is a work to be done by our churches that few have any idea of.... We shall have to give of our means to support laborers in the harvest field, and we shall rejoice in the sheaves gathered in. But while this is right, there is a work, as yet untouched, that must be done. The mission of Christ was to heal the sick, encourage the hopeless, bind up the brokenhearted. This work of restoration is to be carried on among the needy suffering ones of humanity.

God calls not only for your benevolence but for your cheerful countenance, your hopeful words, the grasp of your hand. Relieve some of God's afflicted ones. Some are sick, and hope has departed. Bring back the sunlight to them. There are souls who have lost their courage; speak to them, pray for them. There are those who need the bread of life. Read to them from the Word of God. There is a soul sickness no balm can reach, no medicine heal. Pray for these, and bring them to Jesus Christ. And in all your work Christ will be present to make impressions upon human hearts.—Manuscript 105, 1898.

Visit Every Family and Know Their Spiritual Condition—Wherever a church is established, all the members should engage actively in a missionary work. They should visit every family in the neighborhood and know their spiritual condition. If professed Christians had engaged in this work from the time when their names were first placed on the church books, there would not now be such widespread unbelief, such depths of iniquity, such unparalleled wickedness, as is seen in the world at the present time. If every church member had sought to enlighten others, thousands upon thousands would today stand with God's commandment-keeping people.

And not only in the world do we see the result of the church's neglect to work in Christ's lines. By this neglect a condition of things has been brought into the church that has eclipsed the high and holy interests of the work of God. A spirit of criticism and bitterness has come into the church, and the spiritual discernment of many has been dimmed. Because of this the cause of Christ has suffered great loss. Heavenly intelligences have been waiting to cooperate with human agencies, but we have not discerned their presence.

It is now high time that we repent. All the people of God should interest themselves in the work of doing good. They should unite heart and soul in earnest endeavor to uplift and enlighten their fellow men.—Testimonies for the Church 6:296, 297.

Finding Those Who Will Hear—Several years ago, during a former visit to the South, while out on long drives, I sometimes asked who occupied the homes we passed, and I learned that in many of the larger Southern houses were men who bear important responsibilities in the care of great estates. Upon further inquiry, I learned that no one had sought to bring before these men the Word of Life. None had gone to them, with Bible in hand, and said, "We have something precious for you, and we want that you should hear it." Now it has been presented before me repeatedly that this is a line of work that must be done. We are to go out into the highways and into the hedges and carry to the people the message of truth that Christ has given us. We are to compel many to come in.—Manuscript 15, 1909.

Making Contacts Count for Christ—There are many from whom hope has departed. Bring back the sunshine to them. Many have lost their courage. Speak to them words of cheer. Pray for them. There are those who need the bread of life. Read to them from the Word of God. Upon many is a soul sickness which no earthly balm can reach or physician heal. Pray for these souls. Bring them to Jesus. Tell them that there is a balm in Gilead and a Physician there.—Prophets and Kings, 718, 719.

Working for All Classes—Everywhere there is a work to be done for all classes of society. We are to come close to the poor and the depraved, those who have fallen through intemperance. And, at the same time, we are not to forget the higher classes—the lawyers, ministers, senators, and judges, many of whom are slaves to intemperate habits. We are to leave no effort untried to show them that their souls are worth saving, that eternal life is worth striving for.—Testimonies for the Church 7:58.

Called to Different Lines of Service—The Lord is calling upon His people to take up different lines of missionary work, to sow beside all waters. We do but a small part of the work that He desires us to do among our neighbors and friends. By kindness to the poor, the sick, or the bereaved we may obtain an influence over them, so that divine truth will find access to their hearts. No such opportunity for service should be allowed to pass unimproved. It is the highest missionary work that we can do. The presentation of the truth in love and sympathy from house to house is in harmony with the instruction of Christ to His disciples when He sent them out on their first missionary tour.—The Review and Herald, June 6, 1912.

Help Humanity as Did Christ—As He [Christ] passed through the towns and cities, He was like a vital current, diffusing life and joy wherever He went. The followers of Christ are to labor as He did. We are to feed the hungry, clothe the naked, and comfort the suffering and afflicted. We are to minister to the despairing and inspire hope in the hopeless.—The Desire of Ages, 350.

The Work Every Church Should Have Been Doing—The work of gathering in the needy, the oppressed, the suffering, the destitute, is the very work which every church that believes the truth for this time should long since have been doing. We are to show the tender sympathy of the Samaritan in supplying physical necessities, feeding the hungry, bringing the poor that are cast out to our homes, gathering from God every day grace and strength that will enable us to reach to the very depths of human misery and help those who cannot possibly help themselves. In doing this work we have a favorable opportunity to set forth Christ the crucified One.—Testimonies for the Church 6:276.

Sermons Cannot Do It—By personal labor reach the people where they are. Become acquainted with them. This work cannot be done by proxy. Money loaned or given cannot accomplish it. Sermons from the pulpit cannot do it.—Gospel Workers, 188.

Sunshine Bands—There is power in the ministry of song. Students who have learned to sing sweet gospel songs with melody and distinctness can do much good as singing evangelists. They will find many opportunities to use the talent that God has given them in carrying melody and sunshine into many lonely places darkened by sorrow and affliction, singing to those who seldom have church privileges.

Students, go out into the highways and hedges. Endeavor to reach the higher as well as the lower classes. Enter the homes of the rich as well as the poor, and as you have opportunity, ask, "Would you be pleased to have us sing some gospel hymns?" Then as hearts are softened, the way may open for you to offer a few words of prayer for the blessing of God. Not many will refuse to listen. Such ministry is genuine missionary work.—Counsels to Parents, Teachers, and Students, 547, 548.

A Wide Field of Practical Service—There is a wide field for service for women as well as for men. The efficient cook, the seamstress, the nurse—the help of all is needed. Let the members of poor households be taught how to cook, how to make and mend their own clothing, how to nurse the sick, how to care properly for the home. Even the children should be taught to do some little errand of love and mercy for those less fortunate than themselves.

Other lines of usefulness will open before those who are willing to do the duty nearest them. It is not learned, eloquent speakers that are needed now, but humble, Christlike men and women.

Work disinterestedly, lovingly, patiently, for all with whom you are brought in contact. Show no impatience. Utter not one unkind word. Let the love of Christ be in your hearts, the law of kindness on your lips.—The Review and Herald, August 7, 1913.

Using Our Holidays to Run Errands for the Lord—There are other lines of work. Some are capable of reading the Scriptures and communicating to others that which we believe. These may be channels of light and a precious comfort to some poor discouraged souls who seem to be unable to grasp hope and exercise faith. Others should search and study how they can be doing errands for the Lord. If those whose employment takes the most of their time, excepting Sundays or holidays, instead of spending this time in their own pleasure, use it in blessing others, they will be of service in the cause of God. Your example will help others to do something that will tell to the glory of God. Heed the words of the inspired apostle, "Whether therefore ye eat, or drink, or whatsoever ye do, do all to the glory of God." Thus a living principle will be brought into your daily active life, of being good and doing good....

It will not be possible for all to give their whole time to the work, because of the labor they must do to earn their daily living. Yet these have their holidays and times that they can devote to Christian work, and do good in this way if they cannot give much of their means.—Letter 12, 1892.

The hours so often spent in amusement that refreshes neither body nor soul should be spent in visiting the poor, the sick, and the suffering, or in seeking to help someone who is in need.—Testimonies for the Church 6:276.

Welfare Ministry on the Sabbath—According to the fourth commandment the Sabbath was dedicated to rest and religious worship. All secular employment was to be suspended, but works of mercy and benevolence were in accordance with the purpose of the Lord. They were not to be limited to time or place. To relieve the afflicted, to comfort the sorrowing, is a labor of love that does honor to God's holy day.—Redemption: or the Teachings of Christ, 4:46.

Early-Day Methods of Visitation—Let those who feel the burden of souls resting upon them go out and do house-to-house work, and teach the people precept upon precept, here a little, and there a little, gradually leading them into the full light of Bible truth. This is what we had to do in the early days of the message. As earnest efforts are put forth, the Lord will let His blessing rest upon the workers and upon those who are seeking for an understanding of the truth as it is in the Word of God.

There are precious truths, glorious truths, in God's Word, and it is our privilege to bring these truths before the people. In those parts of the field where many cannot attend meetings far away from their homes, we can bring the truth to them personally and can work with them in simplicity.

What light there is in the Word! In Isaiah we read, "Cry aloud, spare not, lift up thy voice like a trumpet, and shew My people their transgressions." This is the work we are to do. Note the expression, "My people." Why should the prophet say, "My people"? They were not walking in accordance with the light of truth, but God desired to save them from their sins. The truth was to be brought to them anew in its simplicity.

The message of the third angel must go to all people, and Christ has declared that it is to be proclaimed in the highways and in the byways. "Cry aloud, spare not," He commands. This means that wherever they shall present the truth, whether before a public congregation or from house to house, they are to present it as it is revealed in God's Word.—Manuscript 15, 1909.

Not to Wait for Souls to Come to Us—We are not to wait for souls to come to us; we must seek them out where they are. When the Word has been preached in the pulpit, the work has but just began. There are multitudes who will never be reached by the gospel unless it is carried to them.—Christ's Object Lessons, 229.

Labor from house to house, not neglecting the poor, who are usually passed by. Christ said, "He hath anointed Me to preach the gospel to the poor," and we are to go and do likewise.—The Review and Herald, June 11, 1895.

"I Am Lost! and You Never Warned Me!"—Go to the homes of those even who manifest no interest. While mercy's sweet voice invites the sinner, work with every energy of heart and brain, as did Paul, "who ceased not to warn every one night and day with tears." In the day of God how many will confront us and say, "I am lost! I am lost! And you never warned me; you never entreated me to come to Jesus. Had I believed as you did, I would have followed every Judgment-bound soul within my reach with prayers and tears and warnings."—The Review and Herald, June 24, 1884.

Relationship of Visitation Evangelism to Our Own Spirituality—Visit your neighbors in a friendly way, and become acquainted with them....Those who do not take up this work, those who act with the indifference that some have manifested, will soon lose their first love and will begin to censure, criticise, and condemn their own brethren.—The Review and Herald, May 13, 1902.

The Work Not Dull or Uninteresting—All who commune with God will find abundance of work to do for Him. Those who go forth in the spirit of the Master, seeking to reach souls with the truth, will not find the work of drawing souls to Christ a dull, uninteresting drudgery. They are charged with a work as God's husbandmen, and they will become more and more vitalized as they give themselves to the service of God. It is a joyous work to open the Scriptures to others.—Testimonies for the Church 9:118.

Make Others Happy—Be joyful in God. Christ is light, and in Him is no darkness at all. Look toward the light. Accustom yourselves to speak the praise of God. Make others happy. This is your first work. It will strengthen the best traits of character. Throw the windows of the soul wide open heavenward, and let the sunshine of Christ's righteousness in. Morning, noon, and night your hearts may be filled with the bright rays of heaven's light.—The Review and Herald, April 7, 1904.

Rekindle the Spirit of Evangelism of 1844[This, Ellen G. White's last message to the General Conference in session in 1913, was read to the Conference by the president, A. G. Daniells, Tuesday morning, May 27.]—Recently in the night season my mind was impressed by the holy spirit with the thought that if the Lord is coming as soon as we believe he is, we ought to be even more active than we have been in years past in getting the truth before the people.

In this connection my mind reverted to the activity of the Advent believers in 1843 and 1844. At that time there was much house-to-house visitation, and untiring efforts were made to warn the people of the things that are spoken in God's Word. We should be putting forth even greater effort than was put forth by those who proclaimed the first angel's message so faithfully. We are rapidly approaching the end of this earth's history; and as we realize that Jesus is indeed coming soon, we shall be aroused to labor as never before. We are bidden to sound an alarm to the people.—The General Conference Bulletin, May 27, 1913, p. 164.

Bring This Work Into Practice Again—As, like the disciples, you go from place to place, telling the story of the Saviour's love, you will make friends and will see the fruit of your labor. All true, humble, loving, faithful workers will be sustained and strengthened by power from on high. They will win their way to the hearts of the people as they follow Christ's example. The sick will be ministered to, the afflicted prayed for. There will be heard the voice of singing and the voice of prayer. The Scriptures will be opened to testify of truth. And with signs following, the Lord will confirm the word spoken.

This class of work has gone out of fashion. Let it be once more brought into practice. The fields are white all ready to harvest.

The Lord desires many more to go out into the harvest field. He will be with those who study His Word and obey His commands. He will impart to them His grace. Go forth in the name of Christ, remembering that He is your companion, that every prayer, every word, every song, is heard by Him. The message of the soon coming of the Lord with power and great glory will bring conviction to many hearts.—The Review and Herald, February 4, 1904.

[81]
Chapter 10—Kindness the Key to Hearts

Many Reached Only by Love and Kindness—Those who engage in house-to-house labor will find opportunities for ministry in many lines. They should pray for the sick and should do all in their power to relieve them from suffering. They should work among the lowly, the poor, and the oppressed. We should pray for and with the helpless ones who have not strength of will to control the appetites that passion has degraded. Earnest, persevering effort must be made for the salvation of those in whose hearts an interest is awakened. Many can be reached only through acts of disinterested kindness. Their physical wants must first be relieved. As they see evidence of our unselfish love, it will be easier for them to believe in the love of Christ.

Missionary nurses are best qualified for this work, but others should be connected with them. These, although not specially educated and trained in nursing, can learn from their fellow workers the best manner of labor.

Talk, Pharisaism, and self-praise are abundant; but these will never win souls to Christ. Pure, sanctified love, such love as was expressed in Christ's lifework, is as a sacred perfume. Like Mary's broken box of ointment, it fills the whole house with fragrance. Eloquence, knowledge of truth, rare talents, mingled with love, are all precious endowments. But ability alone, the choicest talents alone, cannot take the place of love.—Testimonies for the Church 6:83, 84.

With Love Which Springs From the Heart—Love is the basis
[82] of godliness. Whatever the profession, no man has pure love to God unless he has unselfish love for his brother. But we can never come into possession of this spirit by *trying* to love others. What is needed is the love of Christ in the heart. When self is merged in Christ, love springs forth spontaneously. The completeness of Christian character is attained when the impulse to help and bless others

springs constantly from within—when the sunshine of heaven fills the heart and is revealed in the countenance.

It is not possible for the heart in which Christ abides to be destitute of love. If we love God because He first loved us, we shall love all for whom Christ died. We cannot come in touch with divinity without coming in touch with humanity; for in Him who sits upon the throne of the universe, divinity and humanity are combined. Connected with Christ, we are connected with our fellow men by the golden links of the chain of love. Then the pity and compassion of Christ will be manifest in our life. We shall not wait to have the needy and unfortunate brought to us. We shall not need to be entreated to feel for the woes of others. It will be as natural for us to minister to the needy and suffering as it was for Christ to go about doing good.

Wherever there is an impulse of love and sympathy, wherever the heart reaches out to bless and uplift others, there is revealed the working of God's Holy Spirit.—Christ's Object Lessons, 384, 385.

Christ's Love and Sympathy Drew the People—It was the outcast, the publican and sinner, the despised of the nations, that Christ called, and by His loving-kindness compelled to come unto Him. The one class that He would never countenance was those who stood apart in their self-esteem, and looked down upon others.—The Ministry of Healing, 164.

To Love as Christ Loved—The love that is inspired by the love we have for Jesus will see in every soul, rich and poor, a value that cannot be measured by human estimate. The world sinks into insignificance in comparison with the value of one soul. The love of God revealed for man is beyond any human computation. It is infinite. And the human agent who is a partaker of the divine nature will love as Christ loves, will work as Christ worked. There will be an inborn compassion and sympathy which will not fail or be discouraged. This is the spirit that should be encouraged to live in every heart and be revealed in every life. This love can only exist and be kept refined, holy, pure, and elevated through the love in the soul for Jesus Christ, nourished by daily communion with God. All this coldness on the part of Christians is a denial of the faith. But this spirit will melt away before the bright beams of Christ's love in the

[83]

follower of Christ. Willingly, naturally, he will obey the injunction, "Love one another as I have loved you."—Manuscript 60, 1897.

Pray for Sympathetic Hearts—As surely as we believe in Christ and do His will, not exalting self, but walking in all humility of mind, so surely will the Lord be with us.... Pray that He will give you a heart of flesh, a heart that can feel the sorrows of others, that can be touched with human woe. Pray that He will give you a heart that will not permit you to turn a deaf ear to the widow or the fatherless. Pray that you may have bowels of mercy for the poor, the infirm, and the oppressed. Pray that you may love justice and hate robbery, and make no difference in the bestowal of your favors, except to consider the cases of the needy and the unfortunate. Then the promises recorded in Isaiah 58 will be fulfilled to you.—Letter 24, 1889.

Speaking a Word of Courage—Never, never become heartless, cold, unsympathetic, and censorious. Never lose an opportunity to say a word to encourage and inspire hope.—Testimonies for the Church 5:613.

In working for the victims of evil habits, instead of pointing them to the despair and ruin toward which they are hastening, turn their eyes to Jesus. Fix them upon the glories of the heavenly. This will do more for the saving of body and soul than will all the terrors of the grave when kept before the helpless and apparently hopeless.—The Ministry of Healing, 62.

No One Reclaimed by Reproach—It is always humiliating to have one's errors pointed out. None should make the experience more bitter by needless censure. No one was ever reclaimed by reproach; but many have thus been repelled, and have been led to steel their hearts against conviction. A tender spirit, a gentle, winning deportment may save the erring and hide a multitude of sins.—The Ministry of Healing, 166.

Encourage a Love of Hospitality—As you regard your eternal interest, arouse yourselves, and begin to sow good seed. That which ye sow shall ye also reap. The harvest is coming—the great reaping time, when we shall reap what we have sown. There will be no failure in the crop. The harvest is sure. Now is the sowing time. Now make efforts to be rich in good works, "ready to distribute, willing to communicate; laying up in store for themselves a good foundation against the time to come, that they may lay hold on eternal life." I implore you, my brethren, in every place, rid yourselves of your icy coldness. Encourage in yourselves a love of hospitality, a love to help those who need help.—The Review and Herald, April 20, 1886.

Revive the Spirit of the Good Samaritan—The spirit of the good Samaritan has not been largely represented in our churches. Many in need of help have been passed by, as the priest and Levite passed by the wounded and bruised stranger who had been left to die by the wayside. The very ones who needed the power of the divine Healer to cure their wounds have been left uncared for and unnoticed. Many have acted as if it were enough to know that Satan had his trap all set for a soul, and they could go home and care not for the lost sheep. It is evident that those who manifest such a spirit have not been partakers of the divine nature, but of the attributes of the enemy of God.—Testimonies for the Church 6:294, 295.

Sympathy as Well as Charity—I have been shown that among those who accept present truth there are many whose dispositions and characters need converting. Everyone who claims to be a Christian should examine himself, and see if he is as kind and considerate of his fellow beings as he desires his fellow beings to be of him. When this is done there will be a showing that is after the divine similitude.

The Lord is honored by our acts of mercy, by the exercise of thoughtful consideration for the unfortunate and distressed. The widow and the fatherless need more than our charity. They need sympathy and watchcare and compassionate words and a helping hand to place them where they can learn to help themselves. All deeds done for those who need help are as if done to Christ. In our study to know how to help the unfortunate we should study the way in which Christ worked. He did not refuse to work for those who made mistakes; His works of mercy were done for every class, the righteous and the unrighteous. For all alike He healed disease and gave lessons of instruction if they humbly asked Him.

Those who claim to believe in Christ are to represent Christ in deeds of kindness and mercy. Such will never know until the day of judgment what good they have done in seeking to follow the example of the Saviour.—Letter 140, 1908.

Kindness the Key to Greater Evangelism—If we would humble ourselves before God, and be kind and courteous and tenderhearted and pitiful, there would be one hundred conversions to the truth where now there is only one.—Testimonies for the Church 9:189.

Chapter 11—How to Visit and What to Do

Come Close to Your Neighbors—Go to your neighbors one by one, and come close to them till their hearts are warmed by your unselfish interest and love. Sympathize with them, pray for them, watch for opportunities to do them good, and as you can, gather a few together and open the Word of God to their darkened minds.—The Review and Herald, March 13, 1888.

Help Where Help is Needed Most—There are those all around you who have woes, who need words of sympathy, love, and tenderness, and our humble, pitying prayers. Some are suffering under the iron hand of poverty, some with disease, and others with heartaches, despondency, and gloom. Like Job, you should be eyes to the blind and feet to the lame, and you should inquire into the cause which you know not and search it out with the object in view to relieve their necessities and help just where they most need help.—Testimonies for the Church 3:530.

First meet the temporal necessities of the needy and relieve their physical wants and sufferings, and you will then find an open avenue to the heart, where you may plant the good seeds of virtue and religion.—Testimonies for the Church 4:227.

A Persuasive Approach—Approach the people in a persuasive, kindly manner, full of cheerfulness and love for Christ.... No human tongue can express the preciousness of the ministration of the Word and the Holy Spirit. No human expression can portray to the finite mind the value of understanding and by living faith receiving the blessing that is given as Jesus of Nazareth passes by.—Letter 60, 1903.

Maintain Proper Attitude Toward People—It is a delicate matter to deal with minds. Only He who reads the heart knows how to bring men to repentance. Only His wisdom can give us success in reaching the lost. You may stand up stiffly, feeling, "I am holier than thou," and it matters not how correct your reasoning or how true your words; they will never touch hearts. The love of Christ, manifested in word and act, will win its way to the soul, when the reiteration of precept or argument would accomplish nothing.—The Ministry of Healing, 163, 164.

Show Heartfelt Sympathy—We need more of Christlike sympathy; not merely sympathy for those who appear to us to be faultless, but sympathy for poor, suffering, struggling souls, who are often overtaken in fault, sinning and repenting, tempted and discouraged. We are to go to our fellow men, touched, like our merciful High Priest, with the feeling of their infirmities.—The Ministry of Healing, 164.

Work in a Way That Will Remove Prejudice—My brethren and sisters, visit those who live near you, and by sympathy and kindness seek to reach their hearts. Be sure to work in a way that will remove prejudice instead of creating it. And remember that those who know the truth for this time and yet confine their efforts to their own churches, refusing to work for their unconverted neighbors, will be called to account for unfulfilled duties.—Testimonies for the Church 9:34, 35.

[89]
Get Into the Home When You Can—Come close to the people; get into the families when you can; do not wait for the people to hunt up the shepherd.—Letter 8, 1895.

The Three Important Steps in House-to-House Ministry—The burden now is to convince souls of the truth. This can best be done by personal efforts, by bringing the truth into their houses, praying with them, and opening to them the Scriptures.—The Review and Herald, December 8, 1885.

Importance of the Handshake—Much depends upon the manner in which you meet those whom you visit. You can take hold of a person's hand in greeting in such a way as to gain his confidence at once, or in so cold a manner that he will think you have no interest in him.—Gospel Workers, 189.

Christian Politeness Needed—There are enough who want to be Christians, and if we will let the leaven begin to work, it will take one and then another, just as the spirit of God will work with us and we will see that we can reach the people, not by our own smartness, but by the Spirit of God. Yet we want the ability and power that God has given us to be brought into use. We do not want to be novices forever; we want to know how to conduct ourselves properly; we want Christian politeness. And we want to carry it with us in all our work. We do not want any of the sharp corners which may be in our character to be made prominent, but we want to work in humility, so we will forget them, and better characteristics will come in. We want cheerfulness in our work.—Manuscript 10, 1888.

Power of Courtesy—The cultivation of a uniform courtesy, a willingness to do to others as we would wish them to do to us, would annihilate half the ills of life. The spirit of self-aggrandizement is the spirit of Satan; but the heart in which the love of Christ is cherished, will possess that charity which seeketh not her own.—Patriarchs and Prophets, 133.

Proper Attitude Toward Poor—You don't want to hold yourselves as though it were a condescension to come in contact with poor families. Talk as though they were as good a piece of humanity as you are. They have little enough light and joy, and why not carry additional joy and light to shine in upon them and fill their hearts. What we want is the tender sympathy of Jesus Christ, and then we can melt our way right into their hearts. We want to clothe ourselves, not with pomposity, but with plain simple dress, so that they will feel that we are an equal with them and as though we considered that they were worth saving, and we can melt our way into their hearts.

Now, brethren and sisters, we want the iron taken out of our souls, and we want it taken out of our manner of work. We can educate workers in every church.—Manuscript 10, 1888.

Tactful as Was Christ—He had tact to meet the prejudiced minds, and surprise them with illustrations that won their attention. Through the imagination He reached the heart.—The Desire of Ages, 254.

Talk Courage—Do not utter one despondent word, for such words please Satan. Talk of Christ's goodness and tell of His power. Words of hope and trust and courage are as easily spoken as words of complaint. "Rejoice in the Lord alway: and again I say, Rejoice."—The Review and Herald, April 7, 1904.

Come to the Point—Now, when we go into the house we should not begin to talk of frivolous things, but come right to the point and say, I want you to love Jesus, for He has first loved you.... Take along the publications and ask them to read. When they see that you are sincere they will not despise any of your efforts. There is a way to reach the hardest hearts. Approach in the simplicity, and sincerity, and humility that will help us to reach the souls of them for whom Christ died.—Manuscript 10, 1888.

Present Christ by the Fireside—To all who are working with Christ I would say, Wherever you can gain access to the people by the fireside, improve your opportunity. Take your Bible, and open before them its great truths. Your success will not depend so much upon your knowledge and accomplishments as upon your ability to find your way to the heart. By being social and coming close to the people, you may turn the current of their thoughts more readily than by the most able discourse. The presentation of Christ in the family, by the fireside, and in small gatherings in private houses is often more successful in winning souls to Jesus than are sermons delivered in the open air, to the moving throng, or even in halls or churches.—Gospel Workers, 193.

Tell How You Found Jesus—Visit your neighbors and show an interest in the salvation of their souls. Arouse every spiritual energy to action. Tell those whom you visit that the end of all things is at hand. The Lord Jesus Christ will open the door of their hearts and will make upon their minds lasting impressions.

Strive to arouse men and women from their spiritual insensibility. Tell them how you found Jesus and how blessed you have been since you gained an experience in His service. Tell them what blessing comes to you as you sit at the feet of Jesus and learn precious lessons from His Word. Tell them of the gladness and joy that there is in the Christian life. Your warm, fervent words will convince them that you have found the pearl of great price. Let your cheerful, encouraging words show that you have certainly found the higher way. This is genuine missionary work, and as it is done, many will awake as from a dream.—Testimonies for the Church 9:38.

Present Christ and His Melting Love—There are many souls yearning unutterably for light, for assurance and strength beyond what they have been able to grasp. They need to be sought out and labored for patiently, perseveringly. Beseech the Lord in fervent prayer for help. Present Jesus because you know Him as your personal Saviour. Let His melting love, His rich grace, flow forth from human lips. You need not present doctrinal points unless questioned. But take the Word, and with tender, yearning love for souls, show them the precious righteousness of Christ, to whom you and they must come to be saved.—Manuscript 27, 1895.

In all your labor let it appear that you know Jesus. Present His purity and saving grace, so that those for whom you labor may, by beholding, be changed into the divine image. The chain that is let down from the throne of God is long enough to reach to the lowest depths of sin. Hold up a sin-pardoning Saviour before the lost and lonely, for Jesus has made divine intercession in their behalf. He is able to lift them from the pit of sin, that they may be acknowledged as the children of God, heirs with Christ to an immortal inheritance. They may have the life that measures with the life of God.—The Review and Herald, April 11, 1912.

The Power of Sacred Songs—Those who have the gift of song are needed. Song is one of the most effective means of impressing spiritual truth upon the heart. Often by the words of sacred song the springs of penitence and faith have been unsealed. Church members, young and old, should be educated to go forth to proclaim this last message to the world. If they go in humility, angels of God will go with them, teaching them how to lift up the voice in prayer, how to raise the voice in song, and how to proclaim the gospel message for this time.—The Review and Herald, June 6, 1912.

Hearts Touched by Simple Songs—Learn to sing the simplest of songs. These will help you in house-to-house labor, and hearts will be touched by the influence of the Holy Spirit. Christ was often heard singing hymns of praise; and yet I have heard persons say, "Christ never smiled." How mistaken their ideas in regard to the Saviour! There was joy in His heart. We learn from the Word that there is joy among the heavenly angels over one repentant sinner, and that the Lord Himself rejoices over His church with singing.—The Review and Herald, November 11, 1902.

Talk Familiarly and Make Personal Appeals—Personal, individual effort and interest for your friends and neighbors will accomplish more than can be estimated. It is for the want of this kind of labor that souls for whom Christ died are perishing.... Your work may accomplish more real good than the more extensive meetings, if they lack in personal effort. When both are combined, with the blessing of God, a more perfect and thorough work may be wrought; but if we can have but one part done, let it be the individual labor of opening the Scriptures in households, making personal appeals, and talking familiarly with the members of the family, not about things of little importance, but of the great themes of redemption. Let them see that your heart is burdened for the salvation of souls.—The Review and Herald, March 13, 1888.

Effectiveness of the Question Technique—My ministering brethren, do not think that the only work you can do, the only way you can labor for souls, is to give discourses. The best work you can do is to teach, to educate. Whenever you can find an opportunity to do so, sit down with some family, and let them ask questions. Then answer them patiently, humbly. Continue this work in connection with your more public efforts. Preach less, and educate more, by holding Bible readings and by praying with families and little companies.—Gospel Workers, 193.

With a Voice Full of Pathos—Let the voice express sympathy and tenderness. Christ's voice was full of pathos. By persevering effort we can cultivate the voice, ridding it of all harshness. Let us ask in faith for a converted voice, a converted tongue, and for Christlike sympathy and tenderness, that we may win souls to the truth we teach.—The Review and Herald, November 11, 1902.

If They Shut the Door in Your Face, What Then?—"But," says one, "suppose we cannot gain admittance to the homes of the people; and if we do suppose they rise up against the truths that we present. Shall we not feel excused from making further efforts for them?" By no means. Even if they shut the door in your face, do not hasten away in indignation, and make no further effort to save them. Ask God in faith to give you access to those very souls. Cease not your efforts, but study and plan until you find some other means of reaching them. If you do not succeed by personal visits, try sending them the silent messenger of truth. There is so much pride of opinion in the human heart that our publications often gain admittance where the living messenger cannot.—Historical Sketches, 150.

How Christ Met the People—We shall gain much instruction for our work from a study of Christ's methods of labor and His manner of meeting the people. In the gospel story we have the record of how He worked for all classes, and of how as He labored in cities and towns thousands were drawn to His side to hear His teaching. The words of the Master were clear and distinct and were spoken in sympathy and tenderness. They carried with them the assurance that here was truth. It was the simplicity and earnestness with which Christ labored and spoke that drew so many to Him.—The Review and Herald, January 18, 1912.

Not Mechanical in Labor—All who engage in this personal labor should be just as careful not to become mechanical in their manner of working as should the minister who preaches the Word. They should be constantly learning.—Gospel Workers, 193.

Devise New Methods—I address Christians who live in our large cities: God has made you depositories of truth, not that you may retain it, but that you may impart it to others. You should visit from house to house as faithful stewards of the grace of Christ. As you work, devise, and plan, new methods will continually present themselves to your mind, and by use the powers of your intellect will be increased. A lukewarm, slack performance of duty is an injury to the soul for whom Christ has died. If we would find the pearls buried in the debris of the cities, we should go forth ready to do the work required by the Master.—The Review and Herald, June 11, 1895.

New Life and New Plans—Men are needed who pray to God for wisdom, and who, under the guidance of God, can put new life into the old methods of labor and can invent new plans and new methods of awakening the interest of church members and reaching the men and women of the world.—Manuscript 117, 1907.

In the Power of Persuasion, Prayer, and Love—The poor are to be relieved, the sick cared for, the sorrowing and the bereaved comforted, the ignorant instructed, the inexperienced counseled. We are to weep with those that weep and rejoice with those that rejoice. Accompanied by the power of persuasion, the power of prayer, the power of the love of God, this work will not, cannot, be without fruit.—The Ministry of Healing, 143, 144.

Chapter 12—The Effectiveness of Visitation Evangelism

The Place of Visitation Evangelism in Finishing God's Work on Earth—How can the great work of the third angel's message be accomplished? It must be largely accomplished by persevering, individual effort, by visiting the people in their homes.—Historical Sketches, 150.

One of the most effective ways in which light can be communicated is by private, personal effort. In the home circle, at your neighbor's fireside, at the bedside of the sick, in a quiet way you may read the Scriptures and speak a word for Jesus and the truth. Thus you may sow precious seed that will spring up and bring forth fruit.—Testimonies for the Church 6:428, 429.

Repaid a Thousand Times—Wake up, brethren and sisters. Don't be afraid of good works. Be not weary in well-doing, for you shall reap in due time if you faint not.... Encourage in yourselves a love of hospitality, a love to help those who need help.

You may say you have been deceived, bestowing your means upon those unworthy of your charity, and therefore have become discouraged in trying to help the needy. I present Jesus before you.... One soul wrenched from Satan's grasp; one soul you have benefited; one soul encouraged! This will a thousand times pay you for all your efforts. To you Jesus will say, "Inasmuch as ye have done it unto the least of these My brethren, ye have done it unto Me." Should we not gladly do all we can to imitate the life of our divine Lord?—The Review and Herald, April 20, 1886.

Vital to Our Own Eternal Destiny—As you engage in this work you have companions unseen by human eyes. Angels of heaven were beside the Samaritan who cared for the wounded stranger. Angels from the heavenly courts stand by all who do God's service in ministering to their fellow-men. And you have the cooperation of Christ Himself. He is the Restorer, and as you work under His supervision you will see great results. Upon your faithfulness in this work, not only the well-being of others, but your own eternal destiny depends.—Christ's Object Lessons, 388.

Christ Enters the Homes With Them—The Lord desires that the truth shall come close to the people, and this can be accomplished only by personal labor. Much is comprehended in the command, "Go out into the highways and hedges, and compel them to come in, that My house may be filled." There is a work to be done in this line that has not yet been done. Let God's workers teach the truth in families, drawing close to those for whom they labor. If they thus cooperate with God, He will clothe them with spiritual power. Christ will guide them in their work, entering the houses of the people with them and giving them words to speak that will sink deep into the hearts of the listeners. The Holy Spirit will open hearts and minds to receive the rays coming from the Source of all light.—The Review and Herald, December 29, 1904.

Bring Hope to the People—It is impossible for the man who believes in Christ to see the work that needs to be done and yet do nothing. Daily we are to receive from Heaven the healing balm of God's grace to impart to the needy and suffering. Christ's followers are to learn of the woes of the poor in their immediate vicinity and seek to bring them relief. Those who have a dark and disagreeable life are the very ones whom we should bid to hope because Christ is their Saviour. Are there not those who can go from house to house, from family to family, and repeat the A B C of true Christian experience?—The Review and Herald, April 11, 1912.

E. G. White's Experience in Visitation—I remember when the converting power of God came upon me in my childhood I wanted everyone else to get the blessing that I had, and I could not rest till I had told them of it. I began to visit with my young companions and went to their houses to talk with them and tell them my experience, how precious the Saviour was to me, and how I wanted to serve Him, and how I wanted them to serve Him also. So I would talk of the preciousness of Christ, and I would say, "Won't you kneel down and pray with me?" Some would kneel and some would sit in their chairs, but before we gave up, everyone would be on her knees and we would pray together for hours, till the last one would say, "I believe that Jesus has forgiven me my sins." Sometimes the sun would begin to make its appearance in the heavens before I would give up the struggle. There is a great power in Jesus.—Manuscript 10, 1888.

The "First Works" Bring Results—The reason so many fail to have success is that they trust in themselves altogether too much, and do not feel the positive necessity of abiding in Christ, as they go forth to seek and save that which is lost. Until they have the mind of Christ and teach the truth as it is in Jesus, they will not accomplish much....

The atmosphere of the church is so frigid, its spirit is of such an order, that men and women cannot sustain or endure the example of primitive and heaven-born piety. The warmth of their first love is frozen up, and unless they are watered over by the baptism of the Holy Spirit, their candlestick will be removed out of its place, except they repent and do their first works. The first works of the church were seen when the believers sought out friends, relatives, and acquaintances, and with hearts overflowing with love, told the story of what Jesus was to them and what they were to Jesus.—Testimonies to Ministers and Gospel Workers, 167, 168.

You Are a Letter; Deliver It!—The apostle Paul says to the disciples of Jesus, "Ye are manifestly declared to be the epistle of Christ," "known and read of all men." In every one of His children Jesus sends a letter to the world. If you are Christ's follower, He sends in you a letter to the family, the village, the street, where you live. Jesus, dwelling in you, desires to speak to the hearts of those who are not acquainted with Him. Perhaps they do not read the Bible or do not hear the voice that speaks to them in its pages; they do not see the love of God through His works. But if you are a true representative of Jesus, it may be that through you they will be led to understand something of His goodness, and be won to love and serve Him.—Steps to Christ, 119.

The Literature We Leave in the Homes Will Bear Fruit—"Your feet shod with the preparation of the gospel of peace," you will be prepared to walk from house to house carrying the truth to the people. Sometimes you will find it very trying to do work of this kind; but if you go forth in faith, the Lord will go before you, and His light will shine upon your pathway. As you enter the homes of your neighbors to sell or to give away our literature, and in humility to teach them the truth, you will be accompanied by the light of heaven.—The Review and Herald, November 11, 1902.

God will soon do great things for us if we lie humble and believing at His feet.... More than one thousand will soon be converted in one day, most of whom will trace their first convictions to the reading of our publications.—The Review and Herald, November 10, 1885.

The Best Way to Reach Souls—In the very shadows of the houses of God there are multitudes of godless sinners, without a knowledge of the truth, without hope.... In every city, in every settlement where Christians meet to worship God, there are men and women and children to be gathered into the fold. Many never hear a discourse on God's Word. Who will take upon himself a burden for souls? Who will learn from the Great Teacher that the best way to reach souls is by direct, personal appeal to erring individuals, to those who are dead in trespasses and sins, to behold their uplifted, crucified Redeemer, and live? Christians, let your hearts be filled with sympathy and love for those who know not the truth.—Manuscript 81, 1900.

Situations Adapted to Our Talents—If the teachers of His Word are willing, the Lord will lead them into close relation with the people. He will guide them into the homes of those who need and desire the truth, bringing them into the situations best suited to their talents.—Letter 95, 1896.

Talents of All Needed—The Lord has a place for everyone in His great plan. Talents that are not needed are not bestowed. To every man God gives talents, which are to be improved according to His several ability. Supposing the talent is small, God has a place for it; and that one talent, if used, will do the very work God designed that it should do. The talents of the humble cottager are needed in house-to-house labor and can accomplish more in this work than brilliant gifts. And he who uses aright his one talent will be as verily rewarded as he who uses aright five talents. It is for working according to the ability given that God rewards His servants.—Letter 41, 1899.

How to Find Time for Neighborly Visits—If the young men and the young women would solemnly consecrate themselves to God, if they would practice self-denial in the home life, relieving their tired, careworn mothers, what a change would take place in our churches. The mother could find time to make neighborly visits. When opportunity offered, the children could give assistance by doing, when quite young, little errands of mercy and love to bless others. Thus thousands of the homes of the poor and needy could be entered. Books relating to health and temperance could be placed in many homes. The circulation of these books is an important work, for they contain precious knowledge in regard to the treatment of disease—knowledge that would be a great blessing to those who cannot afford to pay for the physician's visits.—Manuscript 119, 1901.

"Do Not Wait to Be Told Your Duty."—Do not wait to be told your duty. Open your eyes and see who are around you; make yourselves acquainted with the helpless, afflicted, and needy. Hide not yourselves from them and seek not to shut out their needs. Who gives the proofs mentioned in James, of possessing pure religion, untainted with selfishness or corruption?—Testimonies for the Church 2:29.

Break the Spell: "Go to Work, Whether You Feel Like It or Not."—My brethren and sisters, do you desire to break the spell that holds you? Would you arouse from this sluggishness that resembles the torpor of death? Go to work, whether you feel like it or not. Engage in personal effort to bring souls to Jesus and the knowledge of the truth. In such labor you will find both a stimulus and a tonic; it will both arouse and strengthen. By exercise your spiritual powers will become more vigorous, so that you can with better success work out your own salvation. The stupor of death is upon many who profess Christ. Make every effort to arouse them. Warn, entreat, expostulate. Pray that the melting love of God may warm and soften their icebound natures. Though they may refuse to hear, your labor will not be lost. In the effort to bless others your own souls will be blessed.—Testimonies for the Church 5:387.

Carrying the Atmosphere of Heaven—Visiting the sick, comforting the poor and the sorrowful for Christ's sake, will bring to the workers the bright beams of the Sun of Righteousness, and even the countenance will express the peace that dwells in the soul. The faces of men and women who talk with God, to whom the invisible world is a reality, express the peace of God. They carry with them the soft and genial atmosphere of heaven, and diffuse it in deeds of kindness and works of love. Their influence is of a character to win souls to Christ. If all could see and understand, and be doers of the words of God, what peace, what happiness, what health of body and peace of soul, would be the result! A warm, kindly atmosphere of love, the pitying tenderness of Christ in the soul cannot be estimated. The price of love is above gold and silver and precious stones, and makes human agents like Him who lived not to please Himself.—Letter 43, 1895.

"Hundreds and Thousands Were Seen Visiting Families."—In visions of the night representations passed before me of a great reformatory movement among God's people. Many were praising God. The sick were healed, and other miracles were wrought. A spirit of intercession was seen, even as was manifested before the great day of Pentecost. Hundreds and thousands were seen visiting families and opening before them the Word of God. Hearts were convicted by the power of the Holy Spirit, and a spirit of genuine conversion was manifest. On every side doors were thrown open to the proclamation of the truth. The world seemed to be lighted with the heavenly influence. Great blessings were received by the true and humble people of God. I heard voices of thanksgiving and praise, and there seemed to be a reformation such as we witnessed in 1844.—Testimonies for the Church 9:126.

Chapter 13—Organizing the Church for Welfare Ministry

God's Purpose in Church Organization—The church of Christ on earth was organized for missionary purposes, and the Lord desires to see the entire church devising ways and means whereby high and low, rich and poor, may hear the message of truth.—Testimonies for the Church 6:29.

To Unite in Exercises of Charity—Wherever the truth has been proclaimed and people have been awakened and converted, the believers are at once to unite in exercises of charity. Wherever Bible truth has been presented, a work of practical godliness is to be begun. Wherever a church is established, missionary work is to be done for the helpless and the suffering.—Testimonies for the Church 6:84, 85.

A Call for Men Who Can Lead—Unless there are those who will devise means of turning to account the time, strength, and brains of the church members, there will be a great work left undone that ought to be done. Haphazard work will not answer. We want men in the church who have ability to develop in the line of organizing and giving practical work to young men and women in the line of relieving the wants of humanity, and working for the salvation of the souls of men, women, youth, and children.—Letter 12, 1892.

Like a Training School—Every church should be a training school for Christian workers. Its members should be taught how to give Bible readings, how to conduct and teach Sabbath school classes, how best to help the poor and to care for the sick, how to work for the unconverted. There should be schools of health, cooking schools, and classes in various lines of Christian help work. There should not only be teaching, but actual work under experienced instructors. Let the teachers lead the way in working among the people, and others, uniting with them, will learn from their example. One example is worth more than many precepts.—The Ministry of Healing, 149.

Preparing Our Youth for Practical Service—The Great Teacher cooperates with all the efforts made to relieve suffering humanity. Teach the students to make a practical application of the lessons they have received. As they witness human woe and the deep poverty of those they are trying to help, they will be stirred with compassion. Their hearts will be softened and subdued by the deep, holy principles revealed in the Word of God. The great Physician cooperates with every effort made in behalf of suffering humanity, to give health to the body and light and restoration to the soul.... We must now see what can be done to educate the students in practical missionary work.—Manuscript 70, 1898.

Teach Practical Missionary Work—On such occasions as our annual camp meetings we must never lose sight of the opportunities afforded for teaching the believers how to do practical missionary work in the place where they may live. In many instances it would be well to set apart certain men to carry the burden of different lines of educational work at these meetings. Let some help the people to learn how to give Bible readings and to conduct cottage meetings. Let others bear the burden of teaching the people how to practice the principles of health and temperance and how to give treatments to the sick. Still others may labor in the interests of our periodical and book work.—Testimonies for the Church 9:82, 83.

Form Bands of Workers—The formation of small companies as a basis of Christian effort has been presented to me by One who cannot err. If there is a large number in the church, let the members be formed into small companies, to work not only for the church members but for unbelievers. If in one place there are only two or three who know the truth, let them form themselves into a band of workers. Let them keep their bond of union unbroken, pressing together in love and unity, encouraging one another to advance, each gaining courage and strength from the assistance of the others.—Testimonies for the Church 7:21, 22.

Well-organized Companies in Every Church—Let there be in every church well-organized companies of workers to labor in the vicinity of that church. Put self behind you, and let Christ go before as your life and power. Let this work be entered into without delay, and the truth will be as leaven in the earth. When such forces are set to work in all our churches, there will be a renovating, reforming, energizing power in the churches, because the members are doing the very work that God has given them to do. Let all our churches be active, zealous, filled with enthusiasm by the Spirit and power of God. It is the intelligent use of the means, the capabilities, the powers, given you by God, consecrated to His service, that will tell in the communities where you may labor. It may be that you will have to make a very small beginning in some places; but do not be discouraged; the work will grow larger, and you will be doing the work of an evangelist. Look at Christ's manner of working, and strive to labor as He did.—The Review and Herald, September 29, 1891.

To Work Under a Name—In all God's work for man He plans that man shall cooperate with Him. To this end the Lord calls upon the church to have a higher piety, a more just sense of duty, a clearer realization of their obligations to their Creator. He calls upon them to be a pure, sanctified, working people. And the Christian help work is one means of bringing this about, for the Holy Spirit communicates with all who are doing God's service.... I would say: Continue to work with tact and ability. Arouse your associates to work under some name whereby they may be organized to cooperate in harmonious action. Get the young men and women in the churches to work.—Testimonies for the Church 6:266, 267.

Youth to Organize and Train for the Closing Work—There are many lines in which the youth can find opportunity for helpful effort. As they organize into bands for Christian service, their cooperation will prove an assistance and encouragement....

In this closing work of the gospel there is a vast field to be occupied; and, more than ever before, the work is to enlist helpers from the common people. Both the youth and those older in years will be called from the field, from the vineyard, and from the workshop, and sent forth by the Master to give His message. Many of these may have had little opportunity for education, but Christ sees in them qualifications that will enable them to fulfill His purpose. If they put their hearts into the work and continue to be learners, He will fit them to labor for Him.

With such preparation as they can gain, thousands upon thousands of the youth and those older in years should be giving themselves to the work. Already many hearts are responding to the call of the Master Worker, and their numbers will increase.

All who engage in ministry are God's helping hand. There is no line of work in which it is possible for the youth to receive greater benefit. They are co-workers with the angels; rather, they are human agencies through whom the angels accomplish their mission. Angels speak through their voices and work by their hands. And the human workers, cooperating with heavenly agencies, have the benefit of their education and experience. As a means of education what "university course" can equal this? With such an army of workers as our youth, rightly trained, might furnish, how soon the message of a crucified, risen, and soon-coming Saviour might be carried to the world!—The Youth's Instructor, March 3, 1908.

A Great Work to Be Done by Men Now Idle—It is not God's purpose that ministers should be left to do the greatest part of the work of sowing the seeds of truth. Men who are not called to the gospel ministry are to be encouraged to labor for the Master according to their several ability. Hundreds of men and women now idle could do acceptable service. By carrying the truth into the homes of their neighbors and friends, they could do a great work for the Master. God is no respecter of persons. He will use humble, devoted Christians who have the love of the truth in their hearts. Let such ones engage in service for him by doing house-to-house work. Sitting by the fireside, such men—if humble, discreet, and godly—can do more to meet the real needs of families than could a minister.—The Review and Herald, August 26, 1902.

The Best Help Ministers Can Give—The best help that ministers can give the members of our churches is not sermonizing but planning work for them. Give each one something to do for others.... If set to work, the despondent will soon forget their despondency; the weak will become strong; the ignorant, intelligent; and all will be prepared to present the truth as it is in Jesus.—Testimonies for the Church 9:82.

Everyone who is added to the ranks by conversion is to be assigned his post of duty. Everyone should be willing to be or to do anything in this warfare.—Testimonies for the Church 7:30.

Let All Cooperate—There has been so much preaching to our churches that they have almost ceased to appreciate the gospel ministry. The time has come when this order of things should be changed. Let the minister call out the individual church members to help him by house-to-house work in carrying the truth into regions beyond. Let all cooperate with the heavenly intelligences in communicating truth to others.—The Review and Herald, June 11, 1895.

All United to Finish the Work—Those who have the spiritual oversight of the church should devise ways and means by which an opportunity may be given to every member of the church to act some part in God's work. Too often in the past this has not been done. Plans have not been clearly laid and fully carried out whereby the talents of all might be employed in active service. There are but few who realize how much has been lost because of this.

The leaders in God's cause, as wise generals, are to lay plans for advance moves all along the line. In their planning they are to give special study to the work that can be done by the laity for their friends and neighbors. The work of God in this earth can never be finished until the men and women comprising our church membership rally to the work and unite their efforts with those of ministers and church officers.—Testimonies for the Church 9:116, 117.

Christ Can Be Represented in All Lawful Callings—All should be taught how to work. Especially should those who are newly come to the faith be educated to become laborers together with God. If this duty is neglected, the work of the minister is incomplete.

But God does not want His people to hang their weight upon the ministers. As a steward of the grace of God, every church member should feel an individual responsibility to have life and root in himself. All who are ordained unto the life of Christ are ordained to work for the salvation of their fellow men. He who loves God supremely and his neighbor as himself cannot rest content with doing nothing.

Did the professed believers in the truth live the truth, they would today all be missionaries. Some would be working in the islands of the sea; some, in the different countries of the world. Some would be serving Christ as home missionaries. Not all are called upon to go abroad. Some may be successful in business lines, and in this work they may represent Christ. They may show to the world that business may be conducted on righteous principles, in strict fidelity to the truth. There may be Christian lawyers, Christian physicians, Christian merchants. Christ may be represented in all lawful callings.—Manuscript 19, 1900.

Example of a Faithful Church—Sabbath morning, November 10, 1900, we entered the San Francisco church, and found it crowded to its utmost capacity. As I stood before the people I thought of the dream and the instruction which had been given me so many years ago, and I was much encouraged. Looking at the people assembled, I felt that I could indeed say, "The Lord has fulfilled His word."

During the past few years the "beehive" [Reference is here made to a revelation in 1876 when the activities of the then relatively new churches in San Francisco and Oakland were represented as two beehives.] in San Francisco has been indeed a busy one. Many lines of Christian effort have been carried forward by our brethren and sisters there. These included visiting the sick and destitute, finding homes for orphans and work for the unemployed, nursing the sick, and teaching the truth from house to house, distributing literature, and conducting classes on healthful living and the care of the sick. A school for the children has been conducted in the basement of the Laguna Street meetinghouse. For a time a workingmen's home and medical mission was maintained. On Market Street, near the city hall, there were treatment rooms, operated as a branch of the St. Helena Sanitarium. In the same locality was a health-food store. Nearer the center of the city, not far from the call building, was conducted a vegetarian cafe, which was open six days in the week and entirely closed on the Sabbath. Along the water front ship mission work was carried on. At various times our ministers conducted meetings in large halls in the city. Thus the warning message was given by many.—The Review and Herald, July 5, 1906.

For This Purpose the Church Is Organized—Someone must fulfill the commission of Christ; someone must carry on the work which He began to do on earth; and the church has been given this privilege. For this purpose it has been organized. Why, then, have not church members accepted the responsibility? There are those who have seen this great neglect; they have seen the needs of many who are in suffering and want; they have recognized in these poor souls those for whom Christ gave His life, and their hearts have been stirred with pity, every energy has been roused to action. They have entered upon a work of organizing those who will cooperate with them in bringing the truth of the gospel before many who are now in vice and iniquity, that they may be redeemed from a life of dissipation and sin.

Those who have been engaged in this Christian help work have been doing what the Lord desires to have done, and He has accepted their labors. That which has been done in this line is a work which every Seventh-day Adventist should heartily sympathize with and endorse, and take hold of earnestly.—Testimonies for the Church 6:295, 296.

Section 5—Relieving Suffering Humanity

Gem Thought

What a busy life Christ led! Day by day He might be seen entering the humble abodes of want and sorrow, speaking hope to the downcast and peace to the distressed. The poor and suffering received the greatest share of His attention. Children loved Him. They were drawn to Him by His ready sympathy. By His simple, loving words He settled many a difficulty arising among them. Often He took them on His knee and talked with them in a way that won their hearts.

His was the medical missionary work that He asks His people to do today. Humble, gracious, tenderhearted, pitiful, He went about doing good, feeding the hungry, lifting up the bowed down, comforting the sorrowing. None who came to Him for aid went away unrelieved. Not a thread of selfishness was woven into the pattern He has left for His children to follow. He lived the life that He would have all live who believe on Him. It was His meat and drink to do the will of His father. To all who came to Him for help He brought faith and hope and life. Wherever He went He carried blessing.

To us Christ's message is, "If any man will come after Me, let him deny himself, and take up his cross, and follow Me."—Manuscript 115, 1902.

And he sent them to preach the kingdom of God, and to heal the sick. Luke 9:2.

Chapter 14—In the Footsteps of the Master

Christ's Pattern of Medical Ministry—For three years the disciples had before them the wonderful example of Christ. Day by day they walked and talked with Him, hearing His words of cheer to the weary and heavy laden and seeing the manifestations of His power in behalf of the sick and afflicted. When the time came for Him to leave them, He gave them power to work as He had worked. He bestowed on them His grace, saying, "Freely ye have received, freely give." They were to go forth into the world to shed abroad the light of His gospel of love and healing. The work He had done they were to do.

And this is the work we also are to do in the world. In sympathy and compassion we are to minister to those in need of help, seeking with unselfish earnestness to lighten the woe of suffering humanity. As we engage in this work we shall be greatly blessed. Its influence is irresistible. By it souls are won to the Redeemer. The practical carrying out of the Saviour's commission demonstrates the power of the gospel. This work calls for laborious effort, but it pays; for by it perishing souls are saved. Through its influence men and women of talent are to be brought to the cross of Christ.

Man has a body as well as a soul to save. Both are to be restored to health by God's simple but efficacious methods, which appeal to men and women of intelligence. Through a belief in the truth souls are awakened to a need of a preparation for life's duties. As the health of the body is restored the powers of the mind are put forth to grasp the great truths of the gospel.—Letter 152, 1901.

First Meet the Temporal Necessities—The suffering and destitute of all classes are our neighbors, and when their wants are brought to our knowledge it is our duty to relieve them as far as possible. A principle is brought out in this parable [of the good Samaritan] that it would be well for the followers of Christ to adopt. First meet the temporal necessities of the needy and relieve their physical wants and sufferings, and you will then find an open avenue to the heart, where you may plant the good seeds of virtue and religion.—Testimonies for the Church 4:226, 227.

A World to Save—Remember that there is a world to save. We are to act our part, standing close by the side of Christ as his colaborers. He is the head; we are His helping hand. He designs that we, by doing medical missionary work, shall undo the heavy burdens and let the oppressed go free. Let us not close our eyes to the misery around us or our ears to the cries of distress which are continually ascending. Christ is the greatest missionary the world has ever known. He came to uplift and cheer the sorrowing and distressed, and in this work we are to cooperate with him.—Manuscript 31, 1901.

Find Christ's Footprints in the Hovels of Poverty—Many feel that it would be a great privilege to visit the scenes of Christ's life on earth, to walk where He trod, to look upon the lake beside which He loved to teach, and the hills and valleys on which His eyes so often rested. But we need not go to Nazareth, to Capernaum, or to Bethany in order to walk in the steps of Jesus. We shall find His footprints beside the sickbed, in the hovels of poverty, in the crowded alleys of the great city, and in every place where there are human hearts in need of consolation. In doing as Jesus did when on earth, we shall walk in His steps.—The Desire of Ages, 640.

The Gospel of Relief From Suffering—Medical missionary work brings to humanity the gospel of release from suffering. It is the pioneer work of the gospel. It is the gospel practiced, the compassion of Christ revealed. Of this work there is great need, and the world is open for it. God grant that the importance of medical missionary work shall be understood and that new fields may be immediately entered.—Manuscript 55, 1901.

Begin in Your Own Neighborhood—Before the true reformer, the medical missionary work will open many doors. No one need wait until called to some distant field before beginning to help others. Wherever you are, you can begin at once. Opportunities are within the reach of everyone. Take up the work for which you are held responsible, the work that should be done in your home and in your neighborhood. Wait not for others to urge you to action. In the fear of God go forward without delay, bearing in mind your individual responsibility to Him who gave His life for you. Act as if you heard

Christ calling upon you personally to do your utmost in His service. Look not to see who else is ready. If you are truly consecrated, God will, through your instrumentality, bring into the truth others whom He can use as channels to convey light to many that are groping in darkness.

All can do something. In an effort to excuse themselves, some say: "My home duties, my children, claim my time and my means." Parents, your children should be your helping hand, increasing your power and ability to work for the Master. Children are the younger members of the Lord's family. They should be led to consecrate themselves to God, whose they are by creation and by redemption. They should be taught that all their powers of body, mind, and soul are His. They should be trained to help in various lines of unselfish service.—Testimonies for the Church 7:62, 63.

Everyone to Do His Best—The Lord desires every worker to do his best. Those who have not had special training in one of our medical institutions may think that they can do very little; but, my dear fellow workers, remember that in the parable of the talents Christ did not represent all the servants as receiving the same number. To one servant was given five talents; to another, two; and to still another, one. If you have but one talent, use it wisely, increasing it by putting it out to the exchangers. Some cannot do as much as others, but everyone is to do all he can to roll back the wave of disease and distress that is sweeping over our world. Come up to the help of the Lord, to the help of the Lord against the mighty powers of darkness. God desires every one of His children to have intelligence and knowledge, so that with unmistakable clearness and power His glory shall be revealed in our world.—The Review and Herald, June 9, 1904.

Laborers Together With God—A grand side of the work of God is revealed by the words "medical missionary." To be a medical missionary means to be a laborer together with God. Medical missionary work, a work that is to be a great help and strength to the cause, is to be carried forward in all carefulness and wisdom. Into this work not one thread is to be drawn that will spoil the beautiful pattern that God designs shall be worked out.—Manuscript 139, 1902.

Proclaiming the Truth to the Sick and the Well—The gospel ministry is an organization for the proclamation of the truth to the sick and to the well. It combines the medical missionary work and the ministry of the Word. By these combined agencies opportunities are given to communicate light and to present the gospel to all classes and all grades of society. God wants the ministers and the church members to take a decided, active interest in the medical missionary work.

To take people right where they are, whatever their position or condition, and help them in every way possible—this is gospel ministry. Those who are diseased in body are nearly always diseased in mind, and when the soul is sick the body also is affected.—Testimonies for the Church 6:300, 301.

The fifty-eighth chapter of Isaiah contains present truth for the people of God. Here we see how medical missionary work and the gospel ministry are to be bound together as the message is given to the world. Upon those who keep the Sabbath of the Lord is laid the responsibility of doing a work of mercy and benevolence. Medical missionary work is to be bound up with the message, and sealed with the seal of God.—Manuscript 22, 1901.

North, South, East, and West—Why has it not been understood from the Word of God that the work being done in medical missionary lines is a fulfillment of the scripture, "Go out quickly into the streets and lanes of the city, and bring in hither the poor, and the maimed, and the halt, and the blind. And the servant said, Lord, it is done as thou hast commanded, and yet there is room. And the Lord said unto the servant, Go out into the highways and hedges, and compel them to come in, that my house may be full."

This is a work that the churches in every locality, north and south and east and west, should do. The churches have been given the opportunity of answering this work. Why have they not done it? Someone must fulfill the commission.

A work which should have been done has been left undone. Those who have been engaged in the medical missionary work have been doing the very class of work the Lord would have done....

Oh, how much, how very much remains to be done, and yet how many that might use their God-given talents aright are doing almost nothing besides caring for and pleasing themselves. But the hand of the Lord is stretched out still, and if they will work today in His vineyard, He will accept their service.—Manuscript 18, 1897.

Keep a Proper Balance—Medical missionary work should be carried forward by the church in well-organized efforts. It should be to the cause of God as the right hand is to the body. But the medical missionary work is not to take on undue importance. It should be done without neglecting other lines of work.—Letter 139, 1898.

The Work of the Right Hand—The right hand is used to open doors through which the body may find entrance. This is the part the medical missionary work is to act. It is to largely prepare the way for the reception of the truth for this time. A body without hands is useless. In giving honor to the body, honor must also be given to the helping hands, which are agencies of such importance that without them the body can do nothing. Therefore the body which treats indifferently the right hand, refusing its aid, is able to accomplish nothing.—Manuscript 55, 1901.

A Part of a Great Whole—The medical missionary work ought always to have existed in the work of reform. But it is never to become the means of separating the workers in the ministry from their work. Christ united these two branches in all his labors. The medical missionary work is part of the great whole, as the arm is part of the body. But the arm is not to say to the head, I have no need of thee. The body has need of the head decidedly, and the arms, in order to do active, aggressive work. The body is not to become the arm. Each member has its appointed work to perform.—Manuscript 105, 1899.

The Prayer of the Medical Missionary—Pastors and teachers are to work intelligently in their lines, instructing church members how to work in medical missionary lines. When the professed followers of Christ have an indwelling Saviour, they will be found doing as Christ did. They will have no opportunity to rust through inaction. They will have enough to do. And the work which they do under the auspices of the church will be their greatest means of communicating light.

The man who is working according to God's plan will pray, "Let it be known this day in my work for suffering humanity that there is a God in Israel, and that I am thy servant. Let it be seen that I am working, not according to my own impulse and wisdom, but according to thy word."

When man places himself in this attitude, and realizes that he is working out God's plan, and that God is working out His plan through him, he is in possession of divine power, which knows nothing of defeat. All the power of counteragencies is of no more account than the chaff of the threshing floor.—Manuscript 115, 1899.

It Will Bring Life to Churches—To my ministering brethren I would say, Prosecute this work with tact and ability. Set to work the young men and the young women in our churches. Combine the medical missionary work with the proclamation of the third angel's message. Make regular, organized efforts to lift the churches out of the dead level into which they have fallen, and have remained for years. Send into the church workers who will set the principles of health reform in their connection with the third angel's message before every family and individual. Encourage all to take a part in work for their fellow men, and see if the breath of life will not quickly return to these churches.—Letter 54, 1898.

Chapter 15—Medical Ministry in the Homes

The Door of Entrance to Homes—Medical missionary work is the pioneer work of the gospel, the door through which the truth for this time is to find entrance to many homes. God's people are to be genuine medical missionaries, for they are to learn to minister to the needs of both soul and body. The purest unselfishness is to be shown by our workers as, with the knowledge and experience gained by practical work, they go out to give treatments to the sick. As they go from house to house they will find access to many hearts. Many will be reached who otherwise never would have heard the gospel message.—The Review and Herald, December 17, 1914.

Christ Will Guide in This Ministry—If you are pressing close to the side of Christ, wearing His yoke, you will daily learn of Him how to carry messages of peace and comfort to the sorrowing and disappointed, the sad and brokenhearted. You can point the discouraged ones to the Word of God and take the sick to the Lord in prayer. As you pray, speak to Christ as you would to a trusted, much-loved friend. Maintain a sweet, free, pleasant dignity as a child of God. This will be recognized.—Testimonies for the Church 6:323, 324.

The Ministry of Christlike Physicians and Nurses—Oh, that all who are afflicted could be ministered to by Christlike physicians and nurses, who could help them to place their weary, pain-racked bodies in the care of the Great Healer, in faith looking to Him for restoration.

Every sincere Christian bows to Jesus as the true physician of souls. When He stands by the bedside of the afflicted there will be many not only converted but healed. If through judicious ministration the patient is led to give his soul to Christ and to bring his thoughts into obedience to the will of God, a great victory is gained.—The Review and Herald, May 9, 1912.

The Missionary Nurse in the Home—The Lord wants wise men and women acting in the capacity of nurses to comfort and help the sick and suffering.... There are many lines of work to be carried forward by the missionary nurse. There are openings for well-trained nurses to go among families and seek to awaken an interest in the truth. In almost every community there are large numbers who do not attend any religious service. If they are reached by the gospel, it must be carried to their homes. Often the relief of their physical needs is the only avenue by which they can be approached. As missionary nurses care for the sick and relieve the distress of the poor, they will find many opportunities to pray with them, to read to them from God's Word, to speak of the Saviour. They can pray with and for the helpless ones who have not strength of will to control the appetites that passion has degraded. They can bring a ray of hope into the lives of the defeated and disheartened. Their unselfish love, manifested in acts of disinterested kindness, will make it easier for these suffering ones to believe in the love of Christ.—Ibid.

Teach the People How to Keep Well—The medical missionary work presents many opportunities for service. Intemperance in eating and ignorance of nature's laws are causing much of the sickness that exists and are robbing God of the glory due him.... Teach the people that it is better to know how to keep well than to know how to cure disease. We should be wise educators, warning all against self-indulgence. As we see the wretchedness, deformity, and disease that have come into the world as a result of ignorance, how can we refrain from doing our part to enlighten the ignorant and relieve the suffering?—The Review and Herald, June 6, 1912.

The Simple Principles All Should Master—God's people are to be genuine medical missionaries. They are to learn to minister to the needs of soul and body. They should know how to give the simple treatments that do so much to relieve pain and remove disease. They should be familiar with the principles of health reform, that they may show others how, by right habits of eating, drinking, and dressing, disease may be prevented and health regained. A demonstration of the value of the principles of health reform will do much toward removing prejudice against our evangelical work. The Great Physician, the originator of medical missionary work, will bless every one who will go forward humbly and trustfully, seeking to impart the truth for this time.—The Review and Herald, May 5, 1904.

A Continual Reform Essential—Reform, continual reform, must be kept before the people, and by our example we must enforce our teachings. True religion and the laws of health go hand in hand. It is impossible to work for the salvation of men and women without presenting to them the need of breaking away from sinful gratifications, which destroy the health, debase the soul, and prevent divine truth from impressing the mind. Men and women must be taught to take a careful review of every habit and practice, and at once put away those things that cause an unhealthy condition of the body, and thus cast a dark shadow over the mind.—The Review and Herald, November 12, 1901.

Teach the Principles of Healthful Cooking—Because the avenues to the soul have been closed by the tyrant Prejudice, many are ignorant of the principles of healthful living. Good service can be done by teaching the people how to prepare healthful food. This line of work is as essential as any that can be taken up. More cooking schools should be established, and some should labor from house to house, giving instruction in the art of cooking wholesome foods. Many, many will be rescued from physical, mental, and moral degeneracy through the influence of health reform. These principles will commend themselves to those who are seeking for light, and such will advance from this to receive the full truth for this time.

God wants His people to receive to impart. As impartial, unselfish witnesses, they are to give to others what the Lord has given them. And as you enter into this work, and by whatever means in your power seek to reach hearts, be sure to work in a way that will remove prejudice instead of creating it. Make the life of Christ your constant study, and labor as He did, following His example.—The Review and Herald, June 6, 1912.

We need a genuine education in the art of cooking.... Form classes, where you may teach the people how to make good bread and how to put together ingredients to make healthful food combinations from the grains and the vegetables.—Manuscript 150, 1905.

Follow a Course That Commends Reform—Many of the views held by Seventh-day Adventists differ widely from those held by the world in general. Those who advocate an unpopular truth should, above all others, seek to be consistent in their own life. They should not try to see how different they can be from others, but how near they can come to those whom they wish to influence, that they may help them to the positions they themselves so highly prize. Such a course will commend the truths they hold.

Those who are advocating a reform in diet should, by the provision they make for their own table, present the advantages of hygiene in the best light. They should so exemplify its principles as to commend it to the judgment of candid minds....

When those who advocate hygienic reform carry the matter to extremes, people are not to blame if they become disgusted. Too often our religious faith is thus brought into disrepute, and in many cases those who witness such exhibitions of inconsistency can never afterward be brought to think that there is anything good in the reform. These extremists do more harm in a few months than they can undo in a lifetime. They are engaged in a work which Satan loves to see go on.... Narrow ideas and overstraining of small points have been a great injury to the cause of hygiene.—Christian Temperance and Bible Hygiene, 55-57.

Personal Views Not to Be Urged—Those who have but a partial understanding of the principles of reform are often the most rigid, not only in carrying out their views themselves, but in urging them on their families and their neighbors. The effect of their mistaken reforms, as seen in their own ill-health, and their efforts to force their views upon others give many a false idea of dietetic reform and lead them to reject it altogether.

Those who understand the laws of health and who are governed by principle will shun the extremes both of indulgence and of restriction. Their diet is chosen, not for the mere gratification of appetite, but for the upbuilding of the body. They seek to preserve every power in the best condition for highest service to God and man. The appetite is under the control of reason and conscience, and they are rewarded with health of body and mind. While they do not urge their views offensively upon others, their example is a testimony in favor of right principles. These persons have a wide influence for good.

There is a real common sense in dietetic reform. The subject should be studied broadly and deeply, and no one should criticize others because their practice is not, in all things, in harmony with his own. It is impossible to make an unvarying rule to regulate everyone's habits, and no one should think himself a criterion for all. Not all can eat the same things. Foods that are palatable and wholesome to one person may be distasteful, and even harmful, to another. Some cannot use milk, while others thrive on it. Some persons cannot digest peas and beans; others find them wholesome. For some the coarser grain preparations are good food, while others cannot use them.—The Ministry of Healing, 318-320.

Light for the Salvation of the World—Those who act as teachers are to be intelligent in regard to disease and its causes, understanding that every action of the human agent should be in perfect harmony with the laws of life. The light God has given on health reform is for our salvation and the salvation of the world. Men and women should be informed in regard to the human habitation, fitted up by our Creator as His dwelling place, and over which He desires us to be faithful stewards. "For ye are the temple of the living God; as God hath said, I will dwell in them, and walk in them; and I will be their God, and they shall be My people."—The Review and Herald, November 12, 1901.

Revives Confidence—Many have no faith in God and have lost confidence in man, but they appreciate acts of sympathy and helpfulness. As they see one with no inducement of earthly praise or compensation coming to their homes, ministering to the sick, feeding the hungry, clothing the naked, comforting the sad, and tenderly pointing all to Him of whose love and pity the human worker is but the messenger—as they see this, their hearts are touched. Gratitude springs up, faith is kindled. They see that God cares for them, and as His Word is opened they are prepared to listen.—The Review and Herald, May 9, 1912.

Many Saved From Degradation—I have been shown that the medical missionary work will discover, in the very depths of degradation, men who once possessed fine minds, richest qualifications, who will be rescued, by proper labor, from their fallen condition. It is the truth as it is in Jesus that is to be brought before human minds after they have been sympathetically cared for and their physical necessities met. The Holy Spirit is working and cooperating with the human agencies that are laboring for such souls, and some will appreciate the foundation upon a rock for their religious faith. There is to be no startling communication of strange doctrine to these subjects whom God loves and pities; but as they are helped physically by the medical missionary workers, the Holy Spirit cooperates with the minister of human agencies to arouse the moral powers. The mental powers are awakened into activity, and these poor souls will, many of them, be saved in the kingdom of God.

Nothing can, or ever will, give character to the work in the presentation of truth to help the people just where they are so well as Samaritan work. A work properly conducted to save poor sinners that have been passed by the churches, will be the entering wedge whereby the truth will find standing room. A different order of things needs to be established among us as a people, and as this class of work is done, there will be created an entirely different atmosphere surrounding the souls of the workers; for the Holy Spirit communicates to all those who are doing God's service, and those who are worked by the Holy Spirit will be a power for God in lifting up, strengthening, and saving the souls that are ready to perish.—Special Testimonies, Series A 11:32.

Zeal and Perseverance Required—Could I arouse our people to Christian effort, could I lead them to engage in medical missionary work with holy zeal and divine perseverance, not in a few places, but in every place, putting forth personal effort for those out of the fold, how grateful I should be! This is true missionary work. In some places it is attended with little success, apparently; but again, the Lord opens the way, and signal success attends the effort. Words are spoken which are as nails fastened in a sure place. Angels from heaven cooperate with human instrumentalities, and sinners are won to the Saviour.—Letter 43, 1903.

Holy and Devout Men and Women Called—Holy and devout persons, both men and women, are wanted now to go forth as medical missionaries. Let them cultivate their physical and mental powers and their piety to the uttermost. Every effort should be made to send forth intelligent workers. The same grace that came from Jesus Christ to Paul and Apollos, which caused them to be distinguished for their spiritual excellencies, can be received now, and will bring into working order many devoted missionaries.—;Special Testimonies Relating to Medical Missionary Work, 8.

Do Not Wait—Workers—gospel medical missionaries—are needed now. You cannot afford to spend years in preparation. Soon doors now open to the truth will be forever closed. Carry the message now. Do not wait, allowing the enemy to take possession of the fields now open before you. Let little companies go forth to do the work to which Christ appointed His disciples. Let them labor as evangelists, scattering our publications, and talking of the truth to those they meet. Let them pray for the sick, ministering to their necessities, not with drugs, but with nature's remedies, and teaching them how to regain health and avoid disease.—Testimonies for the Church 9:172.

[Note: For more detailed counsels regarding medical ministry and the presentation of our health message see *Ministry of Healing, Medical Ministry, Counsels on Diet and Foods*, and *Counsels on Health*.—Compilers.]

Chapter 16—Preparing for Last-Day Crises and Disasters

These Last-Day Conditions Press Us to Prepare—We are living in the time of the end. The fast-fulfilling signs of the times declare that the coming of Christ is near at hand. The days in which we live are solemn and important. The Spirit of God is gradually but surely being withdrawn from the earth. Plagues and judgments are already falling upon the despisers of the grace of God. The calamities by land and sea, the unsettled state of society, the alarms of war, are portentous. They forecast approaching events of the greatest magnitude.

The agencies of evil are combining their forces and consolidating. They are strengthening for the last great crisis. Great changes are soon to take place in our world, and the final movements will be rapid ones.

The condition of things in the world shows that troublous times are right upon us. The daily papers are full of indications of a terrible conflict in the near future. Bold robberies are of frequent occurrence. Strikes are common. Thefts and murders are committed on every hand. Men possessed of demons are taking the lives of men, women, and little children. Men have become infatuated with vice, and every species of evil prevails.—Testimonies for the Church 9:11.

Something Decisive About to Take Place—The present is a time of overwhelming interest to all living. Rulers and statesmen, men who occupy positions of trust and authority, thinking men and women of all classes, have their attention fixed upon the events, taking place about us. They are watching the strained, restless relations that exist among the nations. They observe the intensity that is taking possession of every earthly element, and they recognize that something great and decisive is about to take place—that the world is on the verge of a stupendous crisis.

Angels are now restraining the winds of strife, that they may not blow until the world shall be warned of its coming doom; but a storm is gathering, ready to burst upon the earth; and when God shall bid His angels loose the winds, there will be such a scene of strife as no pen can picture.—Education, 179, 180.

The time is at hand when there will be sorrow in the world that no human balm can heal. The Spirit of God is being withdrawn. Disasters by sea and by land follow one another in quick succession. How frequently we hear of earthquakes and tornadoes, of destruction by fire and flood, with great loss of life and property! Apparently these calamities are capricious outbreaks of disorganized, unregulated forces of nature, wholly beyond the control of man; but in them all, God's purpose may be read. They are among the agencies by which He seeks to arouse men and women to a sense of their danger.—Prophets and Kings, 277.

Large Cities Will Be Swept Away—The work that should long ago have been in active operation to win souls to Christ has not been done. The inhabitants of the ungodly cities so soon to be visited by calamities have been cruelly neglected. The time is near when large cities will be swept away, and all should be warned of these coming judgments. But who is giving to the accomplishment of this work the wholehearted service that God requires? ...

At the present time there is not a thousandth part being done in working the cities that should be done, and that would be done if men and women would do their whole duty.—Manuscript 53, 1910.

O that God's people had a sense of the impending destruction of thousands of cities, now almost given to idolatry!—The Review and Herald, September 10, 1903.

Impending Disasters—Not long ago a very impressive scene passed before me. I saw an immense ball of fire falling among some beautiful mansions, causing their instant destruction. I heard someone say, "We knew that the judgments of God were coming upon the earth, but we did not know that they would come so soon." Others said, "You knew? Why then did you not tell us? We did not know." On every side I heard such words spoken....

Soon grievous troubles will arise among the nations—trouble that will not cease until Jesus comes. As never before we need to press together, serving Him who has prepared His throne in the heavens and whose kingdom ruleth over all. God has not forsaken His people, and our strength lies in not forsaking Him.

The judgments of God are in the land. The wars and rumors of wars, the destruction by fire and flood, say clearly that the time of trouble, which is to increase until the end, is very near at hand. We have no time to lose. The world is stirred with the spirit of war. The prophecies of the eleventh of Daniel have almost reached their final fulfillment.—The Review and Herald, November 24, 1904.

Indescribable—Last Friday morning, just before I awoke, a very impressive scene was presented before me. I seemed to awake from sleep but was not in my home. From the windows I could behold a terrible conflagration. Great balls of fire were falling upon houses, and from these balls fiery arrows were flying in every direction. It was impossible to check the fires that were kindled, and many places were being destroyed. The terror of the people was indescribable. After a time I awoke and found myself at home.—Letter 278, 1906.

Prepare While There Is an Opportunity—As religious aggression subverts the liberties of our nation, those who would stand for freedom of conscience will be placed in unfavorable positions. For their own sake they should, while they have opportunity, become intelligent in regard to disease, its causes, prevention, and cure. And those who do this will find a field of labor anywhere. There will be suffering ones, plenty of them, who will need help, not only among those of our own faith, but largely among those who know not the truth.—Medical Missionary, November, December, 1892.

Ready to Give Immediate Assistance—Poverty and distress in families will come to our knowledge, and afflicted and suffering ones will have to be relieved. We know very little of the human suffering that exists everywhere about us, but as we have opportunity we should be ready to render immediate assistance to those who are under a severe pressure.—Manuscript 25, 1894.

God's Helping Hand in Lessening Suffering—The work of health reform is the Lord's means for lessening suffering in our world and for purifying His church. Teach the people that they can act as God's helping hand by cooperating with the Master Worker in restoring physical and spiritual health.—Testimonies for the Church 9:112, 113.

Every Member to Take Hold of Medical Missionary Work—We have come to a time when every member of the church should take hold of medical missionary work. The world is a lazar house filled with victims of both physical and spiritual disease. Everywhere people are perishing for lack of a knowledge of the truths that have been committed to us. The members of the church are in need of an awakening, that they may realize their responsibility to impart these truths.—Testimonies for the Church 7:62.

A Door of Entrance to the Large Cities—Henceforth medical missionary work is to be carried forward with an earnestness with which it has never yet been carried. This work is the door through which the truth is to find entrance to the large cities.—Testimonies for the Church 9:167.

Every city is to be entered by workers trained to do medical missionary work.—Testimonies for the Church 7:59.

In every large city there should be a corps of organized, well-disciplined workers; not merely one or two, but scores should be set to work.—Letter 34, 1892.

A Part of the Work of Every Church—Medical missionary work should have its representative in every place in connection with the establishment of our churches.—Manuscript 88, 1902.

In every city where we have a church there is need of a place where treatments can be given. Among the homes of our church members there are few that afford room and facilities for the proper care of the sick. A place should be provided where treatment may be given for common ailments. The building might be inelegant and even rude, but it should be furnished with facilities for giving simple treatments.—Testimonies for the Church 6:113.

The medical missionary work should be a part of the work of every church in our land. Disconnected from the church it would soon become a strange medley of disorganized atoms. It would consume, but not produce. Instead of acting as God's helping hand to forward His truth, it would sap the life and force from the church and weaken the message. Conducted independently, it would not only consume talent and means needed in other lines, but in the very work of helping the helpless apart from the ministry of the word, it would place men where they would scoff at Bible truth.—Testimonies for the Church 6:289.

Medical Missionary Ministry in the Closing Crisis—My heart is made sad as I look at our churches, which ought to be connected in heart and soul and practice with the medical missionary work.... I wish to tell you that soon there will be no work done in ministerial lines but medical missionary work. The work of a minister is to minister. Our ministers are to work on the gospel plan of ministering....

You will never be ministers after the gospel order till you show a decided interest in medical missionary work, the gospel of healing and blessing and strengthening. Come up to the help of the Lord, to the help of the Lord against the mighty powers of darkness, that it be not said of you, "Curse ye Meroz, ... curse ye bitterly the inhabitants thereof; because they came not to the help of the Lord." Judges 5:23.—The General Conference Bulletin, April 12, 1901.

Section 6—The Dorcas Movement in the Church

Gem Thought

In Joppa there was a Dorcas, whose skillful fingers were more active than her tongue. She knew who needed comfortable clothing and who needed sympathy, and she freely ministered to the wants of both classes. And when Dorcas died, the church in Joppa realized their loss. It is no wonder that they mourned and lamented, nor that warm teardrops fell upon the inanimate clay. She was of so great value that by the power of God she was brought back from the land of the enemy, that her skill and energy might still be a blessing to others.

Such patient, prayerful, and persevering fidelity as was possessed by these saints of God is rare; yet the church cannot prosper without it. It is needed in the church, in the Sabbath school, and in society. Many come together in church relationship with their natural traits of character unsubdued; and in a crisis, when strong, hopeful spirits are needed, they give up to discouragement and bring burdens on the church; and they do not see that this is wrong. The cause does not need such persons, for they are unreliable; but there is always a call for steadfast, God-fearing workers, who will not faint in the day of adversity.—Testimonies for the Church 5:304.

Now there was at Joppa a certain disciple named Tabitha, which by interpretation is called Dorcas: this woman was full of good works and almsdeeds which she did. Acts 9:36.

Chapter 17—Women Called to the Work

The Dorcas Movement Today—There certainly should be a larger number of women engaged in the work of ministering to suffering humanity, uplifting, educating them how to believe—simply to believe, in Jesus Christ our Saviour. And as souls give themselves to the Lord Jesus, making an entire surrender, they will understand the doctrine....

I am pained because our sisters in America are not more of them doing the work they might do for the Lord Jesus. Abiding in Christ, they would receive courage and strength and faith for the work. Many women love to talk. Why can't they talk the words of Christ to perishing souls? The more closely we are related to Christ, the heart learns the wretchedness of souls that do not know God, and who do not feel the dishonor they are doing to Christ who has bought them with a price.

When the believing women shall feel the burden of souls, and burden of sins not their own, they will be working as Christ worked. They will consider no sacrifice too great to make to win souls to Christ. And everyone who has this love for souls, is born of God; they are ready to follow in His footsteps, and their words and voice would be talents employed in the Master's service; the very nourishment coming from the parent stock to their own souls would flow out in distinct channels of love to souls who are withered and dried up.

In this work is a constant education. The desire to be a blessing discovers the weakness and inefficiency of the worker. This drives the soul to God in prayer, and the Lord Jesus gives light and His Holy Spirit, and they understand that it is Christ who does the melting and breaking of the hard hearts.—Letter 133, 1898.

The Value of Organization—The work you [Addressed to a woman of broad public experience who had joined the Seventh-day Adventist Church.] are doing to help our sisters feel their individual accountability to God is a good and necessary work. Long has it been neglected. But when this work is laid out in clear, simple, definite lines, we may expect that home duties, instead of being neglected, will be done much more intelligently. The Lord would have us ever to urge the worth of the human soul upon those who do not understand its value.

If we can arrange to have regular, organized companies instructed intelligently in regard to the part they should act as servants of the Master, our churches will have a life and vitality that they have long needed. The excellency of the soul Christ has saved will be appreciated. Our sisters generally have a hard time with their increasing families and their unappreciated trials. I have so longed for women who could be educated to help our sisters rise from their discouragement and feel that they could do a work for the Lord. This is bringing rays of sunshine into their own lives, which are reflected into the hearts of others. God will bless you and all who unite with you in this grand work.—Letter 54, 1899.

The Lord Has a Work for Women—The Lord has a work for women as well as for men. They may take their places in His work at this crisis, and He will work through them. If they are imbued with a sense of their duty, and labor under the influence of the Holy Spirit, they will have just the self-possession required for this time. The Saviour will reflect upon these self-sacrificing women the light of His countenance, and will give them a power that exceeds that of men. They can do in families a work that men cannot do, a work that reaches the inner life. They can come close to the hearts of those whom men cannot reach. Their labor is needed.—The Review and Herald, August 26, 1902.

Women Have a High Destiny—Sisters, we may do a noble work for God if we will. Woman does not know her power. God did not intend that her capabilities should be all absorbed in questioning: What shall I eat? what shall I drink? and wherewithal shall I be clothed? There is a higher purpose for woman, a grander destiny. She should develop and cultivate her powers, for God can employ them in the great work of saving souls from eternal ruin.—Testimonies for the Church 4:642.

We may safely say that the dignity and importance of woman's mission and distinctive duties are of a more sacred and holy character than the duties of man.... Let woman realize the sacredness of her work and, in the strength and fear of God, take up her mission.—Testimonies for the Church 3:565.

If we can impress upon the minds of our sisters the good which it is in their power to do through the Lord Jesus Christ, we shall see a large work accomplished.—Letter 119, 1898.

Women Called to Be Messengers of Mercy—We greatly need consecrated women who, as messengers of mercy, will visit the mothers and the children in their homes and help them in the everyday household duties, if need be, before beginning to talk to them regarding the truth for this time. You will find that by this method you will have souls as the result of your ministry.—The Review and Herald, July 12, 1906.

Why Stand Ye Idle?—The Lord of the vineyard is saying to many women who are now doing nothing, "Why stand ye here all the day idle?" They may be instruments of righteousness, rendering holy service. It was Mary who first preached a risen Jesus; and the refining, softening influence of Christian women is needed in the great work of preaching the truth now. If there were twenty women where now there is one who would make the saving of souls their cherished work, we should see many more converted to the truth. Zealous and continued diligence in the cause of God would be wholly successful, and would astonish them with its results. The work must be accomplished through patience and perseverance, and in this is manifested the real devotion to God. He calls for deeds, and not words only.

The work of God is worthy of our best efforts.... Often we are so wrapped up in our selfish interests that our hearts are not allowed to take in the needs and wants of humanity; we are lacking in deeds of sympathy and benevolence, in sacred and social ministering to the needy, the oppressed, and the suffering.—The Signs of the Times, September 16, 1886.

The Work to Be Done—Inaction and delicate idleness is weakening the life forces of young women. There are those who spend hours of precious time in bed, which is not blessing them with increase of strength or relieving others from burdens, but is bringing upon them debility and confirming them in wrong habits. These hours idled away needlessly in bed can never be regained. The sin of time thus lost is marked in the book of records.

There is enough to do in this busy world of ours. There are enough in God's great family who need sympathy and aid. If our own work does not demand our time, there are sick to be visited, the poor to be helped and encouraged.—The Health Reformer, June, 1873.

A Unique Place for Women in the Work—There is a wide field in which our sisters may do good service for the Master in the various branches of the work connected with His cause. Through missionary labor they can reach a class that our ministers cannot.... There is work neglected or done imperfectly that could be thoroughly accomplished by the help that sisters can give. There are so many kinds of work too laborious for women, which our brethren are called to engage in, that many branches of missionary work are neglected. Many things connected with different churches are left undone that women, if properly instructed, could attend to. Our sisters might serve as church clerks, and the church business would not be so sadly neglected. There are many other offices connected with the cause of God which our sisters are better qualified to fill than our brethren, and in which they might do efficient service.—The Review and Herald, December 19, 1878.

Missionary Correspondence—Women can do good work in the missionary field, by writing to friends, and learning their true feelings in relation to the cause of God. Very valuable items are brought to light through this means. The workers should not seek for self-exaltation, but to present the truth in its simplicity wherever they shall have an opportunity.—The Signs of the Times, September 16, 1886.

God's Claim Upon Our Time and Money—We have no right, my Christian sisters, to waste our time, and give example to others who are less able than we to waste their time and energies upon needless ornaments, upon dress or furniture, or to indulge in superfluities in food. We have religious duties to perform, and if we neglect these duties, and give our time to needless things, we will dwarf the intellect and separate the affections from God. The Author of our existence has claims upon our time and our money. He has poor and suffering ones all around us that money may relieve, and cheering, encouraging words bless. Christ identifies Himself with the wants of suffering humanity. As you neglected to visit the widow and orphans tried in the furnace of affliction, suffering want and privation, you did not realize that Christ would mark the circumstances against you in the book of records, as though you had neglected Him.—The Health Reformer, June, 1873.

Engage in Personal Evangelism—A direct necessity is being met by the work of women who have given themselves to the Lord and are reaching out to help a needy, sin-stricken people. Personal evangelistic work is to be done. The women who take up this work carry the gospel to the homes of the people in the highways and the byways. They read and explain the word to families, praying with them, caring for the sick, relieving their temporal necessities.—Testimonies for the Church 6:118.

Chapter 18—Qualifications of Women for Service

The Kind of Women Called to Service—God calls for earnest women workers, workers who are prudent, warmhearted, tender, and true to principle. He calls for persevering women who will take their minds from self and their personal convenience, and will center them on Christ.... Will our sisters arise to the emergency? Will they work for the Master?—Testimonies for the Church 6:118.

Learning in the School of Christ—The Lord has a work for women as well as men to do. They may accomplish a good work for God, if they will first learn in the school of Christ the precious, all-important lesson of meekness. They must not only bear the name of Christ but possess His Spirit. They must walk even as He walked, purifying their souls from everything that defiles. Then they will be able to benefit others by presenting the all-sufficiency of Jesus.—Manuscript 119, 1907.

With Firm Principle and Decided Character—Women of firm principle and decided character are needed, women who believe that we are indeed living in the last days, and that we have the last solemn message of warning to be given to the world. They should feel that they are engaged in an important work in spreading the rays of light which Heaven has shed upon them. When the love of God and His truth is an abiding principle, they will let nothing deter them from duty or discourage them in their work. They will fear God and will not be diverted from their labors in His cause by the temptation of lucrative situations and attractive prospects. They will preserve their integrity at any cost to themselves. These are the ones who will correctly represent the religion of Christ, whose words will be fitly spoken, like apples of gold in pictures of silver. Such persons can in many ways do a precious work for God. He calls upon them to go out into the harvest field and help gather in the sheaves.—The Signs of the Times, September 16, 1886.

Tact, Perception, Ability—Christian women are called for. There is a wide field in which they may do good service for the

Master. There are noble women who have had moral courage to decide in favor of the truth from the weight of evidence. They have tact, perception, and good ability, and could make successful Christian workers.—Ibid.

The Martha and Mary Attributes Blended—All who work for God should have the Martha and the Mary attributes blended—a willingness to minister and a sincere love of the truth. Self and selfishness must be put out of sight.—Testimonies for the Church 6:118.

Gentlewomen Needed—Women are needed who are not self-important, but gentle in manners and lowly of heart, who will work with the meekness of Christ wherever they can find anything to do for the salvation of souls. All who have been made partakers of the heavenly benefits should be earnest and anxious that others who do not have the privileges which they have enjoyed, should have the evidences of the truth presented before them. And they will not merely *desire* that others should have this benefit, but will see that they *do* have it, and will do their part toward the accomplishment of this object.

Those who become colaborers with God will increase in moral and spiritual power, while those who devote their time and energies to serving themselves will dwarf, and wither, and die.—The Signs of the Times, September 16, 1886.

Improvement of Talents—Our sisters ... are not deficient in ability, and if they would put to a right use the talents they already have, their efficiency would be greatly increased.—Testimonies for the Church 4:629, 630.

Courageous and Self-reliant—Many a home is made very unhappy by the useless repining of its mistress, who turns with distaste from the simple, homely tasks of her unpretending domestic life. She looks upon the cares and duties of her lot as hardships, and that which through cheerfulness might be made not only pleasant and interesting but profitable, becomes the merest drudgery. She looks upon the slavery of her life with repugnance, and imagines herself a martyr.

It is true that the wheels of domestic machinery will not always run smoothly; there is much to try the patience and tax the strength. But while mothers are not responsible for circumstances over which they have no control, it is useless to deny that circumstances make a great difference with mothers in their lifework. But their condemnation is when circumstances are allowed to rule and to subvert their principle, when they grow tired and unfaithful to their high trust, and neglect their known duty.

The wife and mother who nobly overcomes difficulties under which others sink for want of patience and fortitude to persevere, not only becomes strong herself in doing her duty, but her experience in overcoming temptations and obstacles qualifies her to be an efficient help to others, both by words and example. Many who do well under favorable circumstances seem to undergo a transformation of character under adversity and trial; they deteriorate in proportion to their troubles. God never designed that we should be the sport of circumstances.—The Health Reformer, August, 1877.

The Elements of Christian Character—Mothers, you are developing character. Your compassionate Redeemer is watching you in love and sympathy, ready to hear your prayers, and render you the assistance which you need in your lifework. Love, joy, peace, long-suffering, gentleness, faith, and charity are the elements of the Christian character. These precious graces are the fruits of the Spirit. They are the Christian's crown and shield. The highest daydreaming and most exalted aspirations can aim at nothing higher. Nothing can give more perfect content and satisfaction. These heavenly attainments are not dependent upon circumstances, nor the will or imperfect judgment of man. The precious Saviour, who understands our heart struggles and the weakness of our natures, pities, and forgives us our errors and bestows upon us the graces which we earnestly desire.—Ibid.

A True Gentlewoman—Do you make mistakes? Do not let this discourage you. The Lord may permit you to make small mistakes in order to save you from making larger mistakes. Go to Jesus, and ask Him to forgive you, and then believe that He does. "If we confess our sins, He is faithful and just to forgive us our sins, and to cleanse us from all unrighteousness."

When unkind, discouraging words are spoken to you, do not retaliate. Do not reply unless you can return a pleasant answer. Say to yourself, "I will not disappoint my Saviour." The Christian woman is a gentlewoman. On her lips is ever the law of kindness. She utters no hasty words. To speak gentle words when you are irritated will bring sunshine into your hearts and make your path more smooth. A schoolgirl, when asked for a definition of meekness, said, "Meek people are those who give soft answers to rough questions." Christ says, "Blessed are the meek: for they shall inherit the earth." They will be fit subjects for the kingdom of heaven, for they are willing to be taught.—The Review and Herald, April 7, 1904.

Graceful and Dignified—Do not treat life as a romance but as a reality. Perform your smallest duty in the fear and love of God, with faithfulness and cheerfulness. God declares, "He that is faithful in that which is least is faithful also in much."

Study the life that Christ lived while on this earth. He did not neglect the smallest, simplest duty. Perfection marked all that He did. Look to Him for help, and you will be enabled to perform your daily duties with the grace and dignity of one who is seeking for the crown of immortal life.—Ibid. (Counsel addressed to "My Sisters Tempted by Discouragement.")

Faithful in That Which Is Least—My brethren and sisters, do not pass by the little things to look for larger work. You might do successfully the small work but fail utterly in attempting a larger work, and fall into discouragement. Take hold wherever you see that there is a work to be done. It is by doing with your might what your hands find to do that you will develop talent and aptitude for large work. It is by slighting the daily opportunities, neglecting the little things, that so many become fruitless and withered.—The Review and Herald, August 26, 1902.

Attentive to Little Things—We dwell much on the grandeur of Christ's life. We speak of the great things that He accomplished, of the miracles He wrought, of how He spoke peace to the tempestuous waters, restored sight to the blind and hearing to the deaf, and raised the dead to life. But His attention to small things is even higher proof of His greatness. Listen to Him speaking to Martha as she comes to Him with the request that He bid her sister help her with the serving. He tells her not to allow the cares of the household to disturb the peace of her soul. "Martha, Martha," He says, "thou art careful and troubled about many things: but one thing is needful: and Mary hath chosen that good part, which shall not be taken away from her."—The Review and Herald, April 7, 1904.

Frugal; Collect Every Fragment—"Gather up the fragments, that nothing be lost." He who had all resources at His command gives a lesson that not a fragment should be wasted. He who has plenty should not waste. Let nothing be wasted that can do good to any one. Collect every fragment, for someone will need it. These lessons in regard to spiritual blessings bestowed are to be carefully treasured.—Manuscript 60, 1897.

The Power of Politeness—Every woman should develop a well-balanced mind and a pure character, reflecting only the true, the good, and the beautiful. The wife and mother may bind her husband and children to her heart by unvarying love, shown in gentle words and courteous deportment. Politeness is cheap, but it has power to soften natures which would grow hard and rough without it. Christian politeness should reign in every household. The cultivation of a uniform courtesy, a willingness to do by others as we would like them to do by us, would banish half the ills of life.—The Signs of the Times, August 15, 1906.

[155]

Be Sure We Are Working for Jesus—Our sisters are not excused from taking a part in the work of God. Everyone who has tasted of the powers of the world to come has earnest work to do in some capacity in the Lord's vineyard. Our sisters may manage to keep busy with their fingers constantly employed in manufacturing little dainty articles to beautify their homes or to present to their friends. Great quantities of this kind of material may be brought and laid upon the foundation stone, but will Jesus look upon all this variety of dainty work as a living sacrifice to Himself? Will He pronounce the commendation upon the workers, "I know thy works, and thy labour, and thy patience," and how thou "hast borne, and hast patience, and for My name's sake hast laboured, and hast not fainted"?

Let our sisters inquire, How shall I meet in the Judgment these souls with whom I have or should have become acquainted? Have I studied over their individual cases? Have I so acquainted myself with my Bible that I could open the Scriptures to them? ...

Is it the work God has appointed you as His hired servants, to study the intricate, delicate patterns of embroidery and the many obscure points in this class of work for the purpose of mastering what someone else has done or to show what you can do? Is this

[156] the kind of labor that God will commend you in doing, which so absorbs your interest, your God-given time and talents, that you have no taste or education or aptitude for missionary labor? All this kind of work is hay, wood, and stubble, which the fires of the last day will consume. But where are your offerings to God? Where is your patient labor, your earnest zeal, that brings you into connection with Christ, bearing His yoke, lifting His burdens? Where are the gold, the silver, and the precious stones which you have laid upon the foundation stone, which the fires of the last day cannot consume, because they are imperishable?—The Review and Herald, May 31, 1887.

Jesus Knows Women's Burdens—He who gave back to the widow her only son as he was being carried to the burial, is touched today by the woe of the bereaved mother. He who gave back to Mary and Martha their buried brother, who wept tears of sympathy at the grave of Lazarus, who pardoned Mary Magdalene, who remembered His mother when He was hanging in agony upon the cross, who appeared to the weeping women after His resurrection, and made them His messengers to preach a risen Saviour saying, "Go tell My disciples that I go to My Father and to your Father, to My God and to your God," is woman's best friend today and ready to aid her in her need if she will trust Him.—The Health Reformer, August, 1877.

Chapter 19—The Influence of Christian Women

Wonderful Mission of Women—Seventh-day Adventists are not in any way to belittle woman's work.—Gospel Workers, 453.

Wonderful is the mission of the wives and mothers and the younger women workers. If they will, they can exert an influence for good to all around them. By modesty in dress and circumspect deportment they may bear witness to the truth in its simplicity. They may let their light so shine before all that others will see their good works and glorify their Father which is in heaven. A truly converted woman will exert a powerful transforming influence for good. Connected with her husband, she may aid him in his work and become the means of encouragement and blessing to him. When the will and way are brought into subjection to the Spirit of God, there is no limit to the good that can be accomplished.—Manuscript 91, 1908.

To Act a Part in the Closing Work—Our sisters, the youth, the middle-aged, and those of advanced years may act a part in the closing work for this time; and in doing this as they have opportunity they will obtain an experience of the highest value to themselves. In forgetfulness of self they will grow in grace. By training the mind in this direction they will learn how to bear burdens for Jesus.—The Review and Herald, January 2, 1879.

To Serve With Faithfulness and Discernment—At this time every talent of every worker should be regarded as a sacred trust to be used in extending the work of reform. The Lord instructed me that our sisters who have received a training that has fitted them for positions of responsibility are to serve with faithfulness and discernment in their calling, using their influence wisely and, with their brethren in the faith, obtaining an experience that will fit them for still greater usefulness....

In ancient times the Lord worked in a wonderful way through consecrated women who united in His work with men whom He had chosen to stand as His representatives. He used women to gain great and decisive victories. More than once in times of emergency He brought them to the front and worked through them for the salvation of many lives.—Letter 22, 1911.

The Mother's First Responsibility—The mother's influence never ceases. It is ever active, either for good or for evil; and if she would have her work abide the test of the Judgment, she must make God her trust and labor with an eye single to His glory. Her first duty is to her children, to so mold their characters that they may be happy in this life and secure the future, immortal life. She should not be influenced by what Mrs. So-and-So does, nor by the remarks of Mrs. A. or B. in reference to her being so odd, so different from other people in her dress or in the arrangement of her house for comfort rather than display or in the management of her children.

God has given the mother, in the education of her children, a responsibility paramount to everything else.—Good Health, June, 1880.

[159] **Society Has Claims Upon Women**—It is woman's right to look after the interest of her husband, to have a care for his wardrobe, and to seek to make him happy. It is her right to improve her mind and manners, to be social, cheerful, and happy, shedding sunshine in her family and making it a little heaven. And she may have an interest for more than "me and mine." She should consider that society has claims upon her.—The Health Reformer, June, 1873.

A Work Outside Our Homes—Men and women are not fulfilling the design of God when they simply express affection for their own family circle, for their rich relatives and friends, while they exclude those from their love whom they could comfort and bless by relieving their necessities....

When the Lord bids us do good for others outside our home, He does not mean that our affection for home shall become diminished, and that we shall love our kindred or our country less because He desires us to extend our sympathies. But we are not to confine our affection and sympathy within four walls, and enclose the blessing that God has given us, so that others will not be benefited with us in its enjoyment.—The Review and Herald, October 15, 1895.

Enlarging the Sphere of Usefulness—All have not the same work. There are distinct and individual duties for each to perform; yet with these varied duties there may be a beautiful harmony, binding the work of all together in perfect fitness. Our heavenly Father requires of none to whom He has given but one talent, the improvement of five. But if the one be wisely used, the possessor will soon have gained more, and may continually increase her power of influence and sphere of usefulness by making the best use of the talents which God has given her. Her individuality may be distinctly preserved, and yet she be part of the great whole in advancing the work of reform so greatly needed.

Woman, if she wisely improves her time and her faculties, relying upon God for wisdom and strength, may stand on an equality with her husband as adviser, counselor, companion, and co-worker, and yet lose none of her womanly grace or modesty. She may elevate her own character, and just as she does this she is elevating and ennobling the characters of her family and exerting a powerful though unconscious influence upon others around her.—Good Health, June, 1880.

Learning to Reach Other Women With the Truth—Women can learn what needs to be done to reach other women. There are women who are especially adapted for the work of giving Bible readings, and they are very successful in presenting the Word of God in its simplicity to others. They become a great blessing in reaching mothers and their daughters. This is a sacred work, and those engaged in it should receive encouragement.—Letter 108, 1910.

Responsibility to Gather Sheaves—Let every sister who claims to be a child of God feel a responsibility to help all within her reach. The noblest of all attainments may be gained through practical self-denial and benevolence for others' good. Sisters, God calls you to work in the harvest field and to help gather in the sheaves.... In the various lines of home missionary work the modest, intelligent woman may use her powers to the very highest account.—The Review and Herald, December 10, 1914.

An Influence on the Side of Reform and Truth—Why should not women cultivate the intellect? Why should they not answer the purpose of God in their existence? Why may they not understand their own powers, and realizing that these powers are given of God, strive to make use of them to the fullest extent in doing good to others, in advancing the work of reform, of truth, and of real goodness in the world? Satan knows that women have a power of influence for good or for evil; therefore he seeks to enlist them in his cause. He invents multitudinous fashions, and tempts the women of the present day, as he did Eve to pluck and eat, to adopt and practice these ever-changing, never-satisfying modes.

Sisters and mothers, we have a higher aim, a more noble work, than to study the latest fashion and form garments with needless adorning to meet the standard of this modern Moloch. We may become its slave, and sacrifice upon its altars our own and the present and future happiness of our children. But what do we gain in the end? We have sown to the flesh; we shall reap corruption. Our works cannot bear the inspection of God. We shall see at last how many souls might have been blessed and redeemed from darkness and error by our influence, which, instead, encouraged them in pride and outward display to the neglect of the inward adorning.—Good Health, June, 1880.

Placing Leaven of God's Word in Homes—Women as well as men can engage in the work of hiding the truth where it can work out and be made manifest.... Discreet and humble women can do a good work in explaining the truth to the people in their homes. The Word of God thus explained will begin its leavening work, and through its influence whole families will be converted to the truth.—Letter 86, 1907.

Do Not Become Weary in Missionary Service—My sisters, do not become weary in the distribution of our literature. This is a work you may all engage in successfully if you are but connected with God. Before approaching your friends and neighbors or writing letters of inquiry lift the heart to God in prayer. All who with humble heart take part in this work will be educating themselves as acceptable workers in the vineyard of the Lord.—The Review and Herald, December 10, 1914.

Women Can Reach Hearts—To these our friends who expect soon to go from us to other lands I wish to say: "Remember that you can break down the severest opposition by taking a personal interest in the people whom you meet. Christ took a personal interest in men and women while He lived on this earth. Wherever He went He was a medical missionary. We are to go about doing good, even as He did. We are instructed to feed the hungry, clothe the naked, and comfort the sorrowing."

The sisters can do much to reach the heart and make it tender. Wherever you are, my sisters, work in simplicity. If you are in a home where there are children, show an interest in them. Let them see that you love them. If one is sick, offer to give him treatment; help the careworn, anxious mother to relieve her suffering child.—The Review and Herald, November 11, 1902.

To Unite With Other Women in Temperance Work—The Woman's Christian Temperance Union is an organization with whose efforts for the spread of temperance principles we can heartily unite. The light has been given me that we are not to stand aloof from them, but, while there is to be no sacrifice of principle on our part, as far as possible we are to unite with them in laboring for temperance reforms.... We are to work with them when we can, and we can assuredly do this on the question of utterly closing the saloon.

As the human agent submits his will to the will of God, the Holy Spirit will make the impression upon the hearts of those to whom he ministers. I have been shown that we are not to shun the W.C.T.U. workers. By uniting with them in behalf of total abstinence we do not change our position regarding the observance of the seventh day, and we can show our appreciation of their position regarding the subject of temperance. By opening the door and inviting them to unite with us on the temperance question we secure their help along temperance lines; and they, by uniting with us, will hear new truths which the Holy Spirit is waiting to impress upon hearts.—The Review and Herald, June 18, 1908.

Surprised at Our Indifference—I have had some opportunity to see the great advantage to be gained by connecting with the W.C.T.U. workers, and I have been much surprised as I have seen the indifference of many of our leaders to this organization. I call on my brethren to awake.—Letter 274, 1907.

Appreciate the Good Done by W.C.T.U—Light has been given me that there are those with most precious talents and capabilities in the W.C.T.U. Much time and money has been absorbed among us in ways that bring no returns. Instead of this, some of our best talent should be set at work for the W.C.T.U., not as evangelists, but as those who fully appreciate the good that has been done by this body. We should seek to gain the confidence of the workers in the W.C.T.U. by harmonizing with them as far as possible.... This people have been rich in good works.—Manuscript 91, 1907.

A Telling Influence-Counsel to a Sister—I hope, my sister, that you will have an influence in the Woman's Christian Temperance Union.... Get the oil of grace in the conscious and unconscious influence of words spoken, revealing the fact that you have the light of life to shine forth to others in a direct, positive testimony upon subjects where you can all agree, and this will leave a telling influence. My heart is with your heart in this work of temperance. I speak upon this subject most decidedly, and it has a decided influence upon other minds.—Manuscript 74, 1898.

Doing Missionary Work Without Neglecting Home Duties—Intelligent Christian women may use their talents to the very highest account. They can show by their life of self-denial and by their willingness to work to the best of their ability that they believe the truth and are being sanctified through it. Many need a work of this kind to develop the powers they possess. Wives and mothers should in no case neglect their husbands and their children, but they can do much without neglecting home duties, and all have not these responsibilities.

Who can have so deep a love for the souls of men and women for whom Christ died as those who are partakers of His grace? Who can better represent the religion of Christ than Christian women, women who are earnestly laboring to bring souls to the light of truth? Who else is so well adapted to the work of the Sabbath school? The true mother is the true, teacher of children. If with a heart imbued with the love of Christ, she teaches the children of her class, praying with them and for them, she may see souls converted and gathered into the fold of Christ. I do not recommend that woman should seek to become a voter or officeholder; but as a missionary, teaching the truth by epistolary correspondence, distributing reading matter, conversing with families and praying with the mother and children, she may do much and be a blessing.—The Signs of the Times, September 16, 1886.

Women Not Excused Because of Domestic Cares—Some can do more than others, but all can do something. Women should not feel that they are excused because of their domestic cares. They should become intelligent as to how they can work most successfully and methodically in bringing souls to Christ. If all would realize the importance of doing to the utmost of their ability in the work of God, having a deep love for souls, feeling the burden of the work upon them, hundreds would be engaged as active workers who have hitherto been dull and uninterested, accomplishing nothing, or at most but very little.

In many cases the rubbish of the world has clogged the channels of the soul. Selfishness controls the mind and warps the character. Were the life hid with Christ in God, His service would be no drudgery. If the whole heart were consecrated to God, all would find something to do and would covet a part in the work. They would sow beside all waters, praying and believing that the fruit would appear. The practical, God-fearing workers will be growing upward, praying in faith for grace and heavenly wisdom that they may do the work devolving upon them with cheerfulness and a willing mind. They will seek the divine rays of light that they may brighten the paths of others.—Ibid.

A Beautiful, Character-molding Resolution—Let every individual member of the church ask himself, "What part can I act to win souls to Jesus Christ?" "I will," says one class, "guard myself that my wants shall be so bound about that no needless adornment shall steal away the pence and shillings to gratify pride or display. I will consecrate myself to God, and my desire for selfish gratification shall be killed before it buds and blossoms and bears fruit." This is a good resolution. It will please the Saviour who has purchased you....

One may say, "I have no opportunity to obtain money, but I will set apart myself. I will educate and train myself that no opportunity shall be allowed to pass unimproved. I have always kept myself busy, but after all I have not felt a satisfaction in the way my time has been occupied. I see now as never before that very much of my time has been employed in doing nothing but those things that pleased myself. Now I desire to please God, and I will give a portion of my time in doing real service for the Master. I will visit the sick, I will train myself to have an interest and sympathy for the suffering ones, and I will add if possible some favors to make them more comfortable. Through this means I can reach their hearts and speak a word as the servant of Jesus Christ. Thus I can cultivate the art of ministering, and may win souls to Jesus." Can you not see that Jesus will say, "Well done" to this line of ministry?—Letter 12, 1892.

Section 7—The Poor

Gem Thought

A true Christian is the poor man's friend. He deals with his perplexed and unfortunate brother as one would deal with a delicate, tender, sensitive plant. God wants His workers to move among the sick and suffering as messengers of His love and mercy. He is looking upon us, to see how we are treating one another, whether we are Christlike in our dealing with all, high or low, rich or poor, free or bond....

When you meet those who are careworn and oppressed, who know not which way to turn to find relief, put your hearts into the work of helping them. It is not God's purpose that His children shall shut themselves up to themselves, taking no interest in the welfare of those less fortunate than themselves. Remember that for them as well as for you Christ has died. Conciliation and kindness will open the way for you to help them, to win their confidence, to inspire them with hope and courage.—Letter 30, 1887.

If a brother or sister be naked, and destitute of daily food, and one of you say unto them, Depart in peace, be ye warmed and filled; notwithstanding ye give them not those things which are needful to the body; what doth it profit? Even so faith, if it hath not works, is dead, being alone. James 2, 15-17.

Chapter 20—Ministry to the Poor

The Gospel in Its Greatest Loveliness—Unto the poor the gospel is to be preached. Never does the gospel put on an aspect of greater loveliness than when it is brought to the most needy and destitute regions. To men of every station it delivers its precepts, which regulate their duties, and its promises, which nerve them to the discharge of their duties. Then it is that the light of the gospel shines forth in its most radiant clearness and its greatest power. Truth from the Word of God enters the hovel of the peasant and lights up the rude cottages of the poor, both black and white. Rays from the Sun of Righteousness bring gladness to the sick and suffering. Angels of God are there, and the simple faith shown makes the crust of bread and the cup of water as a banquet of luxury. Those who have been loathed and abandoned are raised through faith and pardon to the dignity of sons and daughters of God. Lifted above all in the world, they sit in heavenly places in Christ Jesus. They have no earthly treasure, but they have found the pearl of great price. The sin-pardoning Saviour receives the poor and ignorant and gives them to eat of the bread which comes down from heaven. They drink of the water of life.—Letter 113, 1901.

[170]

Jesus Associated Himself With the Poor—It has become fashionable to look down upon the poor.... But Jesus, the Master, was poor, and He sympathizes with the poor, the discarded, the oppressed, and declares that every insult shown to them is as if shown to Himself. I am more and more surprised as I see those who claim to be children of God possessing so little of the sympathy, tenderness, and love which actuated Christ. Would that every church, North and South, were imbued with the spirit of our Lord's teaching!—Manuscript 6, 1891.

Christ Came to Minister to the Poor—Christ stood at the head of humanity in the garb of humanity. So full of sympathy and love was His attitude that the poorest was not afraid to come to Him. He was kind to all, easily approached by the most lowly. He went from house to house, healing the sick, feeding the hungry, comforting the mourners, soothing the afflicted, speaking peace to the distressed.—Letter 117, 1903.

"And He came to Nazareth, where He had been brought up: and, as His custom was, He went into the synagogue on the sabbath day, and stood up for to read. And there was delivered unto Him the book of the prophet Esaias. And when He had opened the book, He found the place where it was written, The Spirit of the Lord is upon Me, because He hath anointed Me to preach the gospel to the poor; He hath sent Me to heal the brokenhearted, to preach deliverance to the captives, and recovering of sight to the blind, to set at liberty them that are bruised, to preach the acceptable year of the Lord."

This is a wonderful description of Christ's work. The Pharisees and Sadducees despised the poor. The learned and rich neglected them, as though their wealth and knowledge made them of more value than those who were poor. But Jesus declared that it was His work to give encouragement and comfort and help where it was most needed.—Manuscript 65b, 1898.

How Christ Awakened Soul Hunger—Christ's chief work was in the preaching of the gospel to the poor. He chose to minister to the needy, the ignorant. In simplicity He opened before them the blessings they might receive, and thus He awakened their soul's hunger for the truth, the bread of life. Christ's life is an example to all His followers.—Manuscript 103, 1906.

The Evidence of the Divinity of the Gospel—Christ met with the greatest success among the poor, and with this class every human being, whether learned or unlearned, may find abundance to do. The poor need comfort and sympathy, for there are those who without a helping hand will never recover themselves. In working for these Christ's disciples will fulfill their commission. This is the highest credential of the gospel ministry. Had the gospel been of men, it would have been popular with the rich and mighty; but it pours contempt upon the rich and mighty, and calls upon all who accept it to work the works of Christ, helping those who are destitute, despised, forsaken, afflicted.

Those who take hold of the work for the love of Christ and the love of souls will work in Christ's lines. This world is a lazar house of disease, but Christ came to heal the sick, to comfort the brokenhearted, to proclaim deliverance to the captives, to give sight to the blind. The gospel is the very essence of restoration, and Christ would have us bid the brokenhearted, the hopeless, and the afflicted, take hold His strength; for the acceptable year of the Lord has come.—Manuscript 65b, 1898.

Christianity the Solace of the Poor—There is a connection between the religion of Christ and poverty. Christianity is the solace of the poor. There is a false religion, endangering the souls of all who advance it, that teaches that selfish pleasure and enjoyment is the sum of happiness. But the parable of the rich man and Lazarus shows us that this is false. There came a time when the rich man would have given all he possessed to have exchanged places with Lazarus, once poor, and covered with sores.

In the humanity of Christ there are golden threads that bind the believing, trusting poor man to His own soul of infinite love. He is the great physician. In our world He bore our infirmities and carried our burdens. He is the mighty Healer of all diseases. He was poor, and yet He was the center of all goodness, all blessings. He is a reservoir of power to all to consecrate their powers to the work of becoming sons of God.—Manuscript 22, 1898.

Christ Lifted the Stigma From Poverty—Christ has ever been the poor man's friend. He chose poverty, and honored it by making it His lot. He has stripped from it forever the reproach of scorn by blessing the poor, the inheritors of God's kingdom. Such was His work. By consecrating Himself to a life of poverty He redeemed poverty from its humiliation. He took His position with the poor that He might lift from poverty the stigma that the world had attached to it. He knew the danger of the love of riches. He knew that this love is ruinous to many souls. It places those who are rich where they indulge every wish for grandeur. It teaches them to look down on those who are suffering the pressure of poverty. It develops the weakness of human minds and shows that notwithstanding the abundance of wealth, the rich are not rich toward God.

The characters of many have been molded by the false estimate placed on the worldly rich man. The man possessed of houses and lands, lauded and deceived by the respect given him, may look down upon the poor man, who possesses virtues that the rich man does not. When weighed in the golden scales of the sanctuary, the selfish, covetous rich man will be found wanting, while the poor man, who has depended in faith upon God alone for his virtue and goodness, will be pronounced heir to eternal riches in the kingdom of God.—Manuscript 22, 1898.

World's Great Men Cannot Solve the Problem—In the great cities there are multitudes living in poverty and wretchedness, well-nigh destitute of food, shelter, and clothing; while in the same cities are those who have more than heart could wish, who live luxuriously, spending their money on richly furnished houses, on personal adornment, or worse still, upon the gratification of sensual appetites, upon liquor, tobacco, and other things that destroy the powers of the brain, unbalance the mind, and debase the soul. The cries of starving humanity are coming up before God....

There are not many, even among educators and statesmen, who comprehend the causes that underlie the present state of society. Those who hold the reins of government are not able to solve the problem of moral corruption, poverty, pauperism, and increasing crime. They are struggling in vain to place business operations on a more secure basis. If men would give more heed to the teaching of God's Word, they would find a solution of the problems that perplex them.—Testimonies for the Church 9:12, 13.

God's Plan for Israel to Check Inequality—It was to be impressed upon the minds of all that the poor have as much right to a place in God's world as have the more wealthy. Such were the provisions made by our merciful Creator, to lessen suffering, to bring some ray of hope, to flash some gleam of sunshine, into the life of the destitute and distressed.

The Lord would place a check upon the inordinate love of property and power. Great evils would result from the continued accumulation of wealth by one class and the poverty and degradation of another. Without some restraint the power of the wealthy would become a monopoly, and the poor, though in every respect fully as worthy in God's sight, would be regarded and treated as inferior to their more prosperous brethren. The sense of this oppression would arouse the passions of the poorer class. There would be a feeling of despair and desperation which would tend to demoralize society and open the door to crimes of every description. The regulations that God established were designed to promote social equality. The provisions of the sabbatical year and the jubilee would, in a great measure, set right that which during the interval had gone wrong in the social and political economy of the nation.

These regulations were designed to bless the rich no less than the poor. They would restrain avarice and a disposition for self-exaltation and would cultivate a noble spirit of benevolence; and by fostering good-will and confidence between all classes they would promote social order, the stability of government. We are all woven together in the great web of humanity, and whatever we can do to benefit and uplift others will reflect in blessing upon ourselves. The law of mutual dependence runs through all classes of society. The poor are not more dependent upon the rich than are the rich upon the poor. While the one class ask a share in the blessings which God has bestowed upon their wealthier neighbors, the other need the faithful service, the strength of brain and bone and muscle, that are the capital of the poor....

There are many who urge with great enthusiasm that all men should have an equal share in the temporal blessings of God. But this was not the purpose of the Creator. A diversity of condition is one of the means by which God designs to prove and develop character. Yet He intends that those who have worldly possessions shall regard themselves merely as stewards of His goods, as entrusted with means to be employed for the benefit of the suffering and the needy.

Christ has said that we shall have the poor always with us, and He unites His interest with that of His suffering people. The heart of our Redeemer sympathizes with the poorest and lowliest of His earthly children. He tells us that they are His representatives on earth. He has placed them among us to awaken in our hearts the love that He feels toward the suffering and oppressed. Pity and benevolence shown to them are accepted by Christ as if shown to Himself. An act of cruelty or neglect toward them is regarded as though done to Him.—Patriarchs and Prophets, 534-536.

Christ Sees Opportunity in Man's Extremity—Christ's heart is cheered by the sight of those who are poor in every sense of the term; cheered by His view of the ill-used ones who are meek and of those bowed down with the sorrows of bereavement; cheered by the seemingly unsatisfied hungering after righteousness, by the inability of many to begin. He welcomes, as it were, the very condition of things that would discourage many ministers. He sees an opportunity to help those who are so much in need of help by meeting them where they are.

The Lord Jesus corrects our erring piety, giving the burden of this work for the poor and needy in the rough places to men and women of adaptability who have hearts that can feel for the ignorant and for those who are out of the way. The Lord teaches them how to meet these cases. These workers will be encouraged as they see doors opening for them to enter places where they can do medical missionary work. Having little self-confidence, they give God all the glory, taking none of it to themselves. The Saviour is present to help to make a beginning through those whose hands are rough and unskilled, but whose hearts are susceptible to pity and awakened to do something to relieve the woes so abundant. He works through those who can discern mercy in misery, gain in the loss of all things. When the Light of the world passeth by, privileges appear in all hardships, right and order in confusion, the success and wisdom of God in that which has seemed to be failure in human experience....

Christ pronounces His blessing upon those who hunger and thirst after righteousness. In Luke we read, "Blessed be ye poor." The poor have not a hundredth part of the delusive temptations of the rich. In Matthew we read, "Blessed are the poor in spirit: for theirs is the kingdom of heaven." Poverty of spirit signifies wealth to be supplied by the riches of the grace of God.—Letter 100, 1902.

If Poverty Were Removed From the Earth—Want and poverty there will always be. However high the standard of knowledge and morality may be, whatever heights we may reach in civilization, poverty will always continue, as a display of the riches of the grace of God, a standing memorial to the truth of the words, "Not by might, nor by power, but by My Spirit, saith the Lord of hosts." It would not be for the benefit of Christianity for the Lord to remove poverty from the earth. Thus a door would be closed that is now open for the exercise of faith—a means whereby the hearts of the afflicted can be reached by the gospel of goodness. By Christian liberality souls are reached that could be reached in no other way. It is the helping hand of the gospel.—Letter 83, 1902.

Chapter 21—The Poor in the Church

The Needy of the Household of Faith—Our love for God is to be expressed in doing good to the needy and suffering of the household of faith whose necessities come to our knowledge and require our care. Every soul is under special obligation to God to notice His worthy poor with particular compassion. Under no consideration are these to be passed by.—Testimonies for the Church 6:271.

"As we have therefore opportunity, let us do good unto all men, especially unto them who are of the household of faith."

In a special sense Christ has laid upon His church the duty of caring for the needy among its own members. He suffers His poor to be in the borders of every church. They are always to be among us, and He places upon the members of the church a personal responsibility to care for them.

As the members of a true family care for one another, ministering to the sick, supporting the weak, teaching the ignorant, training the inexperienced, so is the "household of faith" to care for its needy and helpless ones.—The Ministry of Healing, 201.

Two Classes to Care For—There are two classes of poor whom we have always within our borders—those who ruin themselves by their own independent course of action and continue in their transgression, and those who for the truth's sake have been brought into straitened circumstances. We are to love our neighbor as ourselves, and then toward both these classes we shall do the right thing under the guidance and counsel of sound wisdom.

There is no question in regard to the Lord's poor. They are to be helped in every case where it will be for their benefit. God wants His people to reveal to a sinful world that He has not left them to perish. Special pains should be taken to help those who for the truth's sake are cast out from their homes and are obliged to suffer. More and more there will be need of large, open, generous hearts, those who will deny self and will take hold of the cases of these very ones whom the Lord loves. The poor among God's people must not be left without provision for their wants. Some way must be found whereby they may obtain a livelihood. Some will need to be taught to work. Others who work hard, and are taxed to the utmost of their ability to support their families, will need special assistance. We should take an interest in these cases and help them to secure employment. There should be a fund to aid such worthy poor families who love God and keep His commandments.

Care must be taken that the means needed for this work shall not be diverted into other channels. It makes a difference whether we help the poor who through keeping God's commandments are reduced to want and suffering, or whether we neglect these in order to help blasphemers who tread underfoot the commandments of God. And God regards the difference. Sabbathkeepers should not pass by the Lord's suffering, needy ones to take upon themselves the burden of supporting those who continue in transgression of God's law, those who are educated to look for help to anyone who will sustain them. This is not the right kind of missionary work. It is not in harmony with the Lord's plan.

Wherever a church is established its members are to do a faithful work for the needy believers. But they are not to stop here. They are also to aid others, irrespective of their faith. As the result of such effort some of these will receive the special truths for this time.

"If there be among you a poor man of one of thy brethren within any of thy gates in thy land which the Lord thy God giveth thee, thou shalt not harden thine heart, nor shut thine hand from thy poor brother: but thou shalt open thine hand wide unto him, and shalt surely lend him sufficient for his need, in that which he wanteth. Beware that there be not a thought in thy wicked heart, saying, The seventh year, the year of release, is at hand; and thine eye be evil against thy poor brother, and thou givest him nought; and he cry unto the Lord against thee, and it be sin unto thee. Thou shalt surely give him, and thine heart shall not be grieved when thou givest unto him: because that for this thing the Lord thy God shall bless thee in all thy works, and in all that thou puttest thine hand unto. For the poor shall never cease out of the land: therefore I command thee, saying, Thou shalt open thine hand wide unto thy brother, to thy poor, and to thy needy, in thy land." Deuteronomy 15:7-11.

Through circumstances some who love and obey God become poor. Some are not careful; they do not know how to manage. Others are poor through sickness and misfortune. Whatever the cause they are in need, and to help them is an important line of missionary work.—Testimonies for the Church 6:269-271.

Poverty May Result From Adverse Circumstance—It has not always been regarded as a mark of inefficiency when through adverse circumstances pinching want has made it necessity for a brother to incur debts or suffer for food and clothing even though he was unable to lift these debts, struggle as hard as he might. A helping hand has been reached out to such ones, to place them upon their feet, free from embarrassment, that they might do their work in the vineyard of the Lord and not be oppressed with the thought that a cloud of debt was hanging over them.—Manuscript 34, 1894.

The Responsibility of the Church or Churches—It is the duty of each church to make careful, judicious arrangements for the care of its poor and sick.—Letter 169, 1901.

God suffers His poor to be in the borders of every church. They are always to be among us, and the Lord places upon the members of every church a personal responsibility to care for them. We are not to lay our responsibility upon others. Toward those within our own borders we are to manifest the same love and sympathy that Christ would manifest were He in our place. Thus we are to be disciplined, that we may be prepared to work in Christ's lines.

The minister should educate the various families and strengthen the church to care for its own sick and poor. He should set at work the God-given faculties of the people, and if one church is overtaxed in this line, other churches should come to its assistance. Let the church members exercise tact and ingenuity in caring for these, the Lord's people. Let them deny themselves luxuries and needless ornaments, that they may make the suffering needy ones comfortable. In doing this they practice the instruction given in the fifty-eighth chapter of Isaiah, and the blessing there pronounced will be theirs.—Testimonies for the Church 6:272.

Every Church Member to Do His Part—The Lord's people are to be as true as steel to principle. He has pointed out the work devolving on every church member. He declares that the church members are faithfully to do their duty to those within their own borders. They are generously to support their own poor. They are to engage in systematic missionary work, teaching their children to keep the way of the Lord and to do judgment and justice.

But the light which for years has been before the churches has been disregarded. The work that ought to have been done for suffering humanity in every church has not been done. Church members have failed to heed the word of the Lord, and this has deprived them of an experience they should have gained in gospel work.—The Review and Herald, March 4, 1902.

The poor and the needy are to be cared for. These must not be neglected, at whatever cost or sacrifice to ourselves.—The Youth's Instructor, August 26, 1897.

The Church to Bear the Burden—The churches that have the poor among them should not neglect their stewardship and throw the burden of the poor and sick upon the sanitarium. All the members of the several churches are responsible before God for their afflicted ones. They should bear their own burdens. If they have sick persons among them, whom they wish to be benefited by treatment, they should, if able, send them to the sanitarium. In doing this they will not only be patronizing the institution which God has established but will be helping those who need help, caring for the poor as God requires us to do.—Testimonies for the Church 4:551.

When the Lord's Poor Are Neglected—When the Lord's poor are neglected and forgotten or greeted with cold looks and cruel words, let the guilty one bear in mind that he is neglecting Christ in the person of His saints. Our Saviour identifies His interest with that of suffering humanity. As the heart of the parent yearns with pitying tenderness over the suffering one of her little flock, so the heart of our Redeemer sympathizes with the poorest and lowliest of His earthly children. He has placed them among us to awaken in our hearts that love which He feels toward the suffering and oppressed, and He will let His judgments fall upon anyone who wrongs, slights, or abuses them.—Testimonies for the Church 4:620.

Search Out the Needs—Your good wishes we will thank you for, but the poor cannot keep comfortable on good wishes alone. They must have tangible proofs of your kindness in food and clothing. God does not mean that any of His followers should beg for bread. He has given you an abundance that you may supply those of their necessities which by industry and economy they are not able to supply. Do not wait for them to call your attention to their needs. Act as did Job. The thing that he knew not he searched out. Go on an inspecting tour and learn what is needed and how it can be best supplied.—Testimonies for the Church 5:151.

Do Not Wait for Them to Come to Us—Poverty and distress in families will come to our knowledge, and afflicted and suffering ones will have to be relieved.... Do not wait for them to come to you. Examine their wearing apparel and help them if they need help. We should invest means to help young men and young women to obtain an education in sending the gospel to the poor, in aiding those who have ventured by faith to take their position upon the platform of eternal truth, when by so doing they have placed themselves in an embarrassing situation. Where there are cases of special need the minister must be prepared to relieve those who are in poverty for the truth's sake.—Manuscript 25, 1894.

Help for New Converts out of Employment—In our benevolent work special help should be given to those who, through the presentation of the truth, are convicted and converted. We must have a care for those who have the moral courage to accept the truth, who lose their situations in consequence, and are refused work by which to support their families. Provision should be made to aid the worthy poor and to furnish employment for those who love God and keep His commandments. They should not be left without help, to feel that they are forced to work on the Sabbath or starve. Those who take their position on the Lord's side are to see in Seventh-day Adventists a warmhearted, self-denying, self-sacrificing people, who cheerfully and gladly minister to their brethren in need. It is of this class especially that the Lord speaks when He says: "Bring the poor that are cast out to thy house." Isaiah 58:7.—Testimonies for the Church 6:85.

Provide Land for Poor Families—Where the school is established [in Australia] there must be land for orchards and gardens, that students may have physical exercise combined with mental taxation, and half and some wholly pay their way at school. Also ground must be purchased, that families that cannot obtain work in the cities because of the observance of the Sabbath may buy small farms and make their own living. This is a positive necessity in this country.

Education must be given in regard to tilling the soil, and we must expect that the Lord will bless this effort.—Manuscript 23, 1894.

Our Duty to Poor Families—Inquiries are often made in regard to our duty to the poor who embrace the third message; and we ourselves have long been anxious to know how to manage with discretion the cases of poor families who embrace the Sabbath. But while at Roosevelt, New York, August 3, 1861, I was shown some things in regard to the poor.

God does not require our brethren to take charge of every poor family that shall embrace this message. If they should do this, the ministers must cease to enter new fields, for the funds would be exhausted. Many are poor from their own lack of diligence and economy; they know not how to use means aright. If they should be helped, it would hurt them. Some will always be poor. If they should have the very best advantages, their cases would not be helped. They have not good calculation, and would use all the means they could obtain, were it much or little.

Some know nothing of denying self and economizing to keep out of debt and to get a little ahead for a time of need. If the church should help such individuals instead of leaving them to rely upon their own resources, it would injure them in the end, for they look to the church and expect to receive help from them and do not practice self-denial and economy when they are well provided for. And if they do not receive help every time, Satan tempts them, and they become jealous and very conscientious for their brethren, fearing they will fail to do all their duty to them. The mistake is on their own part. They are deceived. They are not the Lord's poor.

The instructions given in the Word of God in regard to helping the poor do not touch such cases, but are for the unfortunate and afflicted. God in His providence has afflicted individuals to test and prove others. Widows and invalids are in the church to prove a blessing to the church. They are a part of the means which God has chosen to develop the true character of Christ's professed followers and to call into exercise the precious traits of character manifested by our compassionate Redeemer.

Many who can but barely live when they are single choose to marry and raise a family when they know they have nothing with which to support them. And worse than this, they have no family government. Their whole course in their family is marked with their loose, slack habits. They have but little control over themselves, and are passionate, impatient, and fretful. When such embrace the message they feel that they are entitled to assistance from their more wealthy brethren; and if their expectations are not met, they complain of the church and accuse them of not living out their faith? Who must be the sufferers in this case? Must the cause of God be sapped, and the treasury in different places exhausted, to take care of these large families of poor? No. The parents must be the sufferers. They will not, as a general thing, suffer any greater lack after they embrace the Sabbath than they did before.

There is an evil among some of the poor which will certainly prove their ruin unless they overcome it. They have embraced the truth with their coarse, rough, uncultivated habits, and it takes some time for them to see and realize their coarseness, and that it is not in accordance with the character of Christ. They look upon others who are more orderly and refined as being proud, and you may hear them say: "The truth brings us all down upon a level." But it is an entire mistake to think that the truth brings the receiver down. It brings him up, refines his taste, sanctifies his judgment, and, if lived out, is continually fitting him for the society of holy angels in the city of God. The truth is designed to bring us all up upon a level.

The more able should ever act a noble, generous part in their deal with their poorer brethren, and should also give them good advice, and then leave them to fight life's battles through. But I was shown that a most solemn duty rests upon the church to have an especial care for the destitute widows, orphans, and invalids.—Testimonies for the Church 1:272-274.

Counsel Regarding a Balanced Work—Christ has not bidden us bestow all our labor and all our gifts upon the poor. We have a work to do in behalf of those who are fulfilling His commission, "Go ye into all the world, and preach the gospel to every creature." The increase of the ministry will require an increase of means....

When you expend money consider, "Am I encouraging prodigality?" When you give to the poor and wretched consider, "Am I helping them, or hurting them?" ...

Think of the necessities of our mission fields throughout the world.... The present time is burdened with eternal interests. We are to unfurl the standard of truth before a world perishing in error. God calls for men to rally under Christ's blood-stained banner, give the Bible to the people, multiply camp meetings in different localities, warn the cities, and send the warning far and near in the highways and byways of the world.—Manuscript 4, 1899.

Chapter 22—The Poor of the World

To Supply the Wants of the Poor—All around us we see want and suffering. Families are in need of food; little ones are crying for bread. The houses of the poor lack proper furniture and bedding. Many live in mere hovels, which are almost destitute of conveniences. The cry of the poor reaches to heaven. God sees; God hears.—Testimonies for the Church 6:385.

While God in His providence has laden the earth with His bounties and filled its storehouses with the comforts of life, want and misery are on every hand. A liberal Providence has placed in the hands of His human agents an abundance to supply the necessities of all, but the stewards of God are unfaithful. In the professed Christian world there is enough expended in extravagant display to supply the wants of all the hungry and to clothe the naked. Many who have taken upon themselves the name of Christ are spending His money for selfish pleasure, for the gratification of appetite, for strong drink and rich dainties, for extravagant houses and furniture and dress, while to suffering human beings they give scarcely a look of pity or a word of sympathy.

What misery exists in the very heart of our so-called Christian countries! Think of the condition of the poor in our large cities. In these cities there are multitudes of human beings who do not receive as much care and consideration as are given to the brutes. There are thousands of wretched children, ragged and half starved, with vice and depravity written on their faces. Families are herded together in miserable tenements, many of them dark cellars reeking with dampness and filth. Children are born in these terrible places. Infancy and youth behold nothing attractive, nothing of the beauty of natural things that God has created to delight the senses. These children are left to grow up molded and fashioned in character by the low precepts, the wretchedness, and the wicked example around them. They hear the name of God only in profanity. Impure words, the fumes of liquor and tobacco, moral degradation of every kind, meet the eye and pervert the senses. And from these abodes of wretchedness piteous cries for food and clothing are sent out by many who know nothing about prayer.

By our churches there is a work to be done of which many have little idea, a work as yet almost untouched. "I was an hungred," Christ says, "and ye gave Me meat: I was thirsty, and ye gave Me drink: I was a stranger, and ye took Me in: naked, and ye clothed Me: I was sick, and ye visited Me: I was in prison, and ye came unto Me." Matthew 25:35, 36. Some think that if they give money to this work, it is all they are required to do, but this is an error. Donations of money cannot take the place of personal ministry. It is right to give our means, and many more should do this; but according to their strength and opportunities, personal service is required of all.

The work of gathering in the needy, the oppressed, the suffering, the destitute, is the very work which every church that believes the truth for this time should long since have been doing. We are to show the tender sympathy of the Samaritan in supplying physical necessities, feeding the hungry, bringing the poor that are cast out to our homes, gathering from God every day grace and strength that will enable us to reach to the very depths of human misery and help those who cannot possibly help themselves. In doing this work we have a favorable opportunity to set forth Christ the crucified One.—Testimonies for the Church 6:274-276.

Begin by Helping Your Neighbors—Every church member should feel it his special duty to labor for those living in his neighborhood. Study how you can best help those who take no interest in religious things. As you visit your friends and neighbors show an interest in their spiritual as well as in their temporal welfare. Present Christ as a sin-pardoning Saviour. Invite your neighbors to your home, and read with them from the precious Bible and from books that explain its truths. This, united with simple songs and fervent prayers, will touch their hearts. Let church members educate themselves to do this work. This is just as essential as to save the benighted souls in foreign countries. While some feel the burden of souls afar off, let the many who are at home feel the burden of precious souls around them and work just as diligently for their salvation.

The hours so often spent in amusement that refreshes neither body nor soul should be spent in visiting the poor, the sick, and the suffering, or in seeking to help someone who is in need.

In trying to help the poor, the despised, the forsaken, do not work for them mounted on the stilts of your dignity and superiority, for in this way you will accomplish nothing. Become truly converted, and learn of Him who is meek and lowly in heart. We must set the Lord always before us. As servants of Christ keep saying, lest you forget it, "I am bought with a price."

God calls not only for your benevolence but for your cheerful countenance, your hopeful words, the grasp of your hand. As you visit the Lord's afflicted ones you will find some from whom hope has departed; bring back the sunshine to them. There are those who need the bread of life; read to them from the Word of God. Upon others there is a soul sickness that no earthly balm can reach or physician heal; pray for these, and bring them to Jesus.

On special occasions some indulge in sentimental feelings which lead to impulsive movements. They may think that in this way they are doing great service for Christ, but they are not. Their zeal soon dies, and then Christ's service is neglected. It is not fitful service that God accepts; it is not by emotional spasms of activity that we can do good to our fellow men. Spasmodic efforts to do good often result in more injury than benefit.—Testimonies for the Church 6:276-277.

Give the Right Kind of Help—Methods of helping the needy should be carefully and prayerfully considered. We are to seek God for wisdom, for He knows better than shortsighted mortals how to care for the creatures He has made. There are some who give indiscriminately to everyone who solicits their aid. In this they err. In trying to help the needy we should be careful to give them the right kind of help. There are those who when helped will continue to make themselves special objects of need. They will be dependent as long as they see anything on which to depend. By giving undue time and attention to these we may encourage idleness, helplessness, extravagance, and intemperance.

When we give to the poor we should consider, "Am I encouraging prodigality? Am I helping or injuring them?" No man who can earn his own livelihood has a right to depend on others.

The proverb, "The world owes me a living," has in it the essence of falsehood, fraud, and robbery. The world owes no man a living who is able to work and gain a living for himself. But if one comes to our door and asks for food, we should not turn him away hungry. His poverty may be the result of misfortune.

We should help those who with large families to support have constantly to battle with feebleness and poverty. Many a widowed mother with her fatherless children is working far beyond her strength in order to keep her little ones with her and provide them with food and clothing. Many such mothers have died from overexertion. Every widow needs the comfort of hopeful, encouraging words, and there are very many who should have substantial aid.—Testimonies for the Church 6:227, 228.

Take Note of Every Case of Need—It is God's purpose that the rich and the poor shall be closely bound together by the ties of sympathy and helpfulness. He bids us interest ourselves in every case of suffering and need that shall come to our knowledge. Think it not lowering to your dignity to minister to suffering humanity....

Many not of our faith are longing for the very help that Christians are in duty bound to give. If God's people would show a genuine interest in their neighbors, many would be reached by the special truths for this time. Nothing will or ever can give character to the work like helping the people just where they are. Thousands might today be rejoicing in the message if those who claim to love God and keep His commandments would work as Christ worked.—Testimonies for the Church 6:279, 280.

The Best Way to Reach Hearts Today—By showing an interest in the wants of suffering humanity we can best reach hearts. The culture of the mind and heart is much more easily accomplished when we feel such tender sympathy in others that we scatter our benefits and privileges to relieve their necessities.—Letter 116, 1897.

We want to represent Christ by reaching out to others. We are to work under the commission Christ gave to His disciples, "Go ye therefore, and teach all nations, baptizing them in the name of the Father, and of the Son, and of the Holy Ghost: teaching them to observe all things whatsoever I have commanded you: and, lo, I am with you alway, even unto the end of the world." This, then, is our work, to reach the people who are neglected, and win them to Christ.

Until recently our people have made but little or no effort to help these. Christ came not to call the righteous, but sinners to repentance. He would have every soul regard the efficacy of His blood as of unlimited value, able to save unto the uttermost all who will be persuaded to come to Him. He would have every individual of our race, formed in His image, remember that God is infinite, and that His love revealed in the atonement of Christ, in favor of all mankind, makes manifest the value He places on humanity. He bids them come to Him and be saved. To the Source of all our mercies we must come. He will use men as His agents to win their fellow men from sin.—Letter 33, 1898.

Chapter 23—Helping the Poor to Help Themselves

Educate the Poor to Be Self-reliant—Men and women of God, persons of discernment and wisdom, should be appointed to look after the poor and needy, the household of faith first. These should report to the church and counsel as to what should be done.

Instead of encouraging the poor to think that they can have their eating and drinking provided free, or nearly so, we should place them where they can help themselves. We should endeavor to provide them with work, and if necessary, teach them how to work. Let the members of poor households be taught how to cook, how to make and mend their own clothing, how to care properly for the home. Let boys and girls be thoroughly taught some useful trade or occupation. We are to educate the poor to become self-reliant. This will be true help, for it will not only make them self-sustaining but will enable them to help others.—Testimonies for the Church 6:278, 279.

A Call to Men of Thought and Means—The question will often arise: What can be done where poverty prevails and is to be contended with at every step? Under these circumstances how can we impress minds with correct ideas of improvement? Certainly the work is difficult; and unless the teachers, the thinking men, and the men who have means will exercise their talents and will lift just as Christ would lift were He in their place an important work will be left undone. The necessary reformation will never be made unless men and women are helped by a power outside of themselves. Those who have talents and capabilities must use these gifts to bless their fellow men, laboring to place them upon a footing where they can help themselves. It is thus that the education gained at our schools should be put to the very best use.

God's entrusted talents are not to be hid under a bushel or under a bed. "Ye are the light of the world," Christ said. Matthew 5:14. As you see families living in hovels, with scant furniture and clothing, without tools, without books or other marks of refinement about their homes, will you become interested in them and endeavor to teach them how to put their energies to the very best use, that there may be improvement, and that their work may move forward?—Testimonies for the Church 6:188, 189.

God's Word Reveals the Solution to the Problem—There are largehearted men and women who are anxiously considering the condition of the poor and what means can be found for their relief. How the unemployed and the homeless can be helped to secure the common blessings of God's providence and to live the life He intended man to live, is a question to which many are earnestly endeavoring to find an answer....

If men would give more heed to the teaching of God's Word, they would find a solution of these problems that perplex them. Much might be learned from the Old Testament in regard to the labor question and the relief of the poor. In God's plan for Israel every family had a home on the land, with sufficient ground for tilling. Thus were provided both the means and the incentive for a useful, industrious, and self-supporting life. And no devising of men has ever improved upon that plan. To the world's departure from it is owing, to a large degree, the poverty and wretchedness that exist today....

In Israel industrial training was regarded as a duty. Every father was required to teach his sons some useful trade. The greatest men in Israel were trained to industrial pursuits. A knowledge of the duties pertaining to housewifery was considered essential for every woman. And skill in these duties was regarded as an honor to women of the highest station.

Various industries were taught in the schools of the prophets, and many of the students sustained themselves by manual labor....

The plan of life that God gave to Israel was intended as an object lesson for all mankind. If these principles were carried out today, what a different place this world would be!—The Ministry of Healing, 183-188.

Multitudes Might Find Homes on the Land—Within the vast boundaries of nature there is still room for the suffering and needy to find a home. Within her bosom there are resources sufficient to provide them with food. Hidden in the depths of the earth are blessings for all who have courage and will and perseverance to gather her treasures. The tilling of the soil, the employment that God appointed to man in Eden, opens a field in which there is opportunity for multitudes to gain a subsistence....

If the poor now crowded into the cities could find homes upon the land, they might not only earn a livelihood but find health and happiness now unknown to them. Hard work, simple fare, close economy, often hardship and privation, would be their lot. But what a blessing would be theirs in leaving the city, with its enticements to evil, its turmoil and crime, misery and foulness, for the country's quiet and peace and purity....

[197]

If they ever become industrious and self-supporting, very many must have assistance, encouragement, and instruction. There are multitudes of poor families for whom no better missionary work could be done than to assist them in settling on the land and in learning how to make it yield them a livelihood.

The need for such help and instruction is not confined to the cities. Even in the country, with all its possibilities for a better life, multitudes of the poor are in great need. Whole communities are devoid of education in industrial and sanitary lines....

Imbruted souls, bodies weak and ill-formed, reveal the results of evil heredity and of wrong habits. These people must be educated from the very foundation. They have led shiftless, idle, corrupt lives, and they need to be trained to correct habits.

How can they be awakened to the necessity of improvement? How can they be directed to a higher ideal of life? How can they be helped to rise? What can be done where poverty prevails, and is to be contended with at every step?—The Ministry of Healing, 188-193.

A Work for Christian Farmers—Christian farmers can do real missionary work in helping the poor to find homes on the land and in teaching them how to till the soil and make it productive. Teach them how to use the implements of agriculture, how to cultivate various crops, how to plant and care for orchards.

Many who till the soil fail to secure adequate returns because of their neglect. Their orchards are not properly cared for, the crops are not put in at the right time, and a mere surface work is done in cultivating the soil. Their ill success they charge to the unproductiveness of the land. False witness is often borne in condemning land that, if properly worked, would yield rich returns. The narrow plans, the

[198]

little strength put forth, the little study as to the best methods, call loudly for reform.—The Ministry of Healing, 193.

Even the poorest can improve their surroundings by rising early and working diligently.... It is by diligent labor, by putting to the wisest use every capability, by learning to waste no time, that they will become successful in improving their premises and cultivating their land.—Testimonies for the Church 6:188, 189.

Establishment of Industries—Attention should be given to the establishment of various industries so that poor families can find employment. Carpenters, blacksmiths, and indeed everyone who understands some line of useful labor should feel a responsibility to teach and help the ignorant and the unemployed.

In ministry to the poor there is a wide field of service for women as well as for men. The efficient cook, the housekeeper, the seamstress, the nurse—the help of all is needed....

Missionary families are needed to settle in the waste places. Let farmers, financiers, builders, and those who are skilled in various arts and crafts go to neglected fields to improve the land, to establish industries, to prepare humble homes for themselves, and to help their neighbors.—The Ministry of Healing, 194.

Help Men to Help Themselves—By instruction in practical lines we can often help the poor most effectively. As a rule those who have not been trained to work do not have habits of industry, perseverance, economy, and self-denial. They do not know how to manage. Often through lack of carefulness and right judgment there is wasted that which would maintain their families in decency and comfort if it were carefully and economically used. "Much food is in the tillage of the poor: but there is that is destroyed for want of judgment."

We may give to the poor, and harm them, by teaching them to be dependent....

Real charity helps men to help themselves.... True beneficence means more than mere gifts. It means a genuine interest in the welfare of others. We should seek to understand the needs of the poor and distressed, and to give them the help that will benefit them most. To give thought and time and personal effort costs far more than merely to give money. But it is the truest charity.—The Ministry of Healing, 194, 195.

Physical Effort and Moral Power Required—Physical effort and moral power are to be united in our endeavors to regenerate and reform. We are to seek to gain knowledge in both temporal and spiritual lines, that we may communicate it to others. We are to seek to live out the gospel in all its bearings, that its temporal and spiritual blessings may be felt all around us.—Testimonies for the Church 6:189.

Unwittingly Injured—We may err in making gifts to the poor which are not a blessing to them, leading them to feel that they need not exert themselves and practice economy, for others will not permit them to suffer. We should not give countenance to indolence or encourage habits of self-gratification by affording means for indulgence.—Historical Sketches, 293.

You may give to the poor, and injure them, because you teach them to be dependent. Instead, teach them to support themselves. This will be true help. The needy must be placed in positions where they can help themselves.—Manuscript 46, 1898.

Not to Be Supported in Idleness—The Word of God teaches that if a man will not work, neither shall he eat. The Lord does not require the hard-working man to support those who are not diligent. There is a waste of time, a lack of effort, which brings to poverty and want. If these faults are not seen and corrected by those who indulge them, all that might be done in their behalf is like putting treasure into a basket with holes. But there is an unavoidable poverty, and we are to manifest tenderness and compassion toward those who are unfortunate.—The Review and Herald, January 3, 1899.

Poor to Seek Counsel—There is a class of poor brethren who are not free from temptation. They are poor managers, they have not wise judgment, they wish to obtain means without waiting the slow process of persevering toil. Some are in such haste to better their condition that they engage in various enterprises without consulting men of good judgment and experience. Their expectations are seldom realized; instead of gaining, they lose, and then come temptation and a disposition to envy the rich. They really want to be benefited by the wealth of their brethren, and feel tried because they are not. But they are not worthy of receiving special help. They have evidence that their efforts have been scattered. They have been changeable in business and full of anxiety and cares which bring but small returns. Such persons should listen to the counsel of those of experience. But frequently they are the last ones to seek advice. They think they have superior judgment and will not be taught.

These are often the very ones who are deceived by those sharp, shrewd peddlers of patent rights whose success depends upon the art of deception. These should learn that no confidence whatever can be put in such peddlers. But the brethren are credulous in regard to the very things they should suspect and shun. They do not take home the instruction of Paul to Timothy: "But godliness with contentment is great gain." "And having food and raiment let us be therewith content." Let not the poor think that the rich are the only covetous ones. While the rich hold what they have with a covetous grasp, and seek to obtain still more, the poor are in great danger of coveting the rich man's wealth.—Testimonies for the Church 1:480, 481.

To Be Willing to Receive Advice—Many lack wise management and economy. They do not weigh matters well and move cautiously. Such should not trust to their own poor judgment, but counsel with their brethren who have experience. Those who lack good judgment and economy are often unwilling to seek counsel. They generally think that they understand how to conduct their temporal business, and are unwilling to follow advice. They make bad moves and suffer in consequence. Their brethren are grieved to see them suffer, and they help them out of difficulty. Their unwise management affects the church. It takes means from the treasury of God which should have been used to advance the cause of present truth.

If these poor brethren would take a humble course and be willing to be advised and counseled by their brethren, and then are brought into straitened places, their brethren should feel it their duty to cheerfully help them out of difficulty. But if they choose their own course and rely upon their judgment, they should be left to feel the full consequences of their unwise course, and learn by dear experience that "in a multitude of counselors there is safety." God's people should be subject one to another. They should counsel with each other, that the lack of one be supplied by the sufficiency of the other.—The Review and Herald, April 18, 1871.

Most Poor Could Help Themselves—There are very few in our land of plenty who are really so poor as to need help. If they would pursue a right course, they could in almost every case be above want. My appeal to the rich is, Deal liberally with your poor brethren, and use your means to advance the cause of God. The worthy poor, those who are made poor by misfortune and sickness, deserve your special care and help. "Finally be ye all of one mind, having compassion one of another; love as brethren, be pitiful, be courteous."—Testimonies for the Church 1:481.

Observe the Golden Rule—God often raises up someone who will shield the poor from being placed in positions that will be loss to them, even if it be given to their disadvantage. This is the duty of man toward his fellow man. To take advantage of a man's ignorance because he cannot discern the outcome of a course of action is not right. It is the duty of his brother to personally set the matter plainly and faithfully before him, in all its bearings, lest he shall act blindly, and cripple the resources justly his. When men observe the golden rule, Do unto others as ye would that they should do unto you, many difficulties now existing would be quickly adjusted.—Letter 85, 1896.

Chapter 24—Poor to Exercise Benevolence

Not the Amount, but the Prompting Love—The poor are not excluded from the privilege of giving. They, as well as the wealthy, may act a part in this work. The lesson that Christ gave in regard to the widow's two mites shows us that the smallest willing offerings of the poor, if given from a heart of love, are as acceptable as the largest donations of the rich. In the balances of the sanctuary the gifts of the poor, made from love of Christ, are estimated, not according to the amount given but according to the love which prompts the sacrifice.—The Review and Herald, October 10, 1907.

Sacrifice Also Required of the Poor—Some who are poor in this world's goods are apt to place all the straight testimony upon the shoulders of the men of property. But they do not realize that they also have a work to do. God requires them to make a sacrifice.—The Review and Herald, April 18, 1871.

She Did What She Could—The Saviour called His disciples to Him and bade them mark the widow's poverty. Then His words of commendation fell upon her ear: "Of a truth I say unto you, that this poor widow hath cast in more than they all." Tears of joy filled her eyes as she felt that her act was understood and appreciated. Many would have advised her to keep her pittance for her own use. Given into the hands of the well-fed priests, it would be lost sight of among the many costly gifts brought to the treasury. But Jesus understood her motive. She believed the service of the temple to be of God's appointment, and she was anxious to do her utmost to sustain it. She did what she could, and her act was to be a monument to her memory through all time, and her joy in eternity. Her heart went with her gift; its value was estimated, not by the worth of the coin, but by the love to God and the interest in His work that had prompted the deed.

Jesus said of the poor widow, She "hath cast in more than they all." The rich had bestowed from their abundance, many of them to be seen and honored by men. Their large donations had deprived them of no comfort, or even luxury; they had required no sacrifice, and could not be compared in value with the widow's mite.

It is the motive that gives character to our acts, stamping them with ignominy or with high moral worth. Not the great things which every eye sees and every tongue praises does God account most precious. The little duties cheerfully done, the little gifts which make no show, and which to human eyes may appear worthless, often stand highest in His sight. A heart of faith and love is dearer to God than the most costly gift. The poor widow gave her living to do the little that she did. She deprived herself of food in order to give those two mites to the cause she loved. And she did it in faith, believing that her heavenly Father would not overlook her great need. It was this unselfish spirit and childlike faith that won the Saviour's commendation.

Among the poor there are many who long to show their gratitude to God for His grace and truth. They greatly desire to share with their more prosperous brethren in sustaining His service. These souls should not be repulsed. Let them lay up their mites in the bank of heaven. If given from a heart filled with love for God, these seeming trifles become consecrated gifts, priceless offerings, which God smiles upon and blesses.—The Desire of Ages, 614-616.

How the Macedonian Church Responded—Paul wrote to the Corinthian church: "Moreover, brethren, we do you to wit of the grace of God bestowed on the churches of Macedonia; how that in a great trial of affliction the abundance of their joy and their deep poverty abounded unto the riches of their liberality. For to their power, I bear record, yea, and beyond their power they were willing of themselves; praying us with much intreaty that we would receive the gift, and take upon us the fellowship of the ministering to the saints. And this they did, not as we hoped, but first gave their own selves to the Lord, and unto us by the will of God. Insomuch that we desired Titus, that as he had begun, so he would also finish in you the same grace also."

There had been a famine at Jerusalem, and Paul knew that many of the Christians had been scattered abroad, and that those who remained would be likely to be deprived of human sympathy and exposed to religious enmity. Therefore he exhorted the churches to send pecuniary assistance to their brethren in Jerusalem. The amount raised by the churches exceeded the expectation of the apostles. Constrained by the love of Christ, the believers gave liberally, and they were filled with joy because they should thus express their gratitude to the Redeemer and their love for the brethren. This is the true basis of charity according to God's Word.—Testimonies for the Church 6:271, 272.

According to Our Entrusted Talents—Of the church in Macedonia we read that "in a great trial of affliction, the abundance of their joy and their deep poverty abounded unto the riches of their liberality." Then, shall any of us who profess to be Christians think that we shall be excused in doing nothing for the truth because we are poor? We regard the precious light of truth as an inexpressible, inexhaustible treasure. We are to exert an influence in proportion to our entrusted talents, be we rich or poor, high or low, ignorant or learned. We are servants of Jesus Christ, and the Lord expects us to do our best.—The Review and Herald, September 4, 1894.

Not to Be Denied the Blessing of Giving—A responsibility rests upon the ministers of Christ to educate the churches to be liberal. Even the poor are to have a part in presenting their offerings to God. They are to be sharers of the grace of Christ in denying self to help those whose need is more pressing than their own. Why should the poor saints be denied the blessing of giving to aid those who are still poorer than themselves? The work of educating the people along these lines has been neglected, and the churches have failed to give for the necessity of poorer churches, and thus the blessing has been withheld that should have been theirs, and will be withheld until they shall have a realizing sense of their neglect.—The Review and Herald, September 4, 1894.

Section 8—The Unfortunate

Gem Thought

In the night of spiritual darkness God's glory is to shine forth through His church in lifting up the bowed down and comforting those that mourn. All around us are heard the wails of a world's sorrow. On every hand are the needy and distressed. It is ours to aid in relieving and softening life's hardships and misery. The wants of the soul, only the love of Christ can satisfy. If Christ is abiding in us, our hearts will be full of divine sympathy. The sealed fountains of earnest, Christlike love will be unsealed.—Prophets and Kings, 718, 719.

Because I delivered the poor that cried, and the fatherless, and him that had none to help him. The blessing of him that was ready to perish came upon me: and I caused the widow's heart to sing for joy. ... I was eyes to the blind, and feet was I to the lame. I was a father to the poor: and the cause which I knew not I searched out.
Job 29: 12-16.

Chapter 25—Our Duty to the Unfortunate

Pity for the Blind, Lame, and Afflicted—Those who have pity for the unfortunate, the blind, the lame, the afflicted, the widows, the orphans, and the needy, Christ represents as commandment keepers, who shall have eternal life.—Testimonies for the Church 3:512.

Frozen Sympathies—In view of what heaven is doing to save the lost, how can those who are partakers of the riches of the grace of Christ withdraw their interest and their sympathies from their fellow men? How can they indulge in pride of rank or caste and despise the unfortunate and the poor?

Yet it is too true that the pride of rank and the oppression of the poor which prevail in the world, exist also among the professed followers of Christ. With many the sympathies that ought to be exercised in full measure toward humanity seem frozen up. Men appropriate to themselves the gifts entrusted to them wherewith to bless others. The rich grind the face of the poor and use the means thus gained to indulge their pride and love of display even in the house of God.... Were it not that the Lord has revealed His love to the poor and lowly who are contrite in heart, this world would be a sad place for the poor man.—The Review and Herald, June 20, 1893.

Make Condition of Unfortunate Brother Our Own—When a man is struggling with honest endeavor to sustain himself and his family, and yet is unable to do this, so that they suffer for necessary food and clothing, the Lord will not pronounce our ministering brethren guiltless if they look on with indifference or prescribe conditions for this brother which are virtually impossible of fulfillment ... We are to make the condition of the unfortunate brother our own.

Any neglect on the part of those who claim to be followers of Christ, a failure to relieve the necessities of a brother or a sister who is bearing the yoke of poverty and oppression, is registered in the books of heaven as shown to Christ in the person of His saints. What a reckoning the Lord will have with many, very many, who present the words of Christ to others but fail to manifest tender sympathy and regard for a brother in the faith who is less fortunate and successful than themselves....

If you knew the circumstances of this brother, and did not make earnest efforts to relieve him, and change his oppression to freedom, you are not working the works of Christ, and are guilty before God. I write plainly, for, from the light given me of God, there is a class of work that is neglected.

There may be great interest taken in the wholesale business of feeding the wretched class who are in poverty. All this I have no objection to, but it is a misdirected zeal if we pass by the cases of these who are of the household of faith and let their cry of distress come up to God because of suffering which we might alleviate, and in thus doing represent Jesus Christ in sympathy and love. The Lord has a controversy with us for this neglect. He cannot say to any man or woman, "Well done," unless they have done well in representing the attributes of Christ—goodness, compassion, and love—to their fellow men.—Manuscript 34, 1894.

Provide Homes for Homeless—Years ago I was shown that God's people would be tested upon this point of making homes for the homeless; that there would be many without homes in consequence of their believing the truth. Opposition and persecution would deprive believers of their homes, and it was the duty of those who had homes to open a wide door to those who had not. I have been shown more recently that God would specially test His professed people in reference to this matter.

Christ for our sakes became poor that we through His poverty might be made rich. He made a sacrifice that He might provide a home for pilgrims and strangers in the world seeking for a better country, even an heavenly. Shall those who are subjects of His grace, who are expecting to be heirs of immortality, refuse, or even feel reluctant, to share their homes with the homeless and needy? Shall we, who are disciples of Jesus, refuse strangers an entrance to our doors because they can claim no acquaintance with the inmates?

Has the injunction of the apostle no force in this age: "Be not forgetful to entertain strangers: for thereby some have entertained angels unawares"? ...

[212] Our heavenly Father lays blessings disguised in our pathway, but some will not touch these for fear they will detract from their enjoyment. Angels are waiting to see if we embrace opportunities within our reach of doing good—waiting to see if we will bless others, that they in their turn may bless us....

I have heard many excuse themselves from inviting to their homes and hearts the saints of God. "Why, I have nothing prepared, I have nothing cooked; they must go to some other place." And at that place there may be some other excuse invented for not receiving those who need hospitality, and the feelings of the visitors are deeply grieved, and they leave with unpleasant impressions in regard to the hospitality of these professed brethren and sisters. If you have no bread, sister, imitate the case brought to view in the Bible. Go to your neighbor and say, "Friend, lend me three loaves; for a friend of mine in his journey is come to me, and I have nothing to set before him." We have not an example of this lack of bread ever being made an excuse to refuse entrance to an applicant. When Elijah came to the widow of Sarepta, she shared her morsel with the prophet of God, and he wrought a miracle, and caused that in that act of making a home for his servant, and sharing her morsel with him, she herself was sustained, and her life and that of her son preserved. Thus will it prove in the case of many, if they do this cheerfully, for the glory of God.—Testimonies for the Church 2:27-29.

Church Body Accountable for Negligence of Members—God will hold the church at _____ responsible, as a body, for the wrong course of its members. If a selfish and unsympathizing spirit is allowed to exist in any of its members toward the unfortunate, the widow, the orphan, the blind, the lame, or those who are sick in body [213] or mind, He will hide His face from His people until they do their duty and remove the wrong from among them. If any professing the name of Christ so far misrepresent their Saviour as to be unmindful of their duty to the afflicted, or if they in any way seek to advantage themselves to the injury of the unfortunate, and thus rob them of means, the Lord holds the church accountable for the sin of its members until they have done all they can to remedy the existing evil. He will not hearken to the prayer of His people while the orphan, the fatherless, the lame, the blind, and the sick are neglected among them.—Testimonies for the Church 3:517, 518.

Heaven Keeps a Faithful Record—Christ regards all acts of mercy, benevolence, and thoughtful consideration for the unfortunate, the blind, the lame, the sick, the widow, and the orphan as done to Himself: and these works are preserved in the heavenly records and will be rewarded. On the other hand, a record will be written in the book against those who manifest the indifference of the priest and the Levite to the unfortunate, and those who take any advantage of the misfortunes of others.—Testimonies for the Church 2:512, 513.

[214] # Chapter 26—Help and Encouragement for Widows

The Claims of Widows and Orphans—Among all whose needs demand our interest, the widow and the fatherless have the strongest claims upon our tender sympathy and care. "Pure religion and undefiled before God and the Father is this, To visit the fatherless and widows in their affliction, and to keep himself unspotted from the world."

The father who has died in the faith, resting upon the eternal promise of God, left his loved ones in full trust that the Lord would care for them. And how does the Lord provide for these bereaved ones? He does not work a miracle in sending manna from heaven; He does not send ravens to bring them food; but He works a miracle upon human hearts. He expels selfishness from the soul; He unseals the fountain of benevolence. He tests the love of His professed followers by committing to their tender mercies the afflicted and bereaved ones, the poor and the orphan. These are in a special sense the little ones whom Christ looks upon, whom it is an offense to Him to neglect. Those who do neglect them are neglecting Christ in the person of His afflicted ones. Every kind act done to them in the name of Jesus is accepted by Him as if done to Himself, for He identifies His interest with that of suffering humanity, and He has entrusted to His church the grand work of ministering to Jesus by helping and blessing the needy and suffering. On all who shall minister to them with willing hearts the blessing of the Lord will rest.—The Review and Herald, June 27, 1893.

[215] **Give Tangible Help; Lighten Widow's Burdens**—Many a widowed mother with her fatherless children is bravely striving to bear her double burden, often toiling far beyond her strength in order to keep her little ones with her and to provide for their needs. Little time has she for their training and instruction, little opportunity to surround them with influences that would brighten their lives. She needs encouragement, sympathy, and tangible help.

God calls upon us to supply to these children, so far as we can, the want of a father's care. Instead of standing aloof, complaining of their faults, and of the trouble they may cause, help them in every way possible. Seek to aid the careworn mother. Lighten her burdens.—The Ministry of Healing, 203.

To Be Channels of God's Bounties—In homes supplied with life's comforts, in bins and granaries filled with the yield of abundant harvests, in warehouses stocked with the products of the loom, and vaults stored with gold and silver, God has supplied means for the sustenance of these needy ones. He calls upon us to be channels of His bounty.—The Ministry of Healing, 202.

Help for the Widow Entrusted to the Prosperous—The poor, the homeless, and the widows are among us. I heard a wealthy farmer describe the situation of a poor widow among them. He lamented her straitened circumstances, and then said: "I don't know how she is going to get along this cold winter. She has close times now." Such have forgotten the Pattern, and by their acts say: "Nay, Lord, we cannot drink of the cup of self-denial, humiliation, and sacrifice which You drank of, nor be baptized with the suffering which You were baptized with. We cannot live to do others good. It is our business to take care of ourselves."

Who should know how the widow should get along unless it be those who have well-filled granaries? The means for her to get along are at hand. And dare those whom God has made His stewards, to whom He has entrusted means, withhold from the needy disciples of Christ? If so, they withhold from Jesus. Do you expect the Lord to rain down grain from heaven to supply the needy? Has He not rather placed it in your hands, to help and bless them through you? Has He not made you His instrument in this good work to prove you and to give you the privilege of laying up a treasure in heaven?—Testimonies for the Church 2:32, 33.

Brethren, for Christ's sake fill up your lives with good works.... All you have belongs to God. Be guarded, lest you selfishly hoard the bounties He has given you for the widow and the fatherless.—Testimonies for the Church 4:627.

Christians Possess an Abundance for the Needy—Christians are not excusable for permitting the widow's cries and the orphan's prayers to ascend to Heaven because of their suffering want while a liberal Providence has placed in the hands of these Christians abundance to supply their need. Let not the cries of the widow and fatherless call down the vengeance of Heaven upon us as a people. In the professed Christian world there is enough expended in extravagant display, for jewels and ornaments, to supply the wants of all the hungry and clothe the naked in our towns and cities; and yet these professed followers of the meek and lowly Jesus need not deprive themselves of suitable food or comfortable clothing. What will these church members say when confronted in the day of God by the worthy poor, the afflicted, the widows and fatherless, who have known pinching want for the meager necessities of life, while there was expended by these professed followers of Christ, for superfluous clothing and needless ornaments expressly forbidden in the Word of God, enough to supply all their wants?—The Review and Herald, November 21, 1878.

Neglect Not Those Close By—With every gift and offering there should be a suitable object before the giver, not to uphold any in idleness, not to be seen of men or to get a great name, but to glorify God by advancing His cause. Some make large donations to the cause of God while their brother who is poor may be suffering close by them, and they do nothing to relieve him. Little acts of kindness performed for their brother in a secret manner would bind their hearts together and would be noticed in heaven. I saw that in their prices and wages the rich should make a difference in favor of the afflicted and widows and the worthy poor among them.—Testimonies for the Church 1:194.

God Hears Widow's Prayer—The laws given to Israel guard especially the interests of those who need help. "Thou shalt neither vex a stranger, nor oppress him: for ye were strangers in the land of Egypt. Ye shall not afflict any widow, or fatherless child. If thou afflict them in any wise, and they cry at all unto Me, I will surely hear their cry; and My wrath shall wax hot, and I will kill you with the sword; and your wives shall be widows, and your children fatherless."

Let those in our churches and those who stand in position of responsibility in our institutions learn from these words how carefully the Lord guards the interests of those who cannot help themselves. He hears the cry of the widow for her fatherless children. He will surely bring into judgment those who disregard the rules that He has laid down to shield them from harm.

And yet, in spite of the warnings that God has given, there are those who are not afraid to do injustice to the widow and the fatherless. The word of the Lord has come to them, but they would not change their course in order to help the needy. They turned their ears away from the plea of the fatherless. The tears and prayers of the widow were nothing to them.—Manuscript 117, 1903.

Visiting the Widow—Visiting the widow and the fatherless which the apostle enjoined is to have a Christian, sanctified sympathy with them in their affliction. They are to sacredly guard their interests, to work for them, to put themselves to inconvenience to do them a favor. They are to give them Christlike counsel; they are to unite with them in prayer and to ever bear in mind that Jesus Christ is present in all these visits, and that a faithful record is kept of the object and the work accomplished. Christians will give evidence that they are converted men and women. They will show that they are Bible readers, Bible believers, and they obey every injunction of the Word of God. They will not seek to create sympathy for themselves by speaking in disfavor of wife or husband. They will not become self-centered, but they will have a heart to do others good and to be a blessing to humanity, for this is Christlike. They will walk circumspectly and reveal the character of Christ. They will in all their dealings with widows and the fatherless do just as they would wish others to do by wife and children were they to leave them husbandless and fatherless.

The facts should be borne in mind by all who claim to be children of God, that there is a Watcher in every business transaction who records every act and deed of the transactor and that this record will stand just as it is written until the great day when every man shall receive according as his works have been, unless their wrongs shall have been repented of and blotted out. Any injustice done to saint or sinner will then be rewarded accordingly. Christ identifies His interest in all the afflictions of his people. God will avenge those who shall treat the widow or the fatherless with oppression, or who shall rob them in any way.—Letter 36, 1888.

No Decrease in Responsibility—Every poor, tried soul needs light, needs tender, sympathizing, hopeful words. Every widow needs the comfort of helpful and encouraging words that others can bestow....

There is a great work to be done in our world, and as we approach the close of earth's history, it does not lessen the least degree; but when the perfect love of God is in the heart, wonderful things will be done. Christ will be in the heart of the believer as a well of water springing up into everlasting life.—The Review and Herald, January 15, 1895.

Chapter 27—The Care of Orphans

Christian Fathers and Mothers Needed—Until death shall be swallowed up in victory there will be orphans to be cared for, who will suffer in more ways than one if the tender compassion and loving-kindness of our church members are not exercised in their behalf. The Lord bids us, "Bring the poor that are cast out to thy house." Christianity must supply fathers and mothers for these homeless ones. The compassion for the widow and the orphan manifested in prayers and deeds will come up in remembrance before God, to be rewarded by and by.—The Review and Herald, June 27, 1893.

Christ Says, Take These Children—Fatherless and motherless children are thrown into the arms of the church, and Christ says to His followers: Take these destitute children, bring them up for Me, and ye shall receive your wages. I have seen much selfishness exhibited in these things. Unless there is some special evidence that they *themselves* are to be benefited by adopting into their family those who need homes, some turn away and answer: No. They do not seem to know or care whether such are saved or lost. That, they think, is not their business. With Cain they say: "Am I my brother's keeper?" They are not willing to be put to inconvenience or to make any sacrifice for the orphans, and they indifferently thrust such ones into the arms of the world, who are sometimes more willing to receive them than are these professed Christians. In the day of God inquiry will be made for those whom Heaven gave them the opportunity of saving. But they wished to be excused, and would not engage in the good work unless they could make it a matter of profit to them. I have been shown that those who refuse these opportunities for doing good will hear from Jesus: "As ye did it not to one of the least of these, ye did it not to Me."—Testimonies for the Church 2:33

Open Your Hearts and Your Homes—My husband and I, though called to arduous labor in the ministry, felt it our privilege to gather into our home children who needed care, and help them to form characters for heaven. We could not adopt infants, for this would have engrossed our time and attention and would have robbed the Lord of the service He required of us in bringing many sons and daughters to Him. But we felt that the Lord's instruction in Isaiah 58 was for us, and that His blessing would attend us in obedience to His word. All can do something for the needy little ones, by helping to place them in homes where they can be cared for.—Manuscript 35, 1896.

There is a wide field of usefulness before all who will work for the Master in caring for these children and youth who have been deprived of the watchful guidance of parents and the subduing influence of a Christian home. Many of them have inherited evil traits of character; and if left to grow up in ignorance, they will drift into associations that lead to vice and crime. These unpromising children need to be placed in a position favorable for the formation of a right character, that they may become children of God.

Are you who profess to be children of God acting your part in teaching these, who so much need to be patiently taught how to come to the Saviour? Are you acting your part as faithful servants of Christ? Are these unformed, perhaps ill-balanced minds cared for with that love which Christ has manifested for us? The souls of children and youth are in deadly peril if left to themselves. They need patient instruction, love, and tender Christian care.

Were there no revelation to point out our duty, the very sight of our eyes, and what we know of the inevitable working of cause and effect, should arouse us to rescue these unfortunate ones. If the members of the church would bring into this work the same energy and tact and skill that they employ in the common business relations of life, if they would seek wisdom from God, and earnestly study how to mold these undisciplined minds, many souls that are ready to perish might be rescued....

Brethren and sisters, I ask you to consider this matter carefully. Think of the wants of the fatherless and motherless. Are not your hearts stirred as you witness their sufferings? See if something cannot be done for the care of these helpless ones. As far as lies in your power, make a home for the homeless. Let everyone stand ready to act a part in helping forward this work. The Lord said to

Peter: "Feed My lambs." This command is to us, and by opening our homes for the orphans we aid in its fulfillment. Let not Jesus be disappointed in you.

Take these children and present them to God as a fragrant offering. Ask His blessing upon them, and then mold and fashion them according to Christ's order. Will our people accept this holy trust? Because of our shallow piety and worldly ambition, shall those for whom Christ has died be left to suffer, to go in wrong paths?—Testimonies for the Church 6:282-284.

They Are God's Property—Orphans who are lent to Christians in trust for God are too often passed by and neglected, and yet they are bought with a price, and are just as valuable in the sight of God as we are.... They must be cared for; they must receive special attention. You cannot expend your means in a better way than by opening your doors to make homes for them. When the Lord sees that you are faithful in doing what you can to relieve human misery, He will move upon others to provide means to care for those who need help. Those who enlarge their hearts in this kind of work do no more than their duty.

Christ is our example. He was the Majesty of heaven, yet He did more for our fellow men than any of us can possibly do. "Ye are labourers together with God." Let not one needless expenditure be made for the gratification of pride and vanity. Put your mites and your larger sums in the bank of heaven, where they will accumulate. Many who have had precious opportunities to wear the yoke of Christ in this most precious line of work have refused to submit to the yoke. It has not been pleasant to practice unselfishness, and they have neglected to make the cases of the poor and unfortunate their own. They do not heed the injunctions of Christ, and improve every talent that the Lord has given them, cooperating with heavenly intelligences in gathering souls who will serve, honor, and glorify the name of Christ.—The Review and Herald, January 15, 1895.

Counsel to Foster Parents—Dear Brother and Sister D: Your late visit and conversation with us have suggested many thoughts, of which I cannot forbear placing a few upon paper. I was very sorry that E had not carried himself correctly at all times; yet, when you consider, you cannot expect perfection in youth at his age. Children have faults, and they need a great deal of patient instruction.

That he should have feelings not always correct is no more than can be expected of a boy of his age. You must remember that he has no father or mother, no one to whom he can confide his feelings, his sorrows, and his temptations. Every person feels that he must have some sympathizer. This boy has been tossed about here and there, from pillar to post, and he may have many errors, many careless ways, with considerable independence, and he may lack reverence. But he is quite enterprising, and with right instruction and kind treatment, I have the fullest confidence that he would not disappoint our hopes, but would fully repay all the labor expended on him. Considering his disadvantages, I think he is a very good boy.

When we entreated you to take him we did it because we fully believed it was your duty, and that in doing so you would be blessed. We did not expect that you would do this merely to be benefited by the help that you would receive from the boy, but to benefit him, to do a duty to the orphan—a duty which every true Christian should be seeking and anxiously watching to perform; a duty, a sacrificing duty, which we believed it would do you good to take up, if you did it cheerfully, with a view to being the instrument in the hands of God of saving a soul from the snares of Satan, of saving a son whose father devoted his precious life to pointing souls to the Lamb of God who taketh away the sin of the world....

In regard to E, do not, I entreat of you, forget that he is a child with only a child's experience. Do not measure him, a poor, weak, feeble boy, with yourselves and expect of him accordingly. I fully believe that it is in your power to do the right thing by this orphan. You can present inducements to him so that he will not feel that his task is cheerless, unrelieved by a ray of encouragement. You, my brother and sister, can enjoy yourselves in each other's confidence, you can sympathize with each other, interest and amuse each other, and tell your trials and burdens to each other. You have something to cheer you, while he is alone. He is a thinking boy, but has no one to confide in or to give him a cheering word amid his discouragements and severe trials, which I know he has as well as those more advanced in years.

If you shut yourselves up to each other, it is selfish love, unattended with Heaven's blessing. I have strong hope that you will love the orphan for Christ's sake, that you will feel that your possessions are but worthless unless employed in doing good. Do good; be rich in good works, ready to distribute, willing to communicate, laying up in store for yourselves a good foundation against the time to come, that you may lay hold on eternal life. None will reap the reward of everlasting life but the self-sacrificing. A dying father and mother left their jewels to the care of the church, to be instructed in the things of God and fitted for heaven. When these parents shall look about for their dear ones, and one is found missing because of neglect, what will the church answer? It is in a great degree responsible for the salvation of these orphan children.

In all probability you have failed to gain the boy's confidence and affection by not giving him more tangible proofs of your love by holding out some inducements. If you could not expend money, you could at least in some way encourage him by letting him know you were not indifferent to his case. That the love and affection is to be all on one side is a mistake. How much affection have you educated yourselves to manifest? You are too much shut up to yourselves and do not feel the necessity of surrounding yourselves with an atmosphere of tenderness and gentleness, which comes from true nobility of soul. Brother and Sister F left their children to the care of the church. They had plenty of wealthy relatives who wanted the children; but they were unbelievers, and if allowed to have the care, or become the guardians, of the children, would lead their hearts away from the truth into error, and endanger their salvation. Because these relatives were not allowed to take the children, they were dissatisfied, and have done nothing for them. The confidence of the parents in the church should be considered, and not be forgotten because of selfishness.

We have the deepest interest for these children. One has already developed a beautiful Christian character and married a minister of the gospel. And now, in return for the care and burdens borne for her, she is a true burden bearer in the church. She is sought unto for advice and counsel by the less experienced, and they seek not in vain. She possesses true Christian humility, with becoming dignity, which can but inspire respect and confidence in all who know her. These children are as near to me as my own. I shall not lose sight of them nor cease my care for them. I love them sincerely, tenderly, affectionately.—Testimonies for the Church 2:327-334.

Judged by What They Did Not Do—There are orphans that should be cared for; but some will not venture to undertake this, for it would bring them more work than they care to do, leaving them but little time to please themselves. But when the King shall make investigation these do-nothing, illiberal, selfish souls will learn that heaven is for those who have been workers, those who have denied themselves for Christ's sake. No provisions have been made for those who have ever taken such special care in loving and looking out for themselves. The terrible punishment the King threatened those on His left hand, in this case, is not because of their great crimes. They are not condemned for the things which they did do, but for that which they did not do. You did not do those things Heaven assigned you to do. You pleased yourself, and can take your portion with self-pleasers.—Testimonies for the Church 2:27.

Be Daughters of Benevolence—To my sisters I would say: Be daughters of benevolence. The Son of man came to seek and to save that which was lost. You may have thought that if you could find a child without fault, you would take it and care for it; but to perplex your mind with an erring child, to unlearn it many things and teach it anew, to teach it self-control, is a work which you refuse to undertake. To teach the ignorant, to pity and to reform those who have ever been learning evil, is no slight task; but Heaven has placed just such ones in your way. They are blessings in disguise.—Ibid.

Those With a True Mother's Heart—Mothers who have wisely reared their children feel the burden of responsibility, not only for their own children, but for their neighbor's children. A true mother's heart of sympathy goes out for all with whom she comes in contact. With a determined effort she seeks to turn wayward souls to Christ. In His strength she is enabled to do much. And those who have no children have responsibilities to bear. In most cases they may receive into their homes children who are orphaned and homeless. These they may train for Christ's sake to practice those virtues so much needed in our world.—Manuscript 34, 1899.

Let the condition of helpless little ones appeal to every mother's heart, that she may put into exercise a mother's love for homeless orphan children. Their helplessness appeals to every God-given attribute in human nature.—The Medical Missionary, November, 1894.

In the Loving Atmosphere of a Christian Home—There are the multitudes of children who have been wholly deprived of the guidance of parents and the subduing influence of a Christian home. Let Christians open their hearts and homes to these helpless ones. The work that God has committed to them as an individual duty should not be turned over to some benevolent institution or left to the chances of the world's charity. If the children have no relatives able to give them care, let the members of the church provide homes for them. He who made us ordained that we should be associated in families, and the child nature will develop best in the loving atmosphere of a Christian home.

Many who have no children of their own could do a good work in caring for the children of others. Instead of giving attention to pets, lavishing affection upon dumb animals, let them give their attention to little children, whose characters they may fashion after the divine similitude. Place your love upon the homeless members of the human family. See how many of these children you can bring up in the nurture and admonition of the Lord. Many would thus be greatly benefited themselves.—The Ministry of Healing, 203, 204.

Why the Responsibility Belongs Primarily to the Church—God has placed in our care the poor and the suffering, and these are to be cared for as Christ cared for them. The Lord would have this work done in the different churches, rather than that these unfortunate ones should depend so largely upon institutions; for this will take out of the hands of the churches the very work God has appointed them to do.

When fathers and mothers die and leave their children unprovided for, the orphans should be cared for by the church. Open your hearts, you that have the love of God, and take them into your homes.—Manuscript 105, 1899.

Orphans' Homes—When all is done that can be done in providing for orphans in our own homes, there will still be many needy ones in the world who should be cared for. They may be ragged, uncouth, and seemingly in every way unattractive; but they are bought with a price, and are just as precious in the sight of God as are our own little ones. They are God's property, for whom Christians are responsible. Their souls, God says, "will I require at thine hand."

To care for these needy ones is a good work; yet in this age of the world the Lord does not give us as a people directions to establish large and expensive institutions for this purpose. If, however, there are among us individuals who feel called of God to establish institutions for the care of orphan children, let them follow out their convictions of duty. But in caring for the world's poor, they should appeal to the world for support. They are not to draw upon the people to whom the Lord has given the most important work ever given to men, the work of bringing the last message of mercy before all nations, kindreds, tongues, and people. The Lord's treasury must have a surplus to sustain the work of the gospel in "regions beyond."

Let those who feel the burden of establishing these institutions have wise solicitors to present their necessities and raise funds. Let the people of the world be aroused, let the denominational churches be canvassed by men who feel the necessity that something be done in behalf of the poor and orphans. In every church there are those who fear God. Let these be appealed to, for to them God has given this work....

The design of an orphans' home should be not merely to provide the children with food and clothing but to place them under the care of Christian teachers, who will educate them in the knowledge of God and His Son. Those who work in this line should be men and women who are largehearted and inspired with enthusiasm at the cross of Calvary. They should be men and women who are cultured and self-sacrificing, who will work as Christ worked for the cause of God and the cause of humanity.—Testimonies for the Church 6:286, 287.

Small Homelike Institutions—Such institutions, to be most effective, should be modeled as closely as possible after the plan of a Christian home. Instead of large establishments, bringing great numbers together, let there be small institutions in different places. Instead of being in or near some town or large city, they should be in the country, where land can be secured for cultivation and the children can be brought into contact with nature and can have the benefits of industrial training.

Those in charge of such a home should be men and women who are largehearted, cultured, and self-sacrificing; men and women who undertake the work from love to Christ, and who train the children for Him. Under such care many homeless and neglected ones may be prepared to become useful members of society, an honor to Christ themselves, and in their turn helping others.—The Ministry of Healing, 205-206.

Importance of Seeking Counsel—God will not bless those who work without taking counsel with their brethren. Any Seventh-day Adventist who supposes that in himself he is a complete whole, and that he can at all times safely follow his own mind and judgment, is not to be trusted; for he is not walking in the light as Christ is in the light. There will be many who have not a correct sense of what they are doing. Men need clear ideas, deep spirituality. In His service God desires every man to move sensibly, weighing the motives prompting his movements.—Manuscript 26, 1902.

If We Obeyed God's Instruction—The Word of God abounds with instruction as to how we should treat the widow, the fatherless, and the needy, suffering poor. If all would obey this instruction, the widow's heart would sing for joy; hungry little children would be fed; the destitute would be clothed; and those ready to perish would be revived. Heavenly intelligences are looking on, and when, imbued with zeal for Christ's honor, we place ourselves in the channel of God's providence, these heavenly messengers will impart to us a new spiritual power, so that we shall be able to combat difficulties and triumph over obstacles.—Testimonies for the Church 6:284, 285.

Chapter 28—Adopting Children

Let Families Adopt Children—There is a special work to be done for the children more advanced in years. Let families of our faith who in the churches can do so, adopt these little ones, and they will receive a blessing in so doing.—Letter 205, 1899.

There are persons who have no little ones of their own, who may do good by adopting children. Those who have not the sacred responsibility of proclaiming the Word and laboring directly for the salvation of souls, have duties in other lines of work. If they are consecrated to God, and are qualified to mold and fashion human minds, the Lord will bless them in caring for the children of others.

But let the children of believers have our first consideration. There are among Sabbathkeepers very many large families of children that are not properly cared for. Many parents give evidence that they have not learned of Christ the lessons that would make them safe guardians of children. Their children do not receive proper training. And there are among us many children whom death has deprived of the parents' care. There are those who might take some of these children and seek to mold and fashion their characters according to Bible principles.—Manuscript 35, 1896.

God has a people in this world, and there are many who can adopt children and care for them as God's little ones.—Letter 68, 1899.

Children of Believers—The Lord would have every church consider it a religious obligation resting upon them to adopt the babies of those whose parents have died in the faith. Let families take these little orphans.—Manuscript 44, 1900.

Counsel to a Childless Couple—You have not felt that it was required of you to be interested in others, to make their cases your own, and to manifest an unselfish interest for the very ones who stand most in need of help. You have not reached out to help the most needy, the most helpless.

Had you children of your own to call into exercise care, affection, and love, you would not be so much shut up to yourselves and to your own interests. If those who have no children, and whom God has made stewards of means, would expand their hearts to care for children who need love, care, and affection, and assistance with this world's goods, they would be far happier than they are today. So long as youth who have not a father's pitying care nor a mother's tender love are exposed to the corrupting influences of these last days, it is somebody's duty to supply the place of father and mother to some of them. Learn to give them love, affection, and sympathy.

All who profess to have a Father in heaven, who they hope will care for them, and finally take them to the home He has prepared for them, ought to feel a solemn obligation resting upon them to be friends to the friendless and fathers to the orphans, to aid the widows and be of some practical use in this world by benefiting humanity. Many have not viewed these things in a right light. If they live merely for themselves, they will have no greater strength than this calls for.—Testimonies for the Church 2:328, 329.

Is It God's Will?—The question of adopting a child, especially an infant, involves most serious responsibility. It should not be lightly regarded.... The question for each to settle is, In doing this shall I be merely gratifying my own wishes, or is it a duty the Lord has appointed for me? Is this His way, or a way of my own choosing? All are to be workers for God. Not one is excused. Your talents are not your own, to employ as you shall fancy. Inquire, What would the Lord have me do with His entrusted talents?—Manuscript 35, 1896.

Examine the Motives—We need carefully to search our hearts and study our motives. Selfishness may prompt the desire to do what appears to be an unselfish and praiseworthy act. The reason that many urge for desiring to adopt a child, the longing for something on which to center their affection, reveals the fact that their heart is not centered upon Christ; it is not absorbed in His work.—Manuscript 35, 1896.

Shall Ministers Adopt Children—The question has been asked whether a minister's wife should adopt infant children. I answer: If she has no inclination or fitness to engage in missionary work outside her home, and feels it her duty to take orphan children and care for them, she may do a good work. But let the choice of children be first made from among those who have been left orphans by Sabbathkeeping parents. God will bless men and women as they with willing hearts share their homes with these homeless ones.

But if the minister's wife can herself act a part in the work of educating others, she should consecrate her powers to God as a Christian worker. She should be a true helper to her husband, assisting him in his work, improving her intellect, and helping to give the message. The way is open for humble, consecrated women, dignified by the grace of Christ, to visit those in need of help and shed light into discouraged souls. They can lift up the bowed down by praying with them and pointing them to Christ. Such should not devote their time and strength to one helpless little mortal that requires constant care and attention. They should not thus voluntarily tie their hands.—Testimonies for the Church 6:285.

Perhaps God Has Withheld This Blessing—A well-ordered, well-disciplined family will have a powerful influence for good. But if you have no children of your own, it may be that the Lord has a wise purpose in withholding from you this blessing. It should not be taken as evidence that it is your duty to adopt a child. In some cases this might be advisable. If the Lord bids you take an infant to bring up, then the duty is too plain to be misunderstood. But as a rule it would not be wise for a minister's wife to encumber herself with such a responsibility....

If the companion of a minister is united with her husband in the work of saving souls, it is the highest work she can do. But the care of a little child would absorb her attention, so that she could not attend meetings and labor successfully in visiting and personal effort. Even if she accompanies her husband, the child is too often the burden of thought and conversation, and the visit is made of no effect. Those whom God has called to be colaborers with Him are to have no idols to absorb thought and affection that He would have directed in other lines.—Manuscript 35, 1896.

Ever Keep a Proper Perspective of Responsibility—Great consideration must be exercised in the work that we undertake. We are not to assume large burdens in the care of infant children. This work is being done by others. We have a special work in caring for and educating the children more advanced in years. Let families who can do so adopt the little ones, and they will receive a blessing in so doing.—Testimonies for the Church 6:246, 247.

Chapter 29—The Care of the Aged

Respectfully and Tenderly Cared For—The matter of caring for our aged brethren and sisters who have no homes is constantly being urged. What can be done for them? The light which the Lord has given me has been repeated: It is not best to establish institutions for the care of the aged, that they may be in a company together. Nor should they be sent away from home to receive care. Let the members of every family minister to their own relatives. When this is not possible the work belongs to the church, and it should be accepted both as a duty and as a privilege. All who have Christ's spirit will regard the feeble and aged with special respect and tenderness.—Testimonies for the Church 6:272.

To Remain Among Friends and Relatives—The aged also need the helpful influences of the family. In the home of brethren and sisters in Christ can most nearly be made up to them the loss of their own home. If encouraged to share in the interests and occupations of the household, it will help them to feel that their usefulness is not at an end. Make them feel that their help is valued, that there is something yet for them to do in ministering to others, and it will cheer their hearts and give interest to their lives.

So far as possible let those whose whitening heads and failing steps show that they are drawing near to the grave remain among friends and familiar associations. Let them worship among those whom they have known and loved. Let them be cared for by loving and tender hands....

The presence in our homes of one of these helpless ones is a precious opportunity to cooperate with Christ in His ministry of mercy and to develop traits of character like His. There is a blessing in the association of the old and the young. The young may bring sunshine into the hearts and lives of the aged. Those whose hold on life is weakening need the benefit of contact with the hopefulness and buoyancy of youth. And the young may be helped by the wisdom and experience of the old. Above all, they need to learn the lesson of unselfish ministry. The presence of one in need of sympathy and forbearance and self-sacrificing love would be to many a household a priceless blessing. It would sweeten and refine the home life and call forth in old and young those Christlike graces that would make them beautiful with a divine beauty and rich in heaven's imperishable treasure.—The Ministry of Healing, 204, 205.

Institutions Not the Best Plan—Men should not be employed to give their time and talents to the work of bringing the aged or the orphans together into a company to be fed and clothed. This is not the best way to manage these cases....

Nor is it best to erect buildings for old men and old women, that they may be in a company together. Let them be helped in the very places where they can be helped. Let relations take care of their own poor relations, and let the church take care of its own needy members. This is the very work God would have the church do, and they will obtain a blessing in doing it.—Manuscript 44, 1900.

Chapter 30—Our Responsibility to the Blind

Treat the Blind With Compassion—The Lord desires those connected with the medical missionary work to be true missionaries. In word and action they are to be Christlike. They are not to be merciful only when they feel an impulse to show mercy, nor are they to act selfishly toward the ones who are the most deserving of medical missionary work. The blind, for instance, are to be treated with compassion. Let medical missionaries reflect concerning their actions toward the blind, that they may learn whether as true missionaries for God they could not have done for this unfortunate class of people many things that they have left undone. From what has been presented to me I know that many, many cases have not received the encouragement that Christ would have given them were He in the place of our medical missionaries.

The Lord, He is God. He notices these instances of neglect. Every such wrong action is a misrepresentation of His mercy, lovingkindness, and benevolence.

I am instructed to say, "Watch carefully, prayerfully, conscientiously, lest the mind become so engrossed with many important business transactions that true godliness is overlooked, and love is quenched from the soul, notwithstanding the great and pitiful need of your being God's helping hand to the blind and to all others who are unfortunate." The most friendless demand the most attention. Use your time and strength in learning to be "fervent in spirit," to deal justly, and to love mercy, "serving the Lord." Remember that Christ says, "Inasmuch as ye have done it unto one of the least of these My brethren, ye have done it unto Me."—Manuscript 109, 1902.

While God is a friend to the blind and the unfortunate, He does not excuse their sins. He requires them to overcome, and to perfect Christian character in the name of Jesus, who overcame in their behalf. But Jesus pities our weakness, and He is ready to give strength to bear up in trial and to resist the temptations of Satan if we will cast our burden upon Him.

Angels Guard the Blind—Angels are sent to minister to the children of God who are physically blind. Angels guard their steps and save them from a thousand dangers, which, unknown to them, beset their path. But His Spirit will not attend them unless they cherish a spirit of kindness and seek earnestly to have control over their natures and to bring their passions and every power into submission to God. They must cultivate a spirit of love, and control their words and actions.

I was shown that God requires His people to be far more pitiful and considerate of the unfortunate than they are. "Pure religion and undefiled before God and the Father is this, To visit the fatherless and widows in their affliction, and to keep himself unspotted from the world." Here genuine religion is defined. God requires that the same consideration which should be given to the widow and fatherless be given to the blind and to those suffering under the affliction of other physical infirmities. Disinterested benevolence is very rare in this age of the world.—Testimonies for the Church 3:516.

Guardians of the Unfortunate—If there are those in the church who would cause the blind to stumble, they should be brought to justice; for God has made us guardians of the blind, the afflicted, the widows, and the fatherless. The stumbling block referred to in the Word of God does not mean a block of wood placed before the feet of the blind to cause him to stumble, but it means much more than this. It means any course that may be pursued to injure the influence of their blind brother, to work against his interest, or to hinder his prosperity.

A brother who is blind and poor and diseased, and who is making every exertion to help himself that he may not be dependent, should be encouraged by his brethren in every way possible. But those who profess to be his brethren, who have the use of all their faculties, who are not dependent, but who so far forget their duty to the blind as to perplex and distress and hedge up his way, are doing a work which will require repentance and restoration before God will accept their prayers. And the church of God, who have permitted their unfortunate brother to be wronged, will be guilty of sin until they do all in their power to have the wrong righted.—Testimonies for the Church 3:519, 520.

The Viewpoint of Mercy—I wish that we might all see as God sees. I wish all could realize how God looks upon those men who profess to be followers of Christ, who have the blessing of sight and the advantage of means in their favor, and who yet envy the little prosperity enjoyed by a poor blind man and would benefit themselves, increase their stock of means, at the disadvantage of their afflicted brother. This is regarded of God as the most criminal selfishness and robbery, and is an aggravating sin, which He will surely punish. God never forgets. He does not look upon these things with human eyes and with cold, unfeeling, human judgment. He views things, not from the worldling's standpoint, but from the standpoint of mercy, pity, and infinite love.—Testimonies for the Church 3:514, 515.

Blind Often Mistreated—With those who dare to deal without mercy, God will deal as they have dealt with those who besought them for aid. I have been instructed that the blind have often been dealt with in a merciless way.

True sympathy between man and his fellow man is to be the sign distinguishing those who love and fear God from those who are unmindful of His law.—Manuscript 117, 1903.

Fulfill Your Responsibility to the Unfortunate—It is strange that professed Christian men should disregard the plain, positive teachings of the Word of God and feel no compunctions of conscience. God places upon them the responsibility of caring for the unfortunate, the blind, the lame, the widow, and the fatherless; but many make no effort to regard it. In order to save such, God frequently brings them under the rod of affliction, and places them in positions similar to those occupied by the persons who were in need of their help and sympathy but who did not receive it at their hands.—Testimonies for the Church 3:517.

Section 9—The Outcasts

Gem Thought

There is a work to be accomplished for many to whom it would not be of the least good for you to tell the truth, for they could not comprehend it. But you can reach them through disinterested acts of benevolence. There are outcasts, men who have lost the similitude of God, who must first be cared for, fed, washed, and decently clothed. Then they are not to hear anything but of Christ, His great love and His willingness to save them. Let these perishing souls feel that all you have done for them was done because of your love for their souls.

The Lord uses the human agent. The divine and the human are to unite, becoming laborers together in the work of uplifting and restoring the moral image of God in man.... Move intelligently and perseveringly. Do not be discouraged if you do not at first have all the sympathy and cooperation that you expect. If you work, making the Lord your dependence, be assured that the Lord always helps the humble, meek, and lowly. But you need the working of the Holy Spirit upon your own heart and mind, in order to know how to do Christian help work. Pray much for those you are trying to help. Let them see that your dependence is upon a higher power, and you will win souls.—Letter 24, 1898.

Of some have compassion, making a difference: and others save with fear, pulling them out of the fire; hating even the garment spotted by the flesh. Jude 22, 23.

Chapter 31—Working for Outcasts

The Gospel Invitation to All Classes—Christ illustrated the spiritual blessings of the gospel by a temporal feast, the invitation to the supper. He set forth the wonderful condescension of God in the earnest invitation of the master of the feast to all who would come. The special call of the gospel to be given near the close of earth's history is also presented.

The invitation was to go first to the highways, bidding all come to the marriage supper of the Lamb. That message to the people so highly favored was rejected.

The next call was made to the poorer class—the poor, the halt, the maimed, the blind. These were not exalted by ambitious projects. If they would accept the invitation, they might come. This message was given, and the servants brought the report, "Lord, it is done as thou hast commanded, and yet there is room."

Then the Master said to His workers, "Go and seek in the byways, for the most degraded and the helpless, and compel them to come in, that My house may be filled."—Manuscript 81, 1899.

"Compel them to come in," Christ bids us.... In obedience to this word we must go to the heathen who are near us and to those who are afar off. The "publicans and harlots" must hear the Saviour's invitation. Through the kindness and long-suffering of His messengers the invitation becomes a compelling power to uplift those who are sunken in the lowest depths of sin.—The Ministry of Healing, 164.

Christ Longs to Reshape the Character—However low, however fallen, however dishonored and debased others may be, we are not to despise them and pass them by with indifference; but we should consider the fact that Christ has died for them....Christ longs to reshape the marred human character, to restore the moral image of God in men.—The Review and Herald, October 15, 1895.

He Regards Them as Precious—Every soul is the object of the loving interest of Him who gave His life that He might bring men back to God. This earnest, persevering interest expressed by our heavenly Father teaches us that the helpless and outcast are not to be passed by indifferently. They are the Lord's by creation and by redemption. If we were left to ourselves to judge, we would regard many who are degraded as hopeless. But the Lord sees the value of the silver in them. Though they do not look for help, He regards them as precious. The one who sees beneath the surface knows how to deal with human minds. He knows how to bring men to repentance. He knows that if they see themselves as sinners, they will repent and be converted to the truth. This is the work we are to engage in.—Letter 80, 1898.

Not to Ask—"Are They Worthy?"—To the appeal of the erring, the tempted, the wretched victims of want and sin, the Christian does not ask, Are they worthy? but, How can I benefit them? In the most wretched, the most debased, he sees souls whom Christ died to save, and for whom God has given to His children the ministry of reconciliation.—Thoughts from the Mount of Blessing, 22.

Discovered by Medical Missionary Work—I have been instructed that the medical missionary work will discover, in the very depths of degradation, men who, though they have given themselves up to intemperate, dissolute habits, will respond to the right kind of labor. But they need to be recognized and encouraged. Firm, patient, earnest effort will be required in order to lift them up. They cannot restore themselves. They may hear Christ's call, but their ears are too dull to take in its meaning; their eyes are too blind to see anything good in store for them. They are dead in trespasses and sins. Yet even these are not to be excluded from the gospel feast. They are to receive the invitation: "Come." Though they may feel unworthy, the Lord says: "Compel them to come in." Listen to no excuse. By love and kindness lay right hold of them.... This work, properly conducted, will save many a poor sinner who has been neglected by the churches.—Testimonies for the Church 6:279, 280.

In this work of restoration much painstaking effort will be required. No startling communications of strange doctrines should be made to these souls, but as they are helped physically the truth for this time should be presented. Men and women and youth need to see the law of God with its far-reaching requirements. It is not hardship, toil, or poverty that degrades humanity; it is sin, the transgression of God's law. The efforts put forth to rescue the outcast and degraded will be of no avail unless the claims of the law of God and the need of loyalty to Him are impressed on mind and heart. God has enjoined nothing that is not necessary to bind up humanity with Him. "The law of the Lord is perfect, converting the soul.... The commandment of the Lord is pure, enlightening the eyes." "By the word of Thy lips," says the psalmist, "I have kept me from the paths of the destroyer." Psalm 19:7, 8; 17:4.

Angels are helping in this work to restore the fallen and bring them back to the One who has given His life to redeem them, and the Holy Spirit is cooperating with the ministry of human agencies to arouse the moral powers by working on the heart, reproving of sin, of righteousness, and of judgment.—Testimonies for the Church 6:259, 260.

Working for the Intemperate[Further details and counsel on this topic will be found in The Ministry of Healing, 171-182, and a more recent exhaustive compilation entitled *Temperance*.]—Earnest effort should be made in behalf of those who are in bondage to evil habits. There is everywhere a work to be done for those who through intemperance have fallen. In the midst of churches, religious institutions, and professedly Christian homes, many of the youth are choosing the path to destruction. Through intemperate habits they bring upon themselves disease, and through greed to obtain money for sinful indulgence they fall into dishonest practices. Health and character are ruined. Aliens from God, outcasts from society, these poor souls feel that they are without hope either for this life or for the life to come. The hearts of the parents are broken. Men speak of these erring ones as hopeless, but not so does God regard them. He understands all the circumstances that have made them what they are, and he looks upon them with pity. This is a class that demand help. Never give them occasion to say, "no man cares for my soul."

Among the victims of intemperance are men of all classes and all professions. Men of high station, of eminent talents, of great attainments, have yielded to the indulgence of appetite, until they are helpless to resist temptation. Some of them who were once in the possession of wealth are without home, without friends, in suffering, misery, disease, and degradation. They have lost their self-control.

Unless a helping hand is held out to them they will sink lower and lower.—The Ministry of Healing, 171, 172.

A Battle Fought Again and Again—No random, haphazard, desultory work is to be done. To get fast hold of souls ready to perish means more than praying for a drunkard and then, because he weeps and confesses the pollution of his soul, declaring him saved. Over and over again the battle must be fought.—Testimonies for the Church 8:196.

You must hold fast to those whom you are trying to help, else victory will never be yours. They will be continually tempted to evil. Again and again they will be almost overcome by the craving for strong drink; again and again they may fall; but do not, because of this, cease your efforts.—The Ministry of Healing, 173.

The Work Not in Vain—When some, their human efforts united with the divine, endeavor to reach to the very depths of human woe and misery, God's blessing will rest richly upon them. Even though but few accept the grace of our Lord Jesus Christ, their work will not be in vain; for one soul is precious, very precious, in the sight of God. Christ would have died for one soul in order that that one might live through the eternal ages....

Many souls are being rescued, wrenched from Satan's hand, by faithful workers. Someone must have a burden of soul to find those who have been lost to Christ. The rescue of one soul over whom Satan has triumphed causes joy among the heavenly angels. There are those who have destroyed in themselves the moral image of God. The gospel net must gather in these poor outcasts. Angels of God will cooperate with those who are engaged in this work, who make every effort to save perishing souls, to give them opportunities which many have never had. There is no other way of reaching them but in Christ's way. He ever worked to relieve suffering and teach righteousness. Only thus can sinners be raised from the depths of degradation.—Testimonies for the Church 8:72, 73.

To Labor in Love—The workers must labor in love, feeding, cleansing, and clothing those who need their help. In this way these outcasts are prepared to know that someone cares for their souls. The Lord has shown me that many of these poor outcasts from society will, through the ministration of human agencies, cooperate with divine power and seek to restore the moral image of God in others for whom Christ has paid the price of His own blood. They will be called the elect of God, precious, and will stand next to the throne of God....

The Lord is working to reach the most depraved. Many will know what it means to be drawn to Christ, but will not have moral courage to war against appetite and passion. But the workers must not be discouraged at this; for it is written: "In the latter times some shall depart from the faith, giving heed to seducing spirits, and doctrines of devils." 1 Timothy 4:1. Is it only those rescued from the lowest depths that backslide? There are those in the ministry who have had light and a knowledge of the truth who will not be overcomers. They do not restrict their appetites and passions or deny themselves for Christ's sake. Many poor outcasts, even publicans and sinners, will grasp the hope set before them in the gospel, and will go into the kingdom of heaven before the ones who have had great opportunities and great light, but who have walked in darkness....My brethren and sisters, take your position on the Lord's side, and be earnest, active, courageous co-workers with Christ, laboring with Him to seek and save the lost.—Testimonies for the Church 5:74, 75.

Not to Follow Salvation Army Methods—The Lord has marked out our way of working. As a people we are not to imitate and fall in with Salvation Army methods. This is not the work that the Lord has given us to do. Neither is it our work to condemn them and speak harsh words against them. There are precious, self-sacrificing souls in the Salvation Army. We are to treat them kindly. There are in the Army honest souls, who are sincerely serving the Lord, and who will see greater light, advancing to the acceptance of all truth. The Salvation Army workers are trying to save the neglected, downtrodden ones. Discourage them not. Let them do that class of work by their own methods and in their own way. But the Lord has plainly pointed out the work that Seventh-day Adventists are to do.—Testimonies for the Church 8:184, 185.

Helping the Outcasts Find a New Career—As God's children devote themselves to this work [restoring the fallen], many will lay hold of the hand stretched out to save them. They are constrained to turn from their evil ways. Some of the rescued ones may, through faith in Christ, rise to high places of service, and be entrusted with responsibilities in the work of saving souls. They know by experience the necessities of those for whom they labor, and they know how to help them. They know what means can best be used to recover the perishing. They are filled with gratitude to God for the blessings they have received. Their hearts are quickened by love, and their energies are strengthened to lift up others who can never rise without help. Taking the Bible as their guide and the Holy Spirit as their helper and comforter, they find a new career opening before them. Every one of these souls that is added to the force of workers, provided with facilities and instruction as to how to save souls for Christ, becomes a colaborer with those who brought him the light of truth. Thus God is honored and His truth advanced.—Testimonies for the Church 6:260.

Chapter 32—Cautions Sounded

Slum Work Not to Be Glamorized—Precautions must be taken in this last work that mortals shall undertake. There is danger of so working upon the imagery of the mind that persons who are wholly unfitted to engage in the sacred work of God will consider themselves appointed by Heaven to work for the outcast and fallen. If all the experiences, pleasant and unpleasant were depicted, there would not be so many drawn to this class of work. Many enter the work because they love that which is sensational and exciting. But unless they throw all their energies into this grand, soul-saving work, they reveal that they have not the true missionary spirit.—Manuscript 177, 1899.

Danger in Working for Outcasts—In every effort to keep the soul with all diligence, man needs the keeping power of God. There is danger, constant danger, of contamination in the work among the fallen and degraded. Why, then, do men and women place themselves in contact with this danger who are unprepared to resist temptation, and who have not sufficient strength of character for the work?

Upon the mind of many a young man engaged in the so-called medical missionary work an altogether different effect is produced than the doctor or any of his associates imagine. [Reference is here made to Dr. J. H. Kellogg, who was leading out in a rapidly expanding work for the depraved and outcast.—Compilers.] He is not careful to watch the designs of Satan toward him in his new and exposed career, and gradually he separates from the home life and healthful influences. Before every such youth the danger signal needs to be uplifted. In every place where men and women are working for the degraded someone must bear grave responsibilities, or the workers will become cheap in their attitude, their words, and their principles.

Many will unite in this work, thinking that by so doing they will be helped from their life of sin; and when occasion arises these will think it right to prevaricate, to be dishonest, or to commit any of the sins of which they have been guilty in the past. Beholding this, the workers who are not living in close connection with God will be changed, not from good to a greater good, but from defective to a still more defective character. They will take up with the ways and manners of the open sinner. They will join the evildoers in magnifying every evil report, and in time will lose all love of refinement of speech or manners. Their fear of God and love of righteousness becomes mingled with a kind of religious fever, which is not acceptable in the sight of God.—Manuscript 177, 1899.

More Lost Than Saved—It is dangerous to set young men and young women at work among the abandoned classes. They are placed where they come in contact with every form of impurity, and Satan uses this opportunity to compass their ruin. Thus far more is lost than these workers save. Many of the efforts made for the abandoned result in the loss of the purity of the workers. Those who are engaged in visiting the houses of prostitution place themselves in terrible temptation. This work is always dangerous. It is a scheme of the devil to lead souls into temptation and lustful practices. "Come out from among them, and be ye separate, saith the Lord, and touch not the unclean thing; and I will receive you, and will be a Father unto you, and ye shall be My sons and daughters."

The farther young men and young women keep away from the corrupted and corrupting elements in this world, the better and safer will be their future experience. Medical missionary workers should be cleansed, refined, purified, and elevated. They should stand upon the platform of eternal truth. But I have been instructed that the truth has not been made to appear in its true bearing. The result that is worked out tends to corrupt minds; the sacred is not distinguished from the common.—Letter 162, 1900.

Guard the Work Sacredly—Many things have been presented to me. I was shown that there is a work to be done for the most depraved class, but that this matter must be most carefully guarded, so that the labor put forth shall not be in vain. Young men and young women should not be exposed, as many have been, in meeting the abandoned classes. Decided restraints are to be made, for there are positive dangers to be met. There is need of sacredly guarding the work. In the work for the lower class the strongest precautions should be observed. There are many who should not go into the large cities to work for the most depraved.—Manuscript 17, 1901.

Chapter 33—The Call for a Balanced Work

Maintain Proper Perspective—As the work advances, dangers arise that need to be guarded against. As new enterprises are entered upon, there is a tendency to make some one line all absorbing; that which should have the first place becomes a secondary consideration. The church needs fresh power and vitality, but there is great danger of taking on new lines of work that will waste their energies instead of bringing life into the church.—The Daily Bulletin of the General Conference, March 2, 1899.

Work for the Outcasts Not the Burden of Our Work—Of late [1899] a great interest has been aroused for the poor and outcast classes; a great work has been entered upon for the uplifting of the fallen and degraded. This in itself is a good work. We should ever have the Spirit of Christ, and we are to do the same class of work that He did for suffering humanity. The Lord has a work to be done for the outcasts. There is no question but that it is the duty of some to labor among them and try to save the souls that are perishing. This will have its place in connection with the proclamation of the third angel's message and the reception of Bible truth. But there is a danger of loading down everyone with this class of work, because of the intensity with which it is carried on. There is danger of leading men to center their energies in this line, when God has called them to another work.

The great question of our duty to humanity is a serious one, and much of the grace of God is needed in deciding how to work so as to accomplish the greatest amount of good. Not all are called to begin their work by laboring among the lowest classes. God does not require His workmen to obtain their education and training in order to devote themselves exclusively to these classes. The working of God is manifested in a way which will establish confidence that the work is of His devising, and that sound principles underlie every action. But I have had instruction from God that there is danger of planning for the outcasts in a way which will lead to spasmodic and excitable movements. These will produce no really beneficial results. A class will be encouraged to do a kind of work which will amount to the least in strengthening all parts of the work by harmonious action.

The gospel invitation is to be given to the rich and the poor, the high and the low, and we must devise means for carrying the truth into new places and to all classes of people. The Lord bids us, "Go out into the highways and hedges, and compel them to come in, that My house may be filled." He says, "Begin in the highways; thoroughly work the highways; prepare a company who in unity with you can go forth to do the very work that Christ did in seeking and saving the lost."

Christ preached the gospel to the poor, but He did not confine His labors to this class. He worked for all who would hear His word—not only the publican and the outcasts, but the rich and cultivated Pharisee, the Jewish nobleman, the centurion, and the Roman ruler. This is the kind of work I have ever seen should be done. We are not to strain every spiritual sinew and nerve to work for the lowest classes, and make that work the all in all. There are others whom we must bring to the Master, souls who need the truth, who are bearing responsibilities, and who will work with all their sanctified ability for the high places as well as for the low places.

The work for the poorer classes has no limit. It can never be got through with, and it must be treated as a part of the great whole. To give our first attention to this work, while there are vast portions of the Lord's vineyard open to culture and yet untouched, is to begin in the wrong place. As the right arm is to the body, so is the medical missionary work to the third angel's message. But the right arm is not to become the whole body. The work of seeking the outcasts is important, but it is not to become the great burden of our mission.—Manuscript 3, 1899.

Not Called Upon to Erect Homes for Abandoned Women or Babies—I must speak plainly in regard to some things which must be guarded. We should not enter into the work of maintaining homes for abandoned women or for infants. This responsibility might better be borne by families, who should care for those who need help in these lines.—Letter 11, 1900.

The Lord does not give us direction to erect buildings for the care of babies, although this is a good work, but it is not the work for the present time. Let the world do all it will in this line. Our time and means must be invested in a different line of work. We are to carry the last message of mercy in the very best way to reach those in the churches who are hungering and praying for light.—Letter 232, 1899.

Turn to Fields Ready to Harvest—This work is being made the all-absorbing work, but this is not in God's order. It is a never-ending work, and if it is carried on as it has been in the past, all the power of God's people will be required to counterbalance it, and the work of preparing a people to stand amid the perils of the last days will never be done.

Our work is to put on the armor and make aggressive warfare. Laborers are not to be encouraged to work in the slums and filth of the cities, where they will only secure converts who need watching, and that continually. There are fields all ripe for harvest, and all the time and money is not to be devoted to gathering in those who through indulgence of appetite have trained themselves in pollution. Some of these may be saved. And there are those who can labor in the lowest places of the earth without becoming deteriorated in character. But it is not safe to give young men and young women this class of work to do. The experiment would be a dear one. Thus those who could work in the highways would be disqualified for work of any kind....

Men's feelings may become deeply moved as they see human beings suffering as the result of their own course of action. There are those who are specially impressed to come into direct contact with this class, and the Lord gives them a commission to work in the worst places of the earth, doing what they can to redeem outcasts and place them where they will be under the care of the church. But the Lord has not called Seventh-day Adventists to make this work a specialty. He would not have them in this work engross many workers or exhaust the treasury.—Manuscript 16, 1900.

Support From the World Not From Churches—Constant work is to be done for the outcasts, but this work is not to be made all-absorbing.... No one should now visit our churches and in the present pressure obtain from them means to sustain the work of rescuing outcasts. The means to sustain that work should come, and will come, largely from those not of our faith. Let the churches take up their appointed work of presenting truth from the oracles of God in the highways.—Letter 138, 1898.

The Lord does not lay upon His people all the burden of laboring for a class so hardened by sin that many of them will neither be benefited themselves nor benefit others. If there are men who can take up the work for the most degraded, if God lays upon them a burden to labor for the masses in various ways, let these go forth and gather from the world the means required for doing this work. Let them not depend on the means which God intends shall sustain the work of the third angel's message.—Testimonies for the Church 6:246.

Nations Waiting for the Light—To those who suppose that the Lord has given them the work of caring for the promiscuous mass of outcasts, who have ruined themselves, many of whom will continue to do as they have done in the past, at the same time subsisting on means given them by Seventh-day Adventists, the Lord says, Who gave you this work? There are peoples and nations yet to receive the light of truth for this time. The gospel message is to be exalted and is to become far reaching.

In every place where the message is proclaimed, missionary workers are to go forth with their Bibles in their hands. Souls are to be converted and established in the truth. A meetinghouse is to be built. Light is to shine forth from the believers, who are to be as a city set on a hill. The church is to be in that place a witness to what the truth can do.—Letter 41, 1900.

Section 10—Financial Resources for Welfare Work

Gem Thought

That man might not lose the blessed results of benevolence, our Redeemer formed the plan of enlisting him as His co-worker. By a chain of circumstances which would call forth his charities, He bestows upon man the best means of cultivating benevolence, and keeps him habitually giving to help the poor and to advance His cause. He sends His poor as the representatives of Himself. By their necessities a ruined world are drawing forth from us talents of means and of influence, to present to them the truth, of which they are in perishing need. And as we heed these calls by labor and by acts of benevolence, we are assimilated to the image of Him who for our sakes became poor. In bestowing we bless others, and thus accumulate true riches.—Testimonies for the Church 3:382, 383.

And the multitude of them that believed were of one heart and of one soul: neither said any of them that ought of the things which he possessed was his own; but they had all things common. . . . Neither was there any among them that lacked: for as many as were possessors of lands or houses sold them, and brought the prices of the things that were sold, and laid them down at the apostles' feet: and distribution was made unto every man according as he had need. Acts 4:32-35.

Chapter 34—Our Individual Responsibility

An Individual Work Committed to Christ's Followers—Christ commits to His followers an individual work—a work that cannot be done by proxy. Ministry to the sick and the poor, the giving of the gospel to the lost, is not to be left to committees or organized charities. Individual responsibility, individual effort, personal sacrifice, is the requirement of the gospel.—The Ministry of Healing, 147.

Needs Supplied as We Impart—Christ has bidden us, through the prophet, "Deal thy bread to the hungry," and "satisfy the afflicted soul;" "when thou seest the naked, that thou cover him," and "bring the poor that are cast out to thy house." He has bidden us, "Go ye into all the world, and preach the gospel to every creature." But how often our hearts sink and faith fails us as we see how great is the need and how small the means in our hands. Like Andrew looking upon the five barley loaves and the two little fishes, we exclaim, "What are they among so many?" Often we hesitate, unwilling to give all that we have, fearing to spend and to be spent for others. But Jesus has bidden us, "Give *ye* them to eat." His command is a promise, and behind it is the same power that fed the multitude beside the sea.

In Christ's act of supplying the temporal necessities of a hungry multitude, is wrapped up a deep spiritual lesson for all His workers. Christ received from the Father; He imparted to the disciples; they imparted to the multitude; and the people to one another. So all who are united to Christ will receive from Him the bread of life, the heavenly food, and impart it to others....

The disciples were the channel of communication between Christ and the people. This should be a great encouragement to His disciples today. Christ is the great center, the source of all strength. His disciples are to receive their supplies from Him. The most intelligent, the most spiritually-minded, can bestow only as they receive. Of themselves they can supply nothing for the needs of the soul.

We can impart only that which we receive from Christ, and we can receive only as we impart to others. As we continue imparting we continue to receive; and the more we impart, the more we shall receive. Thus we may be constantly believing, trusting, receiving, and imparting.

The work of building up the kingdom of Christ will go forward, though to all appearance it moves slowly and impossibilities seem to testify against advance. The work is of God, and He will furnish means and will send helpers, true, earnest disciples, whose hands also will be filled with food for the starving multitude. God is not unmindful of those who labor in love to give the word of life to perishing souls, who in their turn reach forth their hands for food for other hungry souls.—The Desire of Ages, 369, 370.

Burden Not to Be Shifted to Organizations—In our work for God there is danger of relying too largely upon what man with his talents and ability can do. Thus we lose sight of the one Master Worker. Too often the worker for Christ fails to realize his personal responsibility. He is in danger of shifting his burden upon organizations, instead of relying upon Him who is the source of all strength. It is a great mistake to trust in human wisdom or numbers in the work of God. Successful work for Christ depends not so much on numbers or talent as upon pureness of purpose, the true simplicity of earnest, dependent faith. Personal responsibilities must be borne, personal duties must be taken up, personal efforts must be made for those who do not know Christ. In the place of shifting your responsibility upon someone whom you think more richly endowed than you are, work according to your ability.—The Desire of Ages, 370.

God Will Provide the Means—The means in our possession may not seem to be sufficient for the work; but if we will move forward in faith, believing in the all-sufficient power of God, abundant resources will open before us. If the work be of God, He Himself will provide the means for its accomplishment. He will reward honest, simple reliance upon Him. The little that is wisely and economically used in the service of the Lord of heaven will increase in the very act of imparting. In the hand of Christ the small supply of food remained undiminished until the famished multitude were satisfied. If we go to the Source of all strength, with our hands of faith outstretched to receive, we shall be sustained in our work, even under the most forbidding circumstances, and shall be enabled to give to others the bread of life.—The Desire of Ages, 369, 371.

Risk Something to Save Souls—There is a fearfulness to venture out and to run risks in this great work, fearing that the expenditure of means would not bring returns. What if means are used, and yet we cannot see that souls have been saved by it? What if there is a dead loss of a portion of our means? Better work and keep at work than to do nothing. You know not which shall prosper, this or that. Men will invest in patent rights and meet with heavy losses, and it is taken as a matter of course. But in the work and cause of God, men are afraid to venture. Money seems to them to be a dead loss that does not bring immediate returns when invested in the work of saving souls. The very means that is now so sparingly invested in the cause of God, and that is selfishly retained, will, in a little while, be cast with all idols to the moles and to the bats. Money will soon depreciate in value very suddenly when the reality of eternal scenes opens to the senses of man.

God will have men who will venture anything and everything to save souls. Those who will not move until they can see every step of the way clearly before them will not be of advantage at this time to forward the truth of God. There must be workers now who will push ahead in the dark as well as in the light, and who will hold up bravely under discouragements and disappointed hopes, and yet work on with faith, with tears and patient hope, sowing beside all waters, trusting the Lord to bring the increase. God calls for men of nerve, of hope, faith, and endurance, to work to the point.—The True Missionary, January, 1874.

Every Dollar Is Needed—The end of all things is at hand, and God calls for men to come into active service and do their duty because He desires it and the world needs their help. Under the guidance of the Holy Spirit men will become discreet in the outlay of means and will expend it according to the greatness and importance of the work which is to be done.... The Lord God of heaven calls upon men to put away their idols, to cut off every extravagant desire, to indulge in nothing that is simply for display and parade, and to study economy in purchasing garments and furniture. Do not expend one dollar of God's money in purchasing needless articles. Your money means the salvation of souls. Then let it not be spent for gems, for gold, or precious stones....

You may give thousands of dollars to the cause, and yet that extra dollar, that extra pound, is called for. Every pound is needed, every shilling can be put to use, and invested in such a way as to bring you imperishable treasure. My dear friends, who love God and would serve Him with wholeheartedness, I entreat of you that you ask yourselves when you are spending money in purchasing goods, "Am I glorifying God, or am I simply gratifying a human desire? Shall I invest this money which I hold in my hand to please myself, to make gifts to my children, or to my friends, or shall I be a co-worker with Christ, a pattern to all who are studying to glorify God?" The rule is given us, "Whether therefore ye eat, or drink, or whatsoever ye do, do all to the glory of God."—Letter 90, 1895.

Chapter 35—Releasing the Streams of Benevolence

To Be God's Almoners—God has placed property in the hands of men in order that they may learn to be merciful, to be His almoners to relieve the suffering of His fallen creatures.—The Signs of the Times, June 20, 1892.

To Keep Hearts Tender and Sympathetic—Acts of generosity and benevolence were designed by God to keep the hearts of the children of men tender and sympathetic and to encourage in them an interest and affection for one another in imitation of the Master, who for our sakes became poor, that we through His poverty might be made rich.—Testimonies for the Church 3:547.

Streams of Beneficence to Be Kept Flowing—The small streams of beneficence must be ever kept flowing into the treasury. God's providence is far ahead, moving onward much faster than our liberalities.—Manuscript 26, 1891.

A Constant Flow of Gifts—The money that God has entrusted to men is to be used in blessing humanity, in relieving the necessities of the suffering and the needy. Men are not to feel that they have done a very wonderful thing when they have endowed certain institutions or churches with large gifts. In the wise providence of God there are constantly presented before them the very ones who need their help. They are to relieve the suffering, clothe the naked, and help many who are in hard and trying circumstances, who are wrestling with all their energies to keep themselves and their families from a pauper's home.—The Review and Herald, January 4, 1898.

We Ask for Others—When we pray, "Give us this day our daily bread," we ask for others as well as ourselves. And we acknowledge that what God gives us is not for ourselves alone. God gives to us in trust, that we may feed the hungry. Of His goodness He has prepared for the poor. And He says, "When thou makest a dinner or a supper, call not thy friends, nor thy brethren, neither thy kinsmen, nor thy rich neighbours.... But when thou makest a feast, call the poor, the maimed, the lame, the blind: and thou shalt be blessed; for they cannot recompense thee: for thou shalt be recompensed at the resurrection of the just."—Thoughts from the Mount of Blessing, 111, 112.

God's Superscription on Every Dollar—Whatever may be the sum of our talents, whether one, two, or five, not a farthing of our money is to be squandered upon vanity, pride, or selfishness. Every dollar of our accumulation is stamped with the image and superscription of God. As long as there are hungry ones in God's world to be fed, naked ones to be clothed, souls perishing for the bread and water of salvation, every unnecessary indulgence, every overplus of capital, pleads for the poor and the naked.—The Signs of the Times, June 20, 1892.

Streams of Beneficence Dried Up—The more means persons expend in dress, the less they can have to feed the hungry and clothe the naked; and the streams of beneficence, which should be constantly flowing, are dried up. Every dollar saved by denying one's self of useless ornaments may be given to the needy or may be placed in the Lord's treasury to sustain the gospel, to send missionaries to foreign countries, to multiply publications to carry rays of light to souls in the darkness of error. Every dollar used unnecessarily deprives the spender of a precious opportunity to do good.—Testimonies for the Church 4:645, 646.

God Calls for Self-Denial—God calls upon the young to deny themselves of needless ornaments and articles of dress, even if they cost but a few dimes, and place the amount in the charity box. He also calls upon those of mature age to stop when they are examining a gold watch or chain or some expensive article of furniture and ask themselves the question: Would it be right to expend so large an amount for that which we could do without or when a cheaper article would serve our purpose just as well? By denying yourselves and lifting the cross for Jesus, who for your sakes became poor, you can do much toward relieving the suffering of the poor among us; and by thus imitating the example of your Lord and Master you will receive His approval and blessing.—Testimonies for the Church 4:511.

Not a Light Matter to Be the Lord's Steward—What if they should see inscribed upon their expensive decorations in their homes, the pictures, and furniture, "Bring the poor that are cast out to thy house"! In the dining room, where the table is laden with abundant food, the finger of God has traced, "Is it not to deal thy bread to the hungry, and that thou bring the poor that are cast out to thy house?"

Let all, old and young, consider that it is not a light matter to be the Lord's steward and to be charged in the books of heaven with using in a selfish manner. The needy, the oppressed, are left in want, while the Lord's money is selfishly squandered in extravagance and luxury. O that all will remember that God is no respecter of persons! It is a great thing to be a steward, faithful and true, before a just impartial God, who will not excuse in any of His stewards any unfairness or any robbery toward Him.—Manuscript 11, 1892.

A Wonderful Reformation Promised—When the grace of Christ is expressed in the words and works of the believers, light will shine forth to those who are in darkness; for while the lips are speaking to the praise of God, the hand will be stretched out in beneficence for the help of the perishing. We read that on the day of Pentecost, when the Holy Spirit descended upon the disciples, no man said that aught that he possessed was his own. All they owned was held for the advance of the wonderful reformation. And thousands were converted in a day. When the same spirit actuates believers today, and they give back to God of His own with the same liberality, a wide and far-reaching work will be accomplished.—Manuscript 95, 1907.

Chapter 36—Specific Funds for Welfare Work

Christians to Act as God's Treasurers—The poor are God's heritage. Christ has given His life for them. He calls upon those whom He has appointed to act as His stewards, to give liberally of the means entrusted to them to relieve the poor and to support His work in the earth. The Lord is rich in resources. He has appointed men to act as His treasurers in this world. That which He has given them they are to use in his service.—Manuscript 146, 1903.

A Thank Offering for the Poor—In every church there should be established a treasury for the poor. Then let each member present a thank offering to God once a week or once a month, as is most convenient. This offering will express our gratitude for the gifts of health, of food, and of comfortable clothing. And according as God has blessed us with these comforts will we lay by for the poor, the suffering, and the distressed. I would call the attention of our brethren specially to this point. Remember the poor. Forgo some of your luxuries, yea, even comforts, and help those who can obtain only the most meager food and clothing. In doing for them you are doing for Jesus in the person of His saints. He identifies Himself with suffering humanity. Do not wait until your imaginary wants are all satisfied. Do not trust to your feelings and give when you feel like it and withhold when you do not feel like it. Give regularly, either ten, twenty, or fifty cents a week, as you would like to see upon the heavenly record in the day of God.—Testimonies for the Church 5:150, 151.

A Self-denial Box at Home—Let everyone have a self-denial box in his home, and when he would spend pennies and shillings in self-gratification let him remember the needy and starving in Africa and India and those close by his own door. There are poor among us. Practice economy, and in every line present your case to God. Ask Him to give you the spirit of Christ, that you may be in every sense of the word Christ's disciples and receive His blessing. As you turn from the worship of self and try to relieve suffering humanity, pray that God will give you a true missionary work to do for souls. Then those who come to worship in the house of God will see a people clothed in modest apparel in harmony with the faith and Word of God. It is these things that steal away the love and trust and confidence of God's people in Him, that mar the religious experience and develop a selfishness that God cannot look upon.—Manuscript 52, 1898.

The Second Tithe—To promote the assembling of the people for religious service, as well as to provide for the poor, a second tithe of all the increase was required. Concerning the first tithe, the Lord had declared, "I have given the children of Levi *all the tenth* in Israel," But in regard to the second He commanded, "Thou shalt eat before the Lord thy God, in the place which He shall choose to place His name there, the tithe of thy corn, of thy wine, and of thine oil, and the firstlings of thy herds and of thy flocks; that thou mayest learn to fear the Lord thy God always." This tithe, or its equivalent in money, they were for two years to bring to the place where the sanctuary was established. After presenting a thank offering to God and a specified portion to the priest, the offerers were to use the remainder for a religious feast, in which the Levite, the stranger, the fatherless, and the widow should participate....

Every third year, however, this second tithe was to be used at home, in entertaining the Levite and the poor, as Moses said, "That they may eat within thy gates, and be filled." This tithe would provide a fund for the uses of charity and hospitality.—Patriarchs and Prophets, 530.

The consecration to God of a tithe of all increase, whether of the orchard and harvest field, the flocks and herds, or the labor of brain or hand; the devotion of a second tithe for the relief of the poor and for other benevolent uses, tended to keep fresh before the people the truth of God's ownership of all and of their opportunity to be channels of His blessings. It was a training adapted to kill out all narrowing selfishness and to cultivate breadth and nobility of character.—Education, 44.

Gifts and Offerings for Welfare Work—Deeds of mercy must be done; the poor and the suffering must be aided. Gifts and offerings should be appropriated for this purpose. Especially in new fields, where the standard of truth has never yet been uplifted, this work must be done.—Special Testimonies, Series A 9:68.

Medical missionaries can find a field in which to relieve the distress of those who are failing under bodily ailments. They should have means so that they may clothe the naked and feed the hungry. Christian help work will do more than the preaching of sermons.—The Review and Herald, December 24, 1895.

It will be necessary that a fund shall be created so that the workers may have means with which to help those who are in poverty and distress, and this practical ministry will open their hearts to respond to the truth.—The Review and Herald, January 28, 1896.

Men are appointed to proclaim the truth in new places. These men must have funds for their support. And they must have a fund to draw upon for the help of the poor and needy whom they meet in their work. The benevolence that they show toward the poor gives influence to their efforts to proclaim the truth. Their willingness to help those in need gains for them the gratitude of those they help and the approval of Heaven.—Letter 32, 1903.

Aided From Special Contributions, Not Regular Church Income—In the sixth chapter of Acts we are shown how when men were to be selected to fill positions in the church, the matter was brought before the Lord, and most earnest prayer was offered for guidance. The widows and fatherless were to be supported by contributions from the church. Their wants were not to be relieved by the church but by special donations. The tithe was to be consecrated to the Lord, and was always to be used for the support of the ministry. Men must be chosen to oversee the work of caring for the poor, to look after the proper distribution of the means in hand, that none among the believers should suffer for the necessaries of life.—Letter 9, 1899.

None Suffer If God's Plans Are Followed—There is nothing, after their recognition of the claims of God, that more distinguishes the laws given by Moses than the liberal, tender, and hospitable spirit enjoined toward the poor. Although God had promised greatly to bless His people, it was not His design that poverty should be wholly unknown among them. He declared that the poor should never cease out of the land. There would ever be those among His people who would call into exercise their sympathy, tenderness, and benevolence.

Then, as now, persons were subject to misfortune, sickness, and loss of property; yet so long as they followed the instruction given by God, there were no beggars among them, neither any who suffered for food.—Patriarchs and Prophets, 530, 531.

Chapter 37—The Wealth of the Gentiles

Not to Take Means From the Cause—The tithe is set apart for a special use. It is not to be regarded as a poor fund. It is to be especially devoted to the support of those who are bearing God's message to the world, and it should not be diverted from this purpose.—Review and Herald, Supplement, December 1, 1896.

The cause of God should not be overlooked that the poor may receive our first attention. Christ once gave His disciples a very important lesson on this point. When Mary poured the ointment on the head of Jesus, covetous Judas made a plea in behalf of the poor, murmuring at what he considered a waste of money. But Jesus vindicated the act, saying: "Why trouble ye her? she hath wrought a good work on Me." "Wheresoever this gospel shall be preached throughout the whole world, this also that she hath done shall be spoken of for a memorial of her." By this we are taught that Christ is to be honored in the consecration of the best of our substance. Should our whole attention be directed to relieving the wants of the poor, God's cause would be neglected. Neither will suffer if His stewards do their duty, but the cause of Christ should come first.—Testimonies for the Church 4:550, 551.

God's claim is to take precedence of any other claim and must be discharged first. Then the poor and the needy are to be cared for.—The Youth's Instructor, August 26, 1897.

To Receive From Outside Sources—God will open the way for us from sources outside our own people. I cannot see how anyone can take exceptions to the receiving of gifts from those not of our faith. They can only do so by taking extreme views and by creating issues which they are not authorized to do.—Special Testimonies to Ministers and Workers 3:43

God Moves Upon Unbelievers to Help—You inquire with respect to the propriety of receiving gifts from Gentiles or the heathen. The question is not strange; but I would ask you, Who is that owns our world? Who are the real owners of houses and lands? Is it not

God? He has an abundance in our world which He has placed in the hands of men, by which the hungry might be supplied with food, the naked with clothing, the homeless with homes. The Lord would move upon worldly men, even idolaters, to give of their abundance for the support of the work, if we would approach them wisely and give them an opportunity of doing those things which it is their privilege to do. What they would give we should be privileged to receive.

We should become acquainted with men in high places, and by exercising the wisdom of the serpent and the harmlessness of the dove we might obtain advantage from them, for God would move upon their minds to do many things in behalf of His people. If proper persons would set before those who have means and influence, the needs of the work of God in a proper light, these men might do much to advance the cause of God in our world. We have put away from us privileges and advantages that we might have had the benefit of, because we chose to stand independent of the world. But we need not sacrifice one principle of truth while taking advantage of every opportunity to advance the cause of God.—Special Testimonies to Ministers and Workers 3:29

Call Upon Great and Good Men to Help Us—There is a world to be warned, and we have been very delicate about calling upon rich men, either church members or worldlings, to aid us in the work. We would that all professed Christians stood with us. We would that their souls might be drawn out in liberality in aiding us in building up the kingdom of God in our world. We should call upon great and good men to help us in our Christian endeavor work. They should be invited to second our efforts in seeking to save that which is lost.—The Origin and Development of the Thanksgiving Plan, 5.

Such Gifts Not to Be Refused—When we show to the world, to angels, and to men that the prosperity of the cause of God is our first consideration, God will bless us. Sometimes He works through unbelievers, and unexpected relief comes. The Lord puts it into the hearts of men to help. The means coming in this way is not to be refused. When means comes from unbelievers it is to be used by the human agent to honor God. Every spiritually-minded, wholehearted giver will rightly apply every God-entrusted talent.

The Lord does not have to depend upon our means. He will not be restricted by the human agent. His way is always the best way, and any help that may come to advance His cause and work in any of our institutions is to be used as coming from Him. Gifts from unbelievers are not to be refused. The money is the Lord's, and is to be received with gratitude. Let God work and send by whom He will.... We believe time is closing. Eternity is at hand. Our supply of means is limited, and the work to be done is great. It is now that faith must be exercised. Our sufficiency is in God.—Manuscript 47, 1899.

Wealthy Will Provide Facilities—Let those who labor in the interests of the cause of God lay the necessities of the work in ----- before the wealthy men of the world. Do this judiciously. Tell them what you are trying to do. Solicit donations from them. It is God's means which they have, means which should be used in enlightening the world.

There are stored up in the earth large treasures of gold and silver. Men's riches have accumulated. Go to these men with a heart filled with love for Christ and suffering humanity and ask them to help you in the work you are trying to do for the Master. As they see that you reveal the sentiments of God's benevolence, a chord will be touched in their hearts. They will realize that they can be Christ's helping hand by doing medical missionary work. They will be led to cooperate with God, to provide the facilities necessary to set in operation the work that needs to be done.—Manuscript 40, 1901.

Impressed by the Spirit to Give—The higher classes have been strangely neglected. In the higher walks of life will be found many who will respond to the truth, because it is consistent, because it bears the stamp of the high character of the gospel. Not a few of the men of ability thus won to the cause will enter energetically into the Lord's work.

The Lord calls upon those who are in positions of trust, those to whom He has entrusted His precious gifts, to use their talents of intellect and means in His service. Our workers should present before these men a plain statement of our plan of labor, telling them what we need in order to help the poor and needy and to establish this work on a firm basis. Some of these will be impressed by the Holy Spirit to invest the Lord's means in a way that will advance

His cause. They will fulfill His purpose by helping to create centers of influence in the large cities.—Testimonies for the Church 7:112.

Money Will Be Given—The experience of apostolic days will come to us if men will be worked by the Holy Spirit. The Lord will withdraw His blessing where selfish interests are indulged, but He will put His people in possession of good throughout the world if they will unselfishly use their ability for the uplifting of humanity. His work is to be a sign of His benevolence, a sign that will win the confidence of the world and bring in resources for the advancement of the gospel.—Special Testimonies, series B 1:20.

It Is God's Money—Why not ask the Gentiles for assistance? I have received instruction that there are men and women in the world who have sympathetic hearts, and who will be touched with compassion as the needs of suffering humanity are presented before them....

The matter has been presented to me in this light. Our work is to be aggressive. The money is the Lord's, and if the wealthy are approached in the right way, the Lord will touch their hearts and impress them to give of their means. God's money is in the hands of these men, and some of them will heed the request for help.

Talk this over, and do all in your power to secure gifts. We are not to feel that it would not be the thing to ask men of the world for means, for it is just the thing to do. This plan was opened before me as a way of coming in touch with wealthy men of the world. Through this means not a few will become interested, and may hear and believe the truth for this time.—Stewardship Series, no. 1, 15, 16.

How to Make the Approach—Multitudes who are prosperous in the world and who never stoop to the common forms of vice are yet brought to destruction through the love of riches....

These men are in need of the gospel. They need to have their eyes turned from the vanity of material things to behold the preciousness of the enduring riches. They need to learn the joy of giving, the blessedness of being coworkers with God.

Persons of this class are often the most difficult of access, but Christ will open ways whereby they may be reached. Let the wisest, the most trustful, the most hopeful laborers seek for these souls. With the wisdom and tact born of divine love, with the refinement and courtesy that result alone from the presence of Christ in the soul, let them work for those who, dazzled by the glitter of earthly riches, see not the glory of the heavenly treasure. Let the workers study the Bible with them, pressing sacred truth home to their hearts. Read to them the words of God: "But of Him are ye in Christ Jesus, who of God is made unto us wisdom, and righteousness, and sanctification, and redemption." "Thus saith the Lord, Let not the wise man glory in his wisdom, neither let the mighty man glory in his might, let not the rich man glory in his riches: but let him that glorieth glory in this, that he understandeth and knoweth Me, that I am the Lord which exercise loving-kindness, judgment, and righteousness, in the earth: for in these things I delight, saith the Lord." "In whom we have redemption through His blood, the forgiveness of sins, according to the riches of His grace." "But my God shall supply all your need according to His riches in glory by Christ Jesus." 1 Corinthians 1:30; Jeremiah 9:23, 24; Ephesians 1:7; Philippians 4:19.

Such an appeal, made in the spirit of Christ, will not be thought impertinent. It will impress the minds of many in the higher classes.

By efforts put forth in wisdom and love, many a rich man may be awakened to a sense of his responsibility and his accountability to God. When it is made plain that the Lord expects them as His representatives to relieve suffering humanity, many will respond and will give of their means and their sympathy for the benefit of the poor. When their minds are thus drawn away from their own selfish interests, many will be led to surrender themselves to Christ. With their talents of influence and means they will gladly unite in the work of beneficence with the humble missionary who was God's agent in their conversion. By a right use of their earthly treasure they will lay up "a treasure in the heavens that faileth not, where no thief approacheth, neither moth corrupteth." They will secure for themselves the treasure that wisdom offers, even "durable riches and righteousness."—Testimonies for the Church 6:256-258.

Chapter 38—Food Sales

Church-sponsored Food Sales Not Condemned—When the State fair was held in Battle Creek, our people took with them onto the grounds three or four cooking stoves and demonstrated how good meals might be prepared without the use of flesh meat. We were told that we set the best table on the ground. Whenever large gatherings are held, it is your privilege to devise plans whereby you can provide those who attend with wholesome food, and you are to make your efforts educational.—Manuscript 27, 1906.

A Unique Experience in Health Education—It was on the occasion of the visit of Barnum's great menagerie to this city on the 28th of June [1877], that the ladies of the Woman's Christian Temperance Union struck a telling blow for temperance and reform by organizing an immense temperance restaurant to accommodate the crowds of people who gathered in from the country to visit the menagerie, thus preventing them from visiting the saloons and groggeries, where they would be exposed to temptation. The mammoth tent, capable of holding five thousand people used by the Michigan Conference for camp meeting purposes, was tendered for the occasion. Beneath this immense canvas temple were erected fifteen or twenty tables for the accommodation of guests.

By invitation the sanitarium set a large table in the center of the great pavilion, bountifully supplied with delicious fruits, grains, and vegetables. This table formed the chief attraction and was more largely patronized than any other. Although it was more than thirty feet long, it became so crowded that it was necessary to set another about two thirds as long, which was also thronged.—Testimonies for the Church 4:275.

Planning for a Banquet—Yesterday I had a two hours' conversation with A and his wife, who are working at the sanitarium here. I think that the interview was a profitable one. They spoke of a plan that they have in mind—to have a banquet at the sanitarium and to invite the prominent residents of St. Helena—lawyers, bankers, and ministers. They hope that thus they can do something to remove the impression that seems to be held by some in St. Helena—that this institution is a place where only imbeciles and decrepit people are cared for. Brother B, manager of the San Francisco Vegetarian Cafe, will come up to take charge of the preparation of the banquet.

I saw no objection to this plan. When the light of health reform first came to us we used, on holiday occasions, to take cooking stoves to the grounds where the people were assembled, and right there bake unleavened bread—gems and rolls. And I think that good was the result of our efforts, though, of course, we had not the health food preparations that we now have. At that time we were just beginning to learn how to live without using flesh meat.

Sometimes we gave entertainments, and we took great care that all that we prepared for the table was palatable and nicely served. In fruit season we would get blueberries and raspberries fresh from the bushes, and strawberries fresh from the vines. We made the table fare an object lesson which showed those present that our diet, even though it was in accordance with the principles of health reform, was far from being a meager one.

Sometimes a short temperance lecture was given in connection with these entertainments, and thus people became acquainted with our principles of living. As far as we knew, all were pleased and all were enlightened. We always had something to say about the necessity of providing wholesome food and of preparing it simply, and yet making it so palatable and appetizing that those eating it would be satisfied. The world is full of the temptation to indulge appetite, and words of warning, earnest and right to the point, have made wonderful changes in families and in individuals.—Letter 166, 1903.

Peril of Making Financial Gain in Sale of Food the Primary Objective—Light was also given that in the cities there would be opportunity to do a work similar to that which we did on the Battle Creek fair grounds. In harmony with this light, hygienic restaurants have been established. But there is grave danger that our restaurant workers will become so imbued with the spirit of commercialism that they will fail to impart the light which the people need. Our restaurants bring us in contact with many people, but if we allow our minds to be engrossed with the thought of financial profit, we shall fail to fulfill the purpose of God. He would have us take advantage of every opportunity to present the truth that is to save men and women from eternal death.—Manuscript 27, 1906.

Christ Reached the People at Their Dinners and Feasts—Christ is our Master. By definite instructions He prepared His followers for their work before leaving them. As soon as He could talk, Christ used the talent of speech, in the family circle and among friends and acquaintances, in a way that was without fault. Not one impure word escaped His lips. Never did He do a wrong action, for He was the Son of God. Although He possessed a human form, yet He was without a taint of sin.

When invited, as His work commenced, to a dinner or feast by Pharisee or publican He accepted the invitation. He was accused by the religious leaders of eating with publicans, and they cast the imputation upon Him that He was like them. But on such occasions Christ controlled the table talk, and gave many precious lessons. Those present listened to Him; for had He not healed their sick, comforted their sorrowing, taken their children in His arms and blessed them? Publicans and sinners were drawn to Him, and when He opened His lips to speak, their attention was riveted on Him.

Christ taught His disciples how to conduct themselves when in the company of those who were not religious and those who were. He taught them by example that when attending any public gathering, they need not want for something to say. But His conversation differed most decidedly from that which had been listened to at feasts in the past. Every word He uttered was a savor of life unto life to His hearers, and they listened with subdued attention, as though desirous of hearing to a purpose.

The respect shown to Christ at the feasts He attended was in marked contrast to the manner in which the scribes and Pharisees were treated, and this made them anxious. Christ gave lessons adapted to the needs of His hearers. It was when He was at a feast that He gave the parable of the great supper, and showed the way in which the invitation of the king was treated....

The great teacher spoke as one having authority. He instructed His disciples in regard to the duties and regulations of true social life, which are the same as the laws of the kingdom of God. Christ spoke His words with great clearness and simplicity, and with no uncertain sound. His words were as apples of gold in pictures of silver.—Manuscript 19, 1899.

Opportunities in Large Gatherings—I was given instruction that as we approach the end there will be large gatherings in our cities, as there has recently been in St. Louis, and that preparations must be made to present the truth at these gatherings. When Christ was upon this earth He took advantage of such opportunities. Wherever a large number of people were gathered for any purpose, His voice was heard, clear and distinct, giving His message. And as a result, after His crucifixion and ascension, thousands were converted in a day. The seed sown by Christ sank deep into hearts, and germinated, and when the disciples received the gift of the Holy Spirit, the harvest was gathered in....

At every large gathering some of our ministers should be in attendance. They should work wisely to obtain a hearing and to get the light of the truth before as many as possible....

We should improve every such opportunity as that presented by the St. Louis Fair. At all similar gatherings there should be present men whom God can use. Leaflets containing the light of present truth should be scattered among the people like the leaves of autumn. To many who attend these gatherings these leaflets would be as the leaves of the tree of life, which are for the healing of the nations.—Letter 296, 1904.

Chapter 39—Forbidden Money-Raising Methods

Lust of Appetite and Love of Pleasure the Wrong Money-raising Appeal—We see the churches of our day encouraging feasting, gluttony, and dissipation, by the suppers, fairs, dances, and festivals gotten up for the purpose of gathering means into the church treasury. Here is a method invented by carnal minds to secure means without sacrificing.

Such an example makes an impression upon the minds of youth. They notice that lotteries and fairs and games are sanctioned by the church, and they think there is something fascinating in this way of obtaining means....

Let us stand clear of all these church corruptions, dissipations, and festivals, which have a demoralizing influence upon young and old. We have no right to throw over them the cloak of sanctity because the means is to be used for church purposes. Such offerings are lame and diseased and bear the curse of God. They are the price of souls. The pulpit may defend festivals, dancing, lotteries, fairs, and luxurious feasts, to obtain means for church purposes, but let us participate in none of these things; for if we do, God's displeasure will be upon us. We do not propose to appeal to the lust of appetite or resort to carnal amusements as an inducement to Christ's professed followers to give of the means which God has entrusted to them. If they do not give willingly, for the love of Christ, the offering will in no case be acceptable to God.—The Review and Herald, November 21, 1878.

The Church Is Desecrated—When money is raised for religious purposes, to what means do many churches resort? To bazaars, suppers, fancy fairs, even to lotteries and like devices. Often the place set apart for God's worship is desecrated by feasting and drinking, buying, selling, and merrymaking. Respect for the house of God and reverence for His worship are lessened in the minds of the youth. The barriers of self-restraint are weakened. Selfishness, appetite, the love of display, are appealed to, and they strengthen as they are indulged.—Testimonies for the Church 9:91.

How Are Unbelievers Impressed?—And what impression is made upon the minds of unbelievers? The holy standard of the Word of God is lowered into the dust. Contempt is cast upon God and upon the Christian name. The most corrupt principles are strengthened by this un-Scriptural way of raising means. And this is as Satan would have it. Men are repeating the sin of Nadab and Abihu. They are using common instead of sacred fire in the service of God. The Lord accepts no such offerings.

All these methods for bringing money into His treasury are an abomination to Him. It is a spurious devotion that prompts all such devising. O what blindness, what infatuation, is upon many who claim to be Christians! Church members are doing as did the inhabitants of the world in the days of Noah, when the imagination of their hearts was only evil continually. All who fear God will abhor such practices as a misrepresentation of the religion of Jesus Christ.—The Review and Herald, December 8, 1896.

Giving for Selfish Considerations—In professedly Christian gatherings Satan throws a religious garment over delusive pleasures and unholy revelings to give them the appearance of sanctity, and the consciences of many are quieted because means are raised to defray church expenses. Men refuse to give for the love of God, but for the love of pleasure and the indulgence of appetite for selfish considerations they will part with their money.

Is it because there is not power in the lessons of Christ upon benevolence, and in His example, and the grace of God upon the heart to lead men to glorify God with their substance, that such a course must be resorted to in order to sustain the church? The injury sustained to the physical, mental, and moral health in these scenes of amusement and gluttony is not small. And the day of final reckoning will show souls lost through the influence of these scenes of gaiety and folly.

It is a deplorable fact that sacred and eternal considerations do not have that power to open the hearts of the professed followers of Christ to make freewill offerings to sustain the gospel, as the tempting bribes of feasting and general merriment. It is a sad reality that these inducements will prevail when sacred and eternal things will have no force to influence the heart to engage in works of benevolence.

The plan of Moses in the wilderness to raise means was highly successful. There was no compulsion necessary. Moses made no grand feast. He did not invite the people to scenes of gaiety, dancing, and general amusement. Neither did he institute lotteries or anything of this profane order to obtain means to erect the tabernacle of God in the wilderness. God commanded Moses to invite the children of Israel to bring the offerings. Moses was to accept gifts of every man that gave willingly from his heart. These freewill offerings came in so great abundance that Moses proclaimed it was enough. They must cease their presents, for they had given abundantly, more than they could use.

Satan's temptations succeed with the professed followers of Christ on the point of indulgence of pleasure and appetite. Clothed as an angel of light, he will quote Scripture to justify the temptations he places before men to indulge the appetite, and in worldly pleasures which suit the carnal heart. The professed followers of Christ are weak in moral power and are fascinated with the bribe which Satan has presented before them, and he gains the victory.

How does God look upon churches that are sustained by such means? Christ cannot accept these offerings, because they were not given through their love and devotion to Him but through their idolatry of self. But what many would not do for the love of Christ they will do for the love of delicate luxuries to gratify the appetite and for love of worldly amusements to please the carnal heart.—The Review and Herald, October 13, 1874.

Motive for Giving Is Chronicled—I was shown that the recording angel makes a faithful record of every offering dedicated to God, and put into the treasury, and also of the final result of the means thus bestowed. The eye of God takes cognizance of every farthing devoted to His cause and of the willingness or reluctance of the giver. The motive in giving is also chronicled. Those self-sacrificing, consecrated ones who render back to God the things that are His, as He requires of them, will be rewarded according to their works.—Testimonies for the Church 2:518, 519.

Section 11—The Fruitage of Welfare Ministry

Gem Thought

People are watching and weighing those who claim to believe the special truths for this time. They are watching to see wherein their life and conduct represent Christ. By humbly and earnestly engaging in the work of doing good to all, God's people will exert an influence that will tell in every town and city where the truth has entered. If all who know the truth will take hold of this work as opportunities are presented, day by day doing little acts of love in the neighborhood where they live, Christ will be manifest to their neighbors. The gospel will be revealed as a living power and not as cunningly devised fables or idle speculations. It will be revealed as a reality, not the result of imagination or enthusiasm. This will be of more consequence than sermons or professions or creeds.—Testimonies for the Church 6:264.

Your giving does not end in meeting the wants of your fellow Christians. It also results in an overflowing tide of thanksgiving to God. Moreover, your very giving proves the reality of your faith, and that means that men thank God that you practice the Gospel that you profess to believe in, as well as for the actual gifts you make to them and to others. And yet further, men will pray for you and feel drawn to you because you have obviously received a generous measure of the grace of God. 2 Corinthians 9:11-14, Phillips version.

Chapter 40—The Influence of Neighborhood Ministry

Let the World See—Let the world see that we are not selfishly narrowed up to our own exclusive interests and religious joys, but that we are liberal, and desire them to share our blessings and privileges, through the sanctification of the truth. Let them see that the religion which we profess does not close up or freeze over the avenues to the soul, making us unsympathizing and exacting. Let all who profess to have found Christ, minister as He did to the benefit of man, cherishing a spirit of wise benevolence. We shall then see many souls following the light that shines from our precept and example.—Testimonies for the Church 4:59.

Christian Help Work Is More Effectual Than Preaching—The good works of the children of God are the most effectual preaching the unbeliever has.—Spiritual Gifts 2:235.

[296] Let them do Christian help work, feeding the hungry and clothing the naked. This will have a far stronger influence for good than the preaching of sermons.—Testimonies for the Church 7:227, 228.

Our ideas of Christian benevolence must be worked out if we would have them enlarged. Practical work will accomplish far more than sermons.—Testimonies for the Church 6:302.

Influence of the Life of Christian Service—The Christian's life will testify that he is governed by other laws than those which the world obeys—laws of a higher order than those that control the lovers of the world. The will of God, our Creator, is to be made manifest in us, not only in the name we bear, but in our life of self-denial. We are to give evidence that we are influenced and controlled by unselfish principles. All our purposes and pursuits should stand in distinct contrast to the selfishness of the world.

Oneness with Christ enables men to wield an influence far above that of the renowned of this world. While copying the example of Christ, they have, with His grace, power to benefit the church and the community. Their influence is felt just in proportion to the distinctness of the line of demarcation which separates them in spirit and principle from the world.

As union is strength, the Source of all power, of all goodness, mercy, and love, takes finite, human beings into copartnership with Himself for the purpose of imparting His divine power to human agencies, to diffuse His influence and extend it far and near. When one is allied to Christ, a partaker of the divine nature, his interest is identified with that of all suffering humanity. As we look aright to the cross of Calvary, every nerve of heart and brain will thrill in sympathy for the human misery in all parts of our world. Those who are created anew in Christ Jesus will realize the wretchedness of sin and the divine compassion of Christ in His infinite sacrifice for fallen man. Communion with Christ imparts to them tenderness of heart; there will be sympathy in their looks, in the tones of the voice; and earnestness of solicitude, love, and energy, in their efforts, which will make them powerful through God in winning souls to Christ.—The Medical Missionary, June, 1891.

The Hallowed Influence of Benevolent Acts—If the world had before them the example that God demands those who believe in Him to set, they would work the works of Christ. If Jesus were set forth, crucified among us, if we viewed the cross of Calvary in the light of God's Word, we would be one with Christ as He was one with the Father. Our faith would be altogether different from the faith now shown. It would be a faith that works by love to God and to our fellow men, and purifies the soul. If this faith were shown by God's people, many more would believe on Christ. A hallowed influence would be exerted by the benevolent actions of God's servants, and they would shine as lights in the world.—Special Testimonies, series A 10:2.

Mightier Than the Sword or Courts of Justice—The love of God in the heart, manifested in true, unselfish missionary labor, will be more mighty than the sword or courts of justice in dealing with the evildoer. The living missionary, with his heart overflowing with the love of God, can break down the barriers. The medical missionary, taking up his appointed work, cannot only relieve bodily maladies, but through the love and grace of Christ can heal the diseased soul, leprous with sin. The hearts of men will often harden under rebuke, but they cannot withstand the love expressed toward them in Christ.—Manuscript 60, 1897.

Loving Ministry Will Allay Prejudice—The glory of heaven is in lifting up the fallen, comforting the distressed. And wherever Christ abides in human hearts He will be revealed in the same way. Wherever it acts the religion of Christ will bless. Wherever it works there is brightness....

Whatever the difference in religious belief, a call from suffering humanity must be heard and answered. Where bitterness of feeling exists because of difference in religion, much good may be done by personal service. Loving ministry will break down prejudice and win souls to God.—Christ's Object Lessons, 386.

We Must Disarm Prejudice—The followers of Christ, as they approach the time of trouble, [should] make every exertion to place themselves in a proper light before the people, to disarm prejudice.—The Great Controversy, 616.

As a means of overcoming prejudice and gaining access to minds medical missionary work must be done.... We are to work as gospel medical missionaries to heal the sin-sick souls by giving them the message of salvation. This work will break down prejudice as nothing else can.—Testimonies for the Church 9:211.

The Witness of the Virtuous, Unselfish Life—The good works of God's people have a more powerful influence than words. By their virtuous life and unselfish acts the beholder is led to desire the same righteousness which produced so good fruit.—The Review and Herald, May 5, 1885.

Deeds Greater Than Creeds—Divine truth exerts little influence upon the world, when it should exert much influence through our practice. The mere profession of religion abounds, but it has little weight. We may claim to be followers of Christ, we may claim to believe every truth in the Word of God; but this will do our neighbor no good unless our belief is carried into our daily life. Our profession may be as high as heaven, but it will save neither ourselves nor our fellow men unless we are Christians. A right example will do more to benefit the world than all our profession.—Christ's Object Lessons, 383.

Influences Emanating From a Loving Home—Those who cultivate love in the home life will form characters after Christ's likeness, and they will be constrained to exert a helpful influence beyond the family circle, in order that they may bless others by kind, thoughtful ministrations, by pleasant words, by Christlike sympathy, by acts of benevolence. They will be quick to discern those who have hungry hearts, and will make a feast for those who are needy and afflicted. Those who have heavenly discernment, who exercise tender regard for every member of the family, will, in doing their whole duty, fit themselves to do a work that will brighten other homes and will teach others by precept and example what it is that will make home happy.—The Review and Herald, October 15, 1895.

Examples of Influence—By their wisdom and justice, by the purity and benevolence of their daily life, by their devotion to the interests of the people—and they, idolaters—Joseph and Daniel proved themselves true to the principles of their early training, true to Him whose representatives they were. These men, both in Egypt and in Babylon, the whole nation honored; and in them a heathen people, and all the nations with which they were connected, beheld an illustration of the goodness and beneficence of God, an illustration of the love of Christ.

What a lifework was that of these noble Hebrews! As they bade farewell to their childhood's home, how little did they dream of their high destiny! Faithful and steadfast, they yielded themselves to the divine guiding, so that through them God could fulfill His purpose.

The same mighty truths that were revealed through these men, God desires to reveal through the youth and the children of today. The history of Joseph and Daniel is an illustration of what He will do for those who yield themselves to Him and with the whole heart seek to accomplish His purpose.

The greatest want of the world is the want of men—men who will not be bought or sold; men who in their inmost souls are true and honest; men who do not fear to call sin by its right name; men whose conscience is as true to duty as the needle to the pole; men who will stand for the right though the heavens fall.—Education, 56, 57.

Chapter 41—Reflex Blessings

The Law of Action and Reaction—Divine wisdom has appointed in the plan of salvation the law of action and reaction, making the work of beneficence, in all its branches, twice blessed. He that gives to the needy blesses others, and is blessed himself in a still greater degree. God could have reached His object in saving sinners without the aid of man, but He knew that man could not be happy without acting a part in the great work in which he would be cultivating self-denial and benevolence. That man might not lose the blessed results of benevolence, our Redeemer formed the plan of enlisting him as His co-worker.—Testimonies for the Church 3:382.

It is as we give ourselves to God for the service of humanity that He gives Himself to us. No one can give place in his own heart and life for the stream of God's blessings to flow to others without receiving in himself a rich reward.—Thoughts from the Mount of Blessing, 81, 82.

Helping Others Will Develop Character—It is in doing the works of Christ, ministering as He did to the suffering and afflicted, that we are to develop Christian character. It is for our good that God has called us to practice self-denial for Christ's sake, to bear the cross, to labor and sacrifice in seeking to save that which is lost. This is the Lord's process of refining, purging away the baser material, that the precious traits of character which were in Christ Jesus, may appear in the believer.... Through the grace of Christ our efforts to bless others are not only the means of our growth in grace, but they will enhance our future eternal happiness. To those who have been co-workers with Christ it will be said, "Well done, thou good and faithful servant: thou hast been faithful over a few things; I will make thee ruler over many things."—The Review and Herald, June 27, 1893.

The spirit of unselfish labor for others gives depth, stability, and Christlike loveliness to the character and brings peace and happiness to its possessor.—Testimonies for the Church 5:607.

The Source of True Happiness—In doing for others a sweet satisfaction will be experienced, an inward peace which will be a sufficient reward. When actuated by a high and noble desire to do others good, they will find true happiness in a faithful discharge of life's manifold duties.—Testimonies for the Church 2:132.

Real happiness is found only in being good and doing good.—The Youth's Instructor, December 5, 1901.

Our happiness will be proportionate to our unselfish works, prompted by divine love, for in the plan of salvation God has appointed the law of action and reaction.—The Signs of the Times, November 25, 1886.

Welfare Work Induces Health—Those who give practical demonstrations of their benevolence by their sympathy and compassionate acts toward the poor, and suffering, and the unfortunate, not only relieve the sufferers, but contribute largely to their own happiness, and are in the way of securing health of soul and body. Isaiah has ... plainly described the work that God will accept and bless His people in doing.—Testimonies for the Church 4:60.

I call your attention to the sure results of heeding the Lord's admonition to care for the afflicted: "Then shall thy light break forth as the morning, and thine health shall spring forth speedily." Is not this what we all crave? Oh, there is health and peace in doing the will of our Heavenly Father. "Thy righteousness shall go before thee; the glory of the Lord shalt be thy rereward. Then shalt thou call, and the Lord shall answer; thou shalt cry, and He shall say, Here I am. If thou take away from the midst of thee the yoke, the putting forth of the finger, and speaking vanity; and if thou draw out thy soul to the hungry, and satisfy the afflicted soul; then shall thy light rise in obscurity, and thy darkness be as the noon day: and the Lord shall guide thee continually, and satisfy thy soul in drought, and make fat thy bones: and thou shalt be like a watered garden, and like a spring of water, whose waters fail not."—The Medical Missionary, June, 1891.

[303]

How Welfare Work Induces Health—The pleasure of doing good to others imparts a glow to the feelings which flashes through the nerves, quickens the circulation of the blood, and induces mental and physical health.—Testimonies for the Church 4:56.

The sympathy which exists between the mind and the body is very great. When one is affected the other responds. The condition of the mind has much to do with the health of the physical system. If the mind is free and happy, under a consciousness of rightdoing and a sense of satisfaction in causing happiness to others, it will create a cheerfulness that will react upon the whole system, causing a freer circulation of the blood and a toning up of the entire body. The blessing of God is a healer, and those who are abundant in benefiting others will realize that wondrous blessing in their hearts and lives.—Testimonies for the Church 4:60.

A Remedy for Disease—Some plead their poor health—they would love to do if they had strength. Such have so long shut themselves up to themselves and thought so much of their own poor feelings and talked so much of their sufferings, trials, and afflictions that it is their present truth. They can think of no one but self, however much others may be in need of sympathy and assistance. You who are suffering with poor health, there is a remedy for you. If thou clothe the naked, and bring the poor that are cast out to thy house, and deal thy bread to the hungry, "then shall thy light break forth as the morning, and thine health shall spring forth speedily." Doing good is an excellent remedy for disease. Those who engage in the work are invited to call upon God, and He has pledged Himself to answer them. Their soul shall be satisfied in drought, and they shall be like a watered garden, whose waters fail not.—Testimonies for the Church 2:29.

This is the recipe that Christ has prescribed for the fainthearted, doubting, trembling soul. Let the sorrowful ones, who walk mournfully before the Lord, arise and help someone who needs help.—Testimonies for the Church 6:266.

Sympathy Productive of Much Good—When human sympathy is blended with love and benevolence and sanctified by the Spirit of Jesus, it is an element which can be productive of great good. Those who cultivate benevolence are not only doing a good work for others and blessing those who receive the good action, but they are benefiting themselves by opening their hearts to the benign influence of true benevolence. Every ray of light shed upon others will be reflected upon our own hearts. Every kind and sympathizing word spoken to the sorrowful, every act to relieve the oppressed, and every gift to supply the necessities of our fellow beings, given or done with an eye to God's glory, will result in blessings to the giver. Those who are thus working are obeying a law of heaven and will receive the approval of God....

Jesus knew the influence of benevolence upon the heart and life of the benefactor, and He sought to impress upon the minds of His disciples the benefits to be derived from the exercise of this virtue. He says: "It is more blessed to give than to receive." He illustrates the spirit of cheerful benevolence, which should be exercised toward friends, neighbors, and strangers, by the parable of the man who journeyed from Jerusalem to Jericho.—Testimonies for the Church 4:56, 57.

In Saving His Neighbor He Saved Himself—A working church is a growing church. The members find a stimulus and a tonic in helping others. I have read of a man who, journeying on a winter's day through deep drifts of snow, became benumbed by the cold, which was almost imperceptibly freezing his vital powers. He was nearly chilled to death and was about to give up the struggle for life, when he heard the moans of a fellow traveler who was also perishing with cold. His sympathy was aroused, and he determined to rescue him. He chafed the ice-cold limbs of the unfortunate man, and after considerable effort raised him to his feet. As the sufferer could not stand, he bore him in sympathizing arms through the very drifts he had thought he could never get through alone.

When he had carried his fellow traveler to a place of safety, the truth flashed home to him that in saving his neighbor he had also saved himself. His earnest efforts to help another had quickened the blood that was freezing in his own veins and sent a healthy warmth to the extremities of his body.

The lesson that in helping others we ourselves receive help, must be urged upon young believers continually, by precept and example, that in their Christian experience they may gain the best results. Let the desponding ones, those disposed to think that the way to eternal life is trying and difficult, go to work to help others. Such efforts, united with prayer for divine light, will cause their own hearts to throb with the quickening influence of the grace of God, their own affections to glow with more divine fervor. Their whole Christian life will be more of a reality, more earnest, more prayerful.—Gospel Workers, 198, 199.

The Church Is Blessed—Let church members during the week act their part faithfully, and on the Sabbath tell their experiences. The meeting will then be as meat in due season, bringing to all present new life and fresh vigor. When God's people see the great need of working as Christ worked for the conversion of sinners, the testimonies borne by them in the Sabbath services will be filled with power. With joy they will bear witness to the preciousness of the experience they have gained in working for others.—Gospel Workers, 199.

Our Own Graces Exercised—Had there been nothing in the world to work at cross purposes with us, patience, forbearance, gentleness, meekness, and longsuffering would not have been called into action. The more these graces are exercised, the more will they be increased and strengthened. The more we deal our temporal bread to the hungry, the oftener we clothe the naked, visit the sick, and relieve the fatherless and the widow in their affliction, the more decidedly shall we realize the blessing of God.—Manuscript 64, 1894.

Why Blessings Are Withheld—The blessing of God cannot come upon those who are idlers in His vineyard. Professed Christians who do nothing neutralize the efforts of real workers by their influence and example. They make the grand and important truths they profess to believe, appear inconsistent, and cause them to have no effect. They misrepresent the character of Christ. How can God let the showers of His grace come upon the churches that are largely composed of this kind of members? They are of no manner of use in the work of God. How can the Master say to such, "Well done, thou good and faithful servant: ... enter thou into the joy of thy Lord," when they have been neither good nor faithful? God cannot speak a falsehood. The power of the grace of God cannot be given in large measure to the churches. It would dishonor His own glorious character to let streams of grace come upon the people who will not wear the yoke of Christ, who will not bear His burdens, who will not deny self, who will not lift the cross of Christ. Because of their slothfulness they are a hindrance to those who would move out in the work if they did not block up the way.—The Review and Herald, July 21, 1896.

Become a Living Stream of Good Deeds—If God and Christ and angels rejoice when even one sinner repents and becomes obedient to Christ, should not man be imbued with the same spirit, and work for time and for eternity with persevering effort to save, not only his own soul, but the souls of others? If you work in this direction with wholehearted interest as the followers of Christ, discharging every duty, improving every opportunity, your own souls will be gradually settling into the mold of a perfect Christian. The heart will not be sere and unfeeling. The spiritual life will not be dwarfed. The heart will glow with the impress of the divine image, for it will be in close sympathy with God. The whole life will flow out with cheerful readiness in channels of love and sympathy for humanity. Self will be forgotten, and the ways of this class will be established in God. In watering others their own souls will be watered. The stream flowing through their souls is from a living spring and is flowing out to others in good deeds, in earnest, unselfish effort for their salvation. In order to be a fruitful tree, the soul must derive its support and nourishment from the Fountain of Life and must be in harmony with the Creator.—The Review and Herald, January 2, 1879.

[308]

The Reason for Barrenness—None of our churches need be barren and unfruitful. But some of our brethren and sisters are in danger of starving to death spiritually even when they are constantly hearing the truth presented by our ministers, for they neglect to impart that which they receive. God requires every one of His stewards to use the talent entrusted to him. He bestows rich gifts upon us in order that we may bestow them freely upon others. He keeps the heart flooded with the light of His presence, in order that we may reveal Christ to our fellow men. How can those who fold their hands in ease, content to do nothing, expect God to continue to supply their necessities? The members of all our churches should labor as those who must give an account.—The Review and Herald, November 11, 1902.

Our Destiny Involved—It is the work that we do or do not do that tells with tremendous power upon our lives and destinies. God requires us to improve every opportunity for usefulness that is offered us. Neglect to do this is perilous to our spiritual growth.—Testimonies for the Church 3:540.

[309] **He Who Lives to Please Himself Is Not a Christian**—"Is it not to deal thy bread to the hungry, and that thou bring the poor that are cast out to thine house? When thou seest the naked that thou cover him; and that thou hide not thyself from thine own flesh?" How much of this hiding has been done! How many have closed the eyes and locked the door of the heart, lest a softening influence should prompt them to works of kindness and charity! The work of Christ never ceases. His tender love and goodness are inexhaustible; His mercy is over all the children of men. The Lord Jesus means that you shall be blessed in imparting to His needy, suffering ones. He has made men His copartners. "We are labourers together with God." Has not Christ, by both precept and example, plainly taught us what we should do? We are to work, imbued with His Spirit, as we look to the cross, ready if He bids us, to leave all for His sake. He who lives to please himself is not a Christian. He has not been created anew in Christ Jesus.

The Christian feels that no other being in the universe has the claim to him which Jesus has. He is a purchased possession, bought by the costly price of the blood of the Lamb. He is to devote himself unreservedly to Christ; his thoughts, his words, and all his works are to be subject to the will of Christ.—The Medical Missionary, June, 1891.

Contentment Here and Eternal Reward Hereafter—In order to be happy, we must strive to attain to that character which Christ exhibited. One marked peculiarity of Christ was His self-denial and benevolence. He came not to seek His own. He went about doing good, and this was His meat and drink. We may, by following [310] the example of the Saviour, be in holy communion with Him; and by daily seeking to imitate His character and follow His example we shall be a blessing to the world and shall secure for ourselves contentment here and an eternal reward hereafter.—Testimonies for the Church 4:227.

Chapter 42—The Present and Eternal Rewards

Service Brings Reward—While the great final reward is given at Christ's coming, truehearted service for God brings a reward even in this life.—Testimonies for the Church 6:305, 306.

Brought Closer to Jesus—When you succor the poor, sympathize with the afflicted and oppressed, and befriend the orphan, you bring yourselves into a closer relationship to Jesus.—Testimonies for the Church 2:25.

A Richer Experience Promised—To practice the principles of love which Christ taught by precept and example will make the experience of everyone who follows him like the experience of Christ.—The Review and Herald, January 15, 1895.

As you open your door to Christ's needy and suffering ones, you are welcoming unseen angels. You invite the companionship of heavenly beings. They bring a sacred atmosphere of joy and peace. They come with praises upon their lips, and an answering strain is heard in heaven. Every deed of mercy makes music there.—The Desire of Ages, 639.

Will Thrill With Satisfaction—There is earnest work for every pair of hands to do. Let every stroke tell for the uplifting of humanity. There are so many that need to be helped. The heart of him who lives, not to please himself, but to be a blessing to those who have so few blessings, will thrill with satisfaction. Let every idler awake and face the realities of life. Take the Word of God and search its pages. If you are doers of this Word, life will indeed be to you a living reality, and you will find that the reward is abundant.—Manuscript 46, 1898.

Perplexing Problems Will Be Solved—If you will seek the Lord and be converted every day, if you will of your own spiritual choice be free and joyous in God, if with gladsome consent of heart to His gracious call, you come wearing the yoke of Christ—the yoke of obedience and service—all your murmurings will be stilled, all your difficulties will be removed, all the perplexing problems that now confront you will be solved.—Thoughts from the Mount of Blessing, 101.

Often Repaid in the Coin of the Realm—The golden rule teaches, by implication, the same truth which is taught elsewhere in the sermon on the mount, that "with what measure ye mete, it shall be measured to you again." That which we do to others, whether it be good or evil, will surely react upon ourselves, in blessing or in cursing. Whatever we give we shall receive again. The earthly blessings which we impart to others may be, and often are, repaid in kind. What we give does, in time of need, often come back to us in fourfold measure in the coin of the realm. But, besides this, all gifts are repaid, even in this life, in the fuller inflowing of His love, which is the sum of all heaven's glory and its treasure.—The Desire of Ages, 194.

God Will Repay—In heaven a book is written for those who interest themselves in the needs of their fellow beings, a book whose record will be revealed in that day when every man will be judged according to the deeds written therein. God will repay every act of injustice done to the poor. Those who manifest indifference or disregard for the unfortunate must not expect to receive the blessing of Him who declared, "Inasmuch as ye have done it unto one of the least of these My brethren, ye have done it unto Me."—Letter 140, 1908.

All Good Deeds Recorded—God has not been unmindful of the good deeds, the self-denying acts, of the church in the past. All are registered on high.—Testimonies for the Church 5:611.

Every faithful, unselfish performance of duty is noticed by the angels and shines in the life record.—Testimonies for the Church 2:132.

Angels are commissioned to be our helpers. They are passing between earth and heaven, bearing upward the record of the doings of the children of men.—The Southern Watchman, April 2, 1903, par. 8.

In Heaven's Imperishable Record—Every act of love, every word of kindness, every prayer in behalf of the suffering and oppressed, is reported before the eternal throne and placed on heaven's imperishable record.—Testimonies for the Church 5:133.

It were well ... to remember the record kept on high—that book in which there are no omissions, no mistakes, and out of which they will be judged. There every neglected opportunity to do service for God is recorded; and there, too, every deed of faith and love is held in everlasting remembrance.—Prophets and Kings, 639.

Reward for Welfare Work—Those who will receive the most abundant reward will be those who have mingled with their activity and zeal, gracious, tender pity for the poor, the orphan, the oppressed, and the afflicted.... There are about us those who have a meek and lowly spirit, the Spirit of Christ, who do many little things to help those around them, and who think nothing of it; they will be astonished at last to find that Christ has noticed the kind word spoken to the disheartened, and taken account of the smallest gift given for the relief of the poor, that cost the giver some self-denial.—The Review and Herald, July 3, 1894.

[314]

God Takes Note of Works of Kindness—Every act of justice, mercy, and benevolence makes melody in heaven. The Father from His throne beholds those who do these acts of mercy and numbers them with His most precious treasures. "And they shall be Mine, saith the Lord of hosts, in that day when I make up My jewels." Every merciful act to the needy, the suffering, is regarded as though done to Jesus.—Testimonies for the Church 2:25.

Rewarded for Little Things Generally Overlooked—At the day of judgment those who have been faithful in their everyday life, who have been quick to see their work and do it, not thinking of praise or profit, will hear the words, "Come, ye blessed of My Father, inherit the kingdom prepared for you from the foundation of the world." Christ does not commend them for the eloquent orations they have made, the intellectual power they have displayed, or the liberal donations they have given. It is for doing little things that are generally overlooked that they are rewarded.—The Youth's Instructor, January 17, 1901.

When the cases of all come in review before God, the question, What did they profess? will not be asked, but, What have they done? Have they been doers of the word? Have they lived for themselves, or have they been exercised in works of benevolence, in deeds of kindness and love, preferring others before themselves, and denying themselves that they might bless others? If the record shows that this has been their life, that their characters have been marked with tenderness, self-denial, and benevolence, they will receive the blessed assurance and benediction from Christ, "Well done." "Come, ye blessed of my Father, inherit the kingdom prepared for you from the foundation of the world."—Testimonies for the Church 3:525.

Right Motivation Essential—It is the motive that gives character to our acts, stamping them with ignominy or with high moral worth. Not the great things which every eye sees and every tongue praises does God account most precious. The little duties cheerfully done, the little gifts which make no show, and which to human eyes may appear worthless, often stand highest in His sight. A heart of faith and love is dearer to God than the most costly gift.—The Desire of Ages, 615.

To Be Judged by Our Motives—Daily review of our acts, to see whether conscience approves or condemns, is necessary for all who wish to reach perfection of Christian character. Many acts which pass for good works, even deeds of benevolence, will, when closely investigated, be found to be prompted by wrong motives.

Many receive applause for virtues which they do not possess. The Searcher of hearts weighs the motives, and often deeds highly applauded by men are recorded by Him as springing from selfishness and base hypocrisy. Every act of our lives, whether excellent and praiseworthy or deserving of censure, is judged by the Searcher of hearts according to the motives which prompted it.—Gospel Workers, 275.

The Two Oars—Faith and Works—If we are faithful in doing our part, in cooperating with Him, God will work through us [to do] the good pleasure of His will. But He cannot work through us if we make no effort. If we gain eternal life, we must work, and work earnestly.... Let us not be deceived by the oft-repeated assertion, "All you have to do is to believe." Faith and works are two oars which we must use equally if we [would] press our way up the stream against the current of unbelief. "Faith, if it hath not works, is dead, being alone." The Christian is a man of thought and practice. His faith fixes its roots firmly in Christ. By faith and good works he keeps his spirituality strong and healthy, and his spiritual strength increases as he strives to work the works of God.—The Review and Herald, June 11, 1901.

Our Crowns May Be Bright or Dim—Although we have no merit in ourselves, in the great goodness and love of God we are rewarded as if the merit were our own. When we have done all the good we can possibly do, we are still unprofitable servants. We have done only what was our duty. What we have accomplished has been wrought solely through the grace of Christ, and no reward is due to us from God on the ground of our merit. But through the merit of our Saviour every promise that God has made will be fulfilled, and every man will be rewarded according to his deeds.

The precious rewards of the future will be proportioned to the work of faith and labor of love in the present life. "He which soweth sparingly shall reap also sparingly; and he which soweth bountifully shall reap also bountifully." We should be most grateful that now in probationary time through the infinite mercy of God we are permitted to sow the seed for our future harvest. We should carefully consider what the harvest will be. Whether the crown of our eternal rejoicing shall be bright or dim depends upon our own course of action. We may make our calling and election sure, and may come into possession of the rich inheritance, or we may defraud ourselves of the far more exceeding and eternal weight of glory.—The Review and Herald, June 27, 1893.

To Meet Those Saved by Our Efforts—When the redeemed stand before God precious souls will respond to their names who are there because of the faithful, patient efforts put forth in their behalf, the entreaties and earnest persuasions to flee to the Stronghold. Thus those who in this world have been laborers together with God will receive their reward.—Testimonies for the Church 8:196, 197.

The redeemed will meet and recognize those whose attention they have directed to the uplifted Saviour. What blessed converse they have with these souls! "I was a sinner," it will be said, "without God and without hope in the world, and you came to me, and drew my attention to the precious Saviour as my only hope." ...

Others will express their gratitude to those who fed the hungry and clothed the naked. "When despair bound my soul in unbelief, the Lord sent you to me," they say, "to speak words of hope and comfort. You brought me food for my physical necessities, and you opened to me the Word of God, awakening me to my spiritual needs. You treated me as a brother. You sympathized with me in my

[317]

sorrows and restored my bruised and wounded soul so that I could grasp the hand of Christ that was reached out to save me. In my ignorance you taught me patiently that I had a Father in heaven who cared for me."—Testimonies for the Church 6:311.

"Come, Ye Blessed of My Father."—When the nations are gathered before Him there will be but two classes, and their eternal destiny will be determined by what they have done or have neglected to do for Him in the person of the poor and the suffering. In that day Christ does not present before men the great work He has done for them in giving His life for their redemption. He presents the faithful work they have done for Him.

To those whom He sets upon His right hand He will say, "Come, ye blessed of My Father, inherit the kingdom prepared for you from the foundation of the world: for I was an hungred, and ye gave Me meat: I was thirsty, and ye gave Me drink: I was a stranger, and ye took Me in: naked, and ye clothed Me: I was sick, and ye visited Me: I was in prison, and ye came unto Me." But those whom Christ commends know not that they have been ministering unto Him. To their perplexed inquiries He answers, "Inasmuch as ye have done it unto one of the least of these My brethren, ye have done it unto Me." ...

Those whom Christ commends in the judgment may have known little of theology, but they have cherished His principles. Through the influence of the divine Spirit they have been a blessing to those about them. Even among the heathen are those who have cherished the spirit of kindness; before the words of life had fallen upon their ears, they have befriended the missionaries, even ministering to them at the peril of their own lives. Among the heathen are those who worship God ignorantly, those to whom the light is never brought by human instrumentality, yet they will not perish. Though ignorant of the written law of God, they have heard His voice speaking to them in nature, and have done the things that the law required. Their works are evidence that the Holy Spirit has touched their hearts, and they are recognized as the children of God.

How surprised and gladdened will be the lowly among the nations, and among the heathen, to hear from the lips of the Saviour, "Inasmuch as ye have done it unto one of the least of these My brethren, ye have done it unto Me." How glad will be the heart of

Infinite Love as His followers look up with surprise and joy at His words of approval.—The Desire of Ages, 637, 638.

Appendix

Personal Experiences of Ellen G. White as a Welfare Worker

[While all through her life Mrs. White was mindful of the needs of those about her, there were times when these needs pressed especially hard. No attempt is made in the following pages to give an exhaustive account, but rather to present some typical experiences concerning which she happened to make a record in her diary or in her letters. These excerpts present the wide field of her welfare ministry, with larger emphasis on two periods in her life experience, one rather early and the other later in her life.

In the "jottings" from the diary of 1859 we see Mrs. White as a thirty-one-year-old mother of three lively boys, carrying the household burdens, writing, traveling, and preaching, and at the same time assisting those around her who were suffering or in need. Through the nineties we observe her in Australia during a period of severe and prolonged depression, with heart-breaking needs on every side. With these the reader will also find a number of statements which help to trace the thread of her welfare activities through her entire life.

The reader will observe that the E. G. White diary entries are recorded in terse diary style, sometimes in short phrases and often in the present tense. Surely it will be also recognized that the purely biographical account as Ellen White recorded her day-by-day activities does not constitute instruction for the church and therefore is not to be considered as authoritative testimony. This is true also of biographical references drawn from the E. G. White letters. Nevertheless, the example of Ellen White does add emphasis to her precept.

The burden of heart carried by Mrs. White, her sense of her responsibility to those in suffering and need about her, and her eagerness to help, though seemingly ever hampered by limited resources, should encourage every Seventh-day Adventist to greater and more enthusiastic participation in *Welfare Ministry*.—Compilers.]

E. G. White Instructed to Set an Example.—After my marriage I was instructed that I must show a special interest in motherless and fatherless children, taking some under my own charge for a time, and then finding homes for them. Thus I would be giving others an example of what they could do.

Although called to travel often, and having much writing to do, I have taken children of three and five years of age, and have cared for them, educated them, and trained them for responsible positions. I have taken into my home from time to time boys from ten to sixteen years of age, giving them motherly care and a training for service. [From the pen of two workers who in their youth spent many months in the White home we have the following comments of what they personally witnessed.—Compilers.

"Not only was Mrs. White a strong counselor for her husband, to guard him against making mistakes that would jeopardize the cause in any part, but she was most careful to carry out in her own course the things she taught to others. For instance, she frequently dwelt in her public talks upon the duty of caring for widows and orphans, citing her hearers to Isaiah 58:7-10; And she exemplified her exhortations by taking the needy to her own home for shelter, food, and raiment. I well remember her having at one time, as members of her family, a boy and girl and a widow and her two daughters. I have, moreover, known her to distribute to poor people hundreds of dollars' worth of new clothes which she bought for that purpose."—J. O. Corliss, The Review and Herald, August 30, 1923.

"Elder White was himself a very philanthropic man. He always lived in a large house, but there were no vacant rooms in it. Although his immediate family was small, his house was always filled with widows and their children, poor friends, poor brethren in the ministry, and those who needed a home. His heart and his pocketbook were always open, and he was ready to help those who needed help. He certainly set a most noble example to our denomination in his largeheartedness and liberality of spirit."—The Medical Missionary,

February, 1894.] I have felt it my duty to bring before our people that work for which those in every church should feel a responsibility.

While in Australia I carried on this same line of work, taking into my home orphan children, who were in danger of being exposed to temptations that might cause the loss of their souls.—The Review and Herald, July 26, 1906.

Ellen G. White in Practical Dorcas Work

(Jottings from E. G. White Diary of 1859)

January 2, Sunday—Sister Augusta Bognes was sent for to assist me to prepare for another journey. Made a coat for Edson. He will accompany us. We tried to comfort Augusta. She is cast down and discouraged, health poor and no one to depend on. She has laid aside her armor and shield of faith. May the Lord strengthen the weak hands and confirm the feeble knees. Gave Sister Irving a warm cloak and dress and a few other things to make over for her.

January 3, Monday—Went to the office. Called in to Brother Loughborough's and to my sister's. Wrote seven pages to Doctor Naramores, then took dinner to my sister's. Had a good interview with my father and mother. Went to the office again after dinner, and wrote four pages to Brother Orton's family. Also wrote four pages to Brother Howland's family and wrote to Sister Ashley, and Brother Collin's family. Paid widow Cranson $1.00 for making a couple of shirts. Paid Sister Bognes $1.00 for making a coat. She was unwilling to take it, but I felt it duty to hand it to her. She is poor and sickly. May the Lord pity and care for her. Said Jesus, "The poor always ye have with you." May the Lord rid us of selfishness and help us to care for other's woes and relieve them.

January 6, Thursday—Make a cap for Edson and a vest. At night am very weary. Give Agnes a half worn dress for her mother. They are poor. The husband and father is sick. Their crops have failed. Have breadstuff to buy and nothing to buy with. Agnes is their main support. She is only seventeen. There are four children now at home. They must suffer unless the church interests themselves in their behalf. May the Lord have mercy upon the needy, and put it in His children's hearts to dispense to them with a liberal hand.

February 3, Thursday—Very sick all day with sick headache. Henry Pierce from Monterey at our house. Send Sister Leander Jones some things for her children and Jenny sends her her best bonnet. May the Lord enable us to see the wants of the poor and give us a ready and willing heart to supply them.

February 28, Monday—Mary Loughborough came here. Stopped with us for dinner. Her baby is sick in the afternoon. Went into Sister Ratel's. Have a pleasant interview. Her babe has on an old torn white dress. The best he has except one that she keeps to put on when she goes out with him. She speaks of her children that died two years since. She does not wish them alive again. The family are all poor. The oldest girl prizes a Bible I gave her, much. She reads out of it to her parents. Sister Ratel's health is very poor. Has spit blood today. I fear she will not fill her place in her family long. She tries to do right. Her husband is a poor, wicked, passionate man and she has great trials. May the Lord sustain her. She begs us to pray for her that she may do right at all times.

March 1, Tuesday—Walked to the office. Called to see Sister Sarah and mother. Sarah gave me a little dress and two aprons for Sister Ratel's babe. I then called on Sister Aurora Lockwood. Had a pleasant interview with her. She is a choice sister, beloved of God and highly respected of all the church.

I rode down to the city and purchased a few things. Bought a little dress for Sister Ratel's babe. Came to the office, assisted them a little there, and then came home to dinner. Sent the little articles to Sister Ratel. Mary Loughborough sends her another dress, so she will do very well now. Oh, that all knew the sweetness of giving to the poor, of helping do others good, and making others happy. The Lord open my heart to do all in my power to relieve those around me. "Give me to feel my brother's woe."

March 8, Tuesday—It is a day when infirmities are striving for the victory. I suffer much pain in my left shoulder and lung. My spirits are depressed. Brother John Andrews leaves today. Comes up to visit us in the eve. Have a pleasant interview. Get together a few things for him to take home. Send Angeline a new calico dress, nine shillings, and a stout pair of calfskin shoes. Father gives the making of the shoes and the making of a pair of boots for Brother John Andrews. I send the little boy a nice little flannel shirt and yarn to knit him a pair of stockings. I send Sister or Mother Andrews a nice large cape, well wadded for her to wear. I make a bag to put them in of towel cloth. Write three small pages to Sister Mary Chase. In it write receipt [recipe] obtained from John's.

March 10, Thursday—Walked to the city and back. Was very weary. Purchased John F. a pair of pants. In the afternoon Sister Irving came in....

For ten weeks the daughter has lived with us, and we paid her nine shillings a week. All but one dollar of this she has handed to her mother. Her clothes are poor, yet she does not appropriate any means to her own use. She forgets herself in her devotion and self-sacrifice to her parents. It was as affecting a scene as I never witnessed. The reluctance of the mother to accept the wages, all the wages of a daughter, through necessity and the willingness and freedom of the daughter to have all go to her poor afflicted parents. The mother and daughter wept, and we wept. We aided them some. Paid half toward a pair of boots for a little brother. One dollar. I paid one-fifty for a pair of shoes for the mother. Husband gave her one dollar in money. Henry gave her ten cents. Edson, ten cents, and little Willie ten. Husband gave her twenty-five more to buy a little luxury for the sick one. We parted with considerable half-worn clothing to make over.

[325]

April 21, Thursday—Work on a rug. Write a letter to Daniel Bourdeau. This morning there is a feeling of sympathy among certain of the flock for Brother Benedict's family. We have contributed a mite for their relief, about seven dollars. Purchased them different things to eat, and carry it to them. Brother and Sister Benedict visited us all day. Had a very interesting and pleasant interview. My mother came to see me, which was a great comfort to me.

Welfare Ministry Through the Years

E. G. White Calls for Help—Dear Brethren and Sisters: The treasury in the Poor Fund, consisting of clothes, et cetera, for those in need, is nearly exhausted. And as there are cases of destitution continually arising, and one new one has arisen recently, I thought it would be well for those who have clothing, bedding, or money to spare to send it on here immediately. We hope there will be no delay, for we are going to assist some that are needy as soon as we get things together. Send your donations to Sr. Uriah Smith or myself.—The Review and Herald, October 30, 1860.

James and Ellen White Combine Prayer and Labor—Before there were any sanitariums among us, my husband and I began work in medical missionary lines. We would bring to our house cases that had been given up by the physicians to die. When we knew not what to do for them we would pray to God most earnestly, and He always sent His blessing. He is the mighty Healer, and He worked with us. We never had time or opportunity to take a medical course, but we had success as we moved out in the fear of God and sought Him for wisdom at every step. This gave us courage in the Lord.

Thus we combined prayer and labor. We used the simple water treatments, and then tried to fasten the eyes of the patients on the Great Healer. We told them what He could do for them. If we can inspire the patients with hope, this is greatly to their advantage. We want all that have any part to act in our sanitariums to have a firm grasp on the power of the Infinite. We believe in Him and in the power of His word. When we do our best for the recovery of the sick, we may then look for Him to be with us, that we may see of His salvation. We put too little confidence in the power of the hand that rules the world.—Manuscript 49, 1908.

In House-to House Ministry—Before our sanitarium there was established my husband and I went from house to house to give treatment. Under God's blessing we saved the lives of many who were suffering.—Letter 45, 1903.

Interest in a Needy Widow—In regard to Nellie L., you know she is a widow with the care of three children, and she is struggling to obtain knowledge that she may engage in the kindergarten work, where she can keep her children with her. Let us not see the poor soul struggle for her life and sacrifice her health to do this. I have thought of the liberal donations that have been made to individuals who have married at Oakland. Would that these friends might use their means and express their sympathies to bless the widow and the fatherless that are deserving of their attention and substantial sympathy. Have not such cases claims upon us?

I will help Nellie one hundred dollars if you will do the same. Two hundred dollars would be a great blessing to her just now. Will you do this for Christ's sake? Will you encourage others to help her to get a start in life? It would be far better to do this than to wait and let Nellie be worn out with anxiety and care and fall in the struggle, leaving her children helpless, motherless, to be cared for by others.

One hundred dollars from you will not be a large sum, but it will be a great blessing to her. Will you do this? Let us do it as a free gift and not let the horror of debt be upon her who is struggling under such discouragements. If you will do this, please collect in my name from Signs Office one hundred dollars for Nellie L. Let us both take stock in this matter and the Lord will bless us. I know she will struggle with all her powers to be self-supporting. Battle Creek, Mich., March 28, 1889 Brother C. H. Jones:

Please pay to the order of ------$100.00 (One Hundred Dollars) as a gift from the Lord who has made me His steward of means. "Ellen G. White" (Letter 28, 1889.)

Pioneering in Australia

Prejudice Removed by Welfare Ministry—We passed through many interesting experiences while in Australia. We helped establish a school from the foundation, going into the eucalyptus woods and camping while the trees were being felled, the grounds cleared, and the school buildings erected.

Prejudice in the community in which the school was established, was broken down by the medical missionary work that we did. The nearest physician lived twenty miles away. I told the brethren that I would allow my secretary, a trained nurse who has been with me for twenty years, to go to visit the sick whenever they called for her. We made a hospital of our home. My nurse treated successfully some most difficult cases that the physicians had pronounced incurable. This labor was not without its reward. Suspicion and prejudice were removed. The hearts of the people were won, and many accepted the truth. At the time we went there it was regarded necessary to keep everything under lock and key, for fear of theft. Only once was anything stolen from us, and that was shortly after our arrival. Now the community is law abiding, and no one thinks of being robbed.—Manuscript 126, 1902.

Personal Interest in the People—We tried to take a personal interest in the people. If we met someone walking as we were driving to the station four and a half miles away, we were glad to let them ride with us in our carriage. We did what we could to develop our land, and encouraged our neighbors to cultivate the soil, that they too might have fruit and vegetables of their own. We taught them how to prepare the soil, what to plant, and how to take care of the growing produce. They soon learned the advantages of providing for themselves in this way. We realized that Christ took a personal interest in men and women while He lived on this earth. He was a medical missionary everywhere He went. We are to go about doing good, even as He did. We are instructed to feed the hungry and clothe the naked, to heal the sick and comfort those that mourn.—Manuscript 126, 1902.

Economizing to Help Others—We live economically in every way and make a study of how every penny is to be laid out.... We make over and over our clothing, patching and enlarging garments in order to make them wear a little longer, so that we can supply with clothing those who are more needy. One of our brethren in Ormondville, who is an intelligent carpenter, could not go forward in baptism because he had not a change of clothing. When he was able to get a cheap suit he was the most grateful man I ever saw, because he could then go forward in the ordinance of baptism.—Letter 89a, 1894.

New Durable Material Bought for Relief Work—Some of our people say to me, "Give away your old clothes, and that will help the poor." Should I give away the garments that I patch and enlarge, the people would not be able to see anything of which they could make use. I buy for them new, strong, durable material. I have visited the factories where they make tweed cloth and have bought a number of remnants that perhaps have a flaw but can be purchased cheap, and will do some good to those to whom we give. I can afford to wear the old garments until they are beyond repair. I have purchased your uncle excellent cloth for pants and vest, and he is now supplied with good respectable clothing. In this way I can supply large families of children with durable garments, which the parents would not think of getting for them.—Ibid.

Purchasing Wood From Needy Farmers—Poverty is so widespread in the colonies that starvation is staring many in the face, and the strangest part of the matter is that the farmers seem so perfectly helpless to devise plans by which to turn their time and money to account.... We purchase wood from our brethren who are farmers, and we try to give their sons and daughters employment. But we need a large charitable fund upon which to draw to keep families from starvation. Those who need our help are not of the tramp order, but are men who have earned in prosperous times as high as twenty and forty dollars per week.... I divided my household stores of provisions with families of this sort, sometimes going eleven miles to relieve their necessities.—Letter 89a, 1894.

Solicitous for a Needy Student—Will you please inquire of Brother ----- in regard to the clothing that he requires, and what he needs please furnish to him, and charge the same to my account. He has not received his trunk, and I fear he may suffer for the want of necessary changes.—Letter 100, 1893.

Helping a Minister Suffering Illness—Brother and Sister A. have been laboring in Ormondville, about one hundred miles from here, with good results.... I met him in Napier, and he told me I was the one who sent him to school in Healdsburg, paying his expenses to obtain an education. I was so thankful to see the result of this investment.

[330]

We sent Brother A.... to the institute at St. Helena.... He is a great sufferer. I have appropriated three hundred dollars to this case, although there are many cases where every dollar is needed, but I feel perfectly clear in helping in this case. It is a case where those who love and fear God must show their sympathy in a tangible manner and bear in mind that Christ identified his interest with suffering humanity.—Letters 79 and 33, 1893.

Mrs. White Meeting the Problems of Depression—Brother M.'s family are industrious workers if they can only get work to do. We will not see them go hungry or destitute of clothing or become discouraged. They are bought, bought by the blood of Christ, and are of value with God. While in this country we will continue to help the poor and distressed as far as possible. Brother M. is in debt on his place; I met the last quarter's interest, seven pounds, for which I expect nothing, but I would not, could not, see the family turned into the street.... We pray most earnestly that the Lord will work in behalf of this dear family.

We are sorely perplexed ourselves to understand our duty to all these suffering ones. So many families are out of employment, and that means destitute, hungry, afflicted, and oppressed. I can see no way but to help these poor souls in their great need, and I shall do this if the Lord will. And He does will. His word is sure, and cannot fail, nor be changed by any of the human devices to evade it.

We must help the needy and the oppressed lest Satan take them out of our hands, out of our ranks, and place them, while under temptation, in his own ranks.—Letter 42, 1894.

Shopping to Meet the Needs of the Poor—I go to Sydney today to the yearly sales to purchase some goods. They have these sales to rid the stores of their old stock. The poor around us are suffering for food and clothing, and I can buy at an advantage by visiting these stores. We economize as much as possible, and there is need enough for it.... There are many poor who are distressed for want of food and clothing who are of the household of faith. Our purses will scarcely suffice to reach the needs of those we know. Jesus says, "Inasmuch as ye have done it unto one of the least of these My brethren, ye have done it unto Me." How precious are these words of comfort to the poor!—Letter 39, 1895.

A Dorcas Society Organized—Sunday has been a busy day for us, planning for the very, very poor and setting in operation some plans which will relieve myself and family from doing everything that is to be done. Sister C., a worthy woman, is prostrated upon her bed with sciatica. She has a son thirteen years of age and an aged mother, who is an invalid with no means of support. The mother has had help from her sons in paying house rent, and as times have become harder and closer this is all they seem able to do. We have also Bro. R. and his wife with four helpless children. He does his level best to support his innocent children, but they are in want all the time. He gets little for his fruit. We now go round to the members of the church to see if they can supply us with old clothes for these destitute families. I have been buying good material at sales to make up for them, as well as supplying them with food.

Some of our family were out on a charity expedition yesterday, and made a little beginning. Some things were collected. There are eight families that we have been helping all that we thought advisable.

A Dorcas society is to open this week to examine and remodel old and new material to help the needy. The members of my family and I have made many donations of money and clothing. The draft upon us has not been small. We do not have to hunt up cases; they hunt us up. These things are forced upon our notice; we cannot be Christians and pass them by, and say, "Be ye warmed and clothed," and do not those things that will warm and clothe them. The Lord Jesus says, "The poor always ye have with you." They are God's legacy to us.—Manuscript 4, 1895.

[332]

Assisting With Food and Clothing—The poor, our family have had to assist in food and clothing, and to help the widow and fatherless by money gifts as well as food and clothing. This is part of our work as Christians which cannot be neglected. Christ said, "The poor always ye have with you," and in this part of the Lord's vineyard that is literally true. Doing good in all its forms is enjoined upon the Lord's missionaries by the Holy Scriptures. Read 2 Corinthians 9. You see, not only is our work to preach, but as we see suffering humanity in the world, we are to help them in their temporal necessities. Thus we will be instruments in the hands of God....

Those who have given themselves to the Lord will yoke up with Christ and will work in Christ's lines, ever looking to Jesus for wisdom and correct judgment as to how to move. Many bring their zeal and natural temperaments into their benevolence; they move by impulse: they give to those to whom they take a notion to give; and others who are every bit as worthy, they, like the priest and Levite, look upon them but do not feel any particular interest, and pass by on the other side, which is the side of indifference and neglect. Doing good in all its forms is enjoined in the Holy Scriptures, but prudence and careful consideration are needed to know how to show mercy and help the really needy. The way that is profitable to both parties is to help them to help themselves; open ways before them in the place of giving them money; find some work for them to do; manifest discretion; and be sure we make such use of means as will do the most good for the Lord's poor in the present and future.—Letter 31b, 1895.

Work Supplied to Needy Families—There were many here who were poor and in need. Men who were trying to serve the Lord and keep His commandments could not provide food for their families, and they begged us to give them something to do. We employed them, and they ate at our table. We gave them suitable wages until their families were fed and comfortably clothed. Then we let them go to find work somewhere else. Some of them we had to provide with a suit of Willie's clothes, to make them fit for Sabbath meetings.—Letter 33, 1897.

Providing Work, Books, and Clothes—Those in this country who receive the truth are mostly poor, and in the winter time it is a hard matter for them to sustain their families. Since I wrote the foregoing, a letter was brought to me from ... a man who was a coachbuilder. He was in great poverty two years ago, and we gave him work. He was obliged to leave his family, a wife and five children, in the suburbs of Sydney, and come to Cooranbong, about ninety miles off, to obtain work. Before this he was in partnership with his brother, who also is a coachbuilder.

But when he embraced the Sabbath he lost his situation, and he worked for small wages, and finally he could get no work. He is an intelligent, refined man, an able teacher in the Sabbath school, and a sincere Christian. We kept him as long as we had work that he could do, and when he left he modestly asked if we could let him have a few books on present truth, for he had none. I gave him about six dollars' worth of books. He also asked if we had any cast-off clothing that we could give him, that his wife might make over for the children. I provided him a box of clothing, for which he was very grateful.—Letter 113, 1897.

As Set Before Her by the Lord—Why do you not search out the cases of such men as Brother_____? He is a Christian gentleman in every sense of the word. He is a man that God loves. Such men as he are precious in the Lord's sight. I know him well.

I interested myself in his case.... I endeavored to anticipate his needs and never to place him where he would have to beg for work. While in Cooranbong I tried to set an example of how the needy should be helped. I tried to work in the way set before me by the Lord.—Letter 105, 1902.

A Dorcas Society in the E. G. White Home—Last evening we had a Dorcas Society in our home, and my workers who help in the preparation of my articles for the papers and do the cooking and sewing, five of them, sat up until midnight, cutting out clothing. They made three pairs of pants for the children of one family. Two sewing machines were running until midnight. I think there was never a happier set of workers than were these girls last evening.

We made up a bundle of clothing for this family, and thought it was about all we could do. Sister C. is now on this errand of mercy to this poor family, cutting out garments from the material provided. There are also other families to be supplied. And now comes another request, and we must supply them with things for winter wear. Thus it has been ever since we came to this country. We shall certainly heed the call to send a box of clothing to these needy ones. I merely tell you these things that you may know that we are surrounded by poverty. The wife of this fisherman is to be baptized next Sabbath. The poor have the gospel preached unto them. The people of this locality have very little of this world's goods.—Letter 113, 1897.

Assisting the Sick and Destitute—The sick call upon us for help, and we go to their assistance. Sister McEnterfer, my helper and nurse, is called upon from miles around to prescribe for them and give them treatment. She has had wonderful success. There is no physician in Cooranbong, but we shall build a hospital or sanitarium soon, where the sick can be brought in and cared for. In the past we have brought them to our own home and cared for them, for we cannot let human beings suffer without doing something to relieve them....

We take no pay for anything we do, but we must have a hospital, which will cost as little as possible, where we can have some conveniences and facilities for caring for the sick.

This is the work of Christ, and this must be our work. We want to follow closely in the footsteps of the Master. We find in this place intelligent people, who once were in comfortable positions, but poverty has come to them. We find these work, and pay them for it, and thus relieve their necessities. This is the very work to be done in order to heal the maladies of the soul as well as of the body. Christ is the mighty Healer of soul and body.

Christ declared, "The poor always have ye with you." Oh, how I long to do more than I am now doing. May the Lord strengthen me, is my prayer, that I may be able to do all He has appointed me to do. Yesterday a box of clothing was sent to a poor but intelligent and industrious family. The father is a fine workman, a coachmaker by trade. He works when he can get work. This is now the third box of clothing we have sent him. Souls are coming into the truth through the influence of this family, and Brother Starr is going to Sydney to baptize several who have been converted to the truth.

I long to see the work advancing. We shall labor on patiently, and the Lord will do the convicting and the converting. We cannot neglect the poor. Christ was poor. He knew privation and want. I use every dollar of my income to advance the work.... We mean to work while the day lasts, for the night cometh in which no man can work.—Letter 111, 1898.

Medical Missionary Work Around Cooranbong—Sr. Sara McEnterfer, in company with Bro. James, my farmer, has just gone to visit Bro. C., who lives six miles from here in the bush. This brother has embraced the truth since we came to Cooranbong....

Now news has come to us that our beloved brother has come down with typhoid fever. Mr. Pringle is the only man in the village who knows anything about giving treatment without drugs; but six weeks ago he was called upon to attend Mr. B., who was also down with typhoid. He has stayed with him night and day, and has now returned to his home, worn out with the strain. So he cannot be depended on to nurse Bro. C.

Sara and Bro. J. have gone up to see what the situation is. If Bro. C. can be moved, he must be brought within our reach, even if he has to be carried on a litter. We cannot let him lie there and die, to leave his wife and children to the mercy of whoever will have mercy upon them....

March 21. Sara has just returned with the good news that Bro. C. is much better. He was attacked, but Mr. Pringle, who was able to visit him, found him a very different subject from Mr. B. Bro. C. is a health reformer, and when his case was given vigorous treatment the fever was mastered. He is weak, but is up and dressed, and is cheerful and happy in the Lord. Sara says that the corn he is growing will help largely to sustain his family. They have a hand mill, and grind this corn over and over until it is fine. From this they make their bread, for they have not money to purchase fine flour. We shall send them some flour. This is the work that has been done in several cases. We have just helped men to help themselves.

Bro. C. has that in him that will not allow him, if he has health, to depend on anyone. But the man who purchased his boat has paid him nothing, for he could not. W. C. White saw Bro. C.'s necessity, and borrowed eight pounds from our blacksmith and loaned it to him, that he might make a beginning. And all are glad and more than astonished to see the beginning he has made. About twelve acres have been declared and planted with sweet corn and field corn. The sweet corn they will eat, and the field corn they will sell. The vegetables that have been grown help a great deal in supporting the family. The little lads are working with their father like little farmers. They are so earnest and full of zeal that it is amusing to look at them and see how happy they are in their work. They have not much society besides their own family connections, but they are in the very best school they could be in.—Letter 48, 1899.

First Attention to Needy Church Members—There are families who have lost their situations which they have held for twenty years. One man and his wife have a large family of children which we have been caring for. I am paying the expenses of four children in school from this one family. We see many cases we must help. These are excellent men we have helped. They have large families, but they are the Lord's poor. One man was a coachbuilder, a cabinetmaker, and a wheelwright, and a gentleman of superior order in the sight of God, who reads the heart of all. This family we provided with clothing from our family for three years. We moved the family to Cooranbong. We hoped to help them get a home this winter. I let them live in my tent, and they put an iron roof on it and have lived in it a year. Everyone loves this man, his wife, and children. We must help them. They have a father and a mother they must support. Three families of this same order are on the school premises, and oh, if we only had money to help them build a cheap wooden home, how glad they would be! I use every penny I have in this helping work. But it makes a difference with me whom I help, whether it is God's suffering poor who are keeping His commandments and lose their situations in consequence or whether it is a blasphemer

[337]

treading under foot the commandments of God. And God regards the difference. We should make these men and women all workers together with God.—Letter 45, 1900.

"We Helped All We Could."—In Australia we have tried to do all we could in this line. We located in Cooranbong, and there, where the people have to send twenty-five miles for a doctor, and pay him twenty-five dollars a visit, we helped the sick and suffering all we could. Seeing that we understood something of disease, the people brought their sick to us, and we cared for them. Thus we entirely broke down the prejudice in that place....

Medical missionary work is the pioneer work. It is to be connected with the gospel ministry. It is the gospel in practice, the gospel practically carried out. I have been made so sorry to see that our people have not taken hold of this work as they should....

All heaven is interested in the work of relieving suffering humanity. Satan is exerting all his powers to obtain control over the souls and bodies of men. He is trying to bind them to the wheels of his chariot. My heart is made sad as I look at our churches, which ought to be connected in heart and soul and practice with the medical missionary work.—The General Conference Bulletin, April 12, 1901.

Mrs. White Retained Broad Sympathies Throughout Life

Drawn Out to President McKinley's Widow—I am not able to sleep past two o'clock A.M. I am awakened often at one o'clock at night with my heart drawn out in tender sympathy for the bereaved wife of President McKinley. One is taken and the other left. The strong one upon whose large affections she could ever lean, is not. While he was in health, fulfilling the duties of his office, an apparently friendly hand was extended, which President McKinley was ready to grasp. That Judas hand held a pistol and shot the President. Amid scenes of pleasant life and enjoyment came sorrow and sadness and suffering and woe. How could he do this terrible murderous action?

My heart is in deep sympathy for the one who is left. I have been repeating over and over, Oh, how short come all words of human sympathy. There are thousands that would speak words to relieve if possible the breaking heart, but they do not understand how feeble are words to comfort the bereaved one, who in her feebleness ever found a human heart in her husband, full of tenderness and compassion and love. The strong human arm upon which the frail suffering wife leaned, is not.

I do not wish that our sister should have less regret and less love for the faithful husband, but that she should now look to her best Friend, One whose love has been expressed to her all her life. I would speak to her the words of Isaiah 61:1-3: "The Spirit of the Lord God is upon Me; because the Lord hath anointed Me to preach good tidings unto the meek; He hath sent me to bind up the brokenhearted, to proclaim liberty to the captives, and the opening of the prison to them that are bound; to proclaim the acceptable year of the Lord, and the day of vengeance of our God; to comfort all that mourn; to appoint unto them that mourn in Zion, to give unto them beauty for ashes, the oil of joy for mourning, the garment of praise for the Spirit of heaviness; that they might be called trees of righteousness, the planting of the Lord."—Diary, 1901.

Ministering to Aged War Veterans—At one time I had some remnants of books and some complete volumes of *Sabbath Readings* stored somewhere in Battle Creek. Please ask Brother Amadon to make diligent search for all these things, and to send to me....

We can use the small volumes of *Sabbath Readings* and other works to good advantage in orphans' homes and in many other places where these little books will be highly valued. We could use some of them in the Soldiers' Home at Yountville, where many hundreds of old soldiers are provided for in large government buildings. We are giving these men every attention possible. Every other Sabbath a party from the sanitarium and the St. Helena churches visits them, to sing religious hymns and to speak to them. They are interested in these meetings, and seem delighted with everything that our people do for them.

We are sending papers to these soldiers and have placed in their library copies of my works, *Christ's Object Lessons*, and some larger books of mine. Many of these men are intelligent. Our brethren and sisters are working this field, and we hope to do much more for the soldiers than we have yet done. Sometimes a talk—a short, pointed, Bible sermon—is given them, and they listen with intense interest.

The gospel songs, the short prayer, and the good talk, taken together, seem to be just what is needed to interest the old men. They say, "We never have had any such work as this done for us before!"

We desire to keep books and papers circulating among these soldiers. Please help us all you can along this line by gathering together something for them to read—books and papers full of Bible truth.—Letter 96, 1903.

A Letter to Fatherless Children

San Jose, California
June 29, 1905
Dear Children,

I must write a few lines to you. We wish that we could step into your home and weep with you and kneel with you in prayer. Will each one of you seek the Lord and serve Him? You can be a great blessing to your mother by doing nothing that will make her heart sad. The Lord Jesus will receive you if you will give your hearts to Him. Do all that is possible to relieve your mother from every care and burden.

The Lord has promised to be a Father to the fatherless. If you will give your hearts to Him, He will give you power to become the sons and daughters of God. If the elder children will relieve the mother by bearing as many burdens as possible, and by treating the younger children kindly, teaching them to do right and not to worry mother, the Lord will greatly bless them.

Give your hearts to the loving Saviour, and do only those things that are pleasing in His sight. Do nothing to grieve your mother. Remember that the Lord loves you, and that each one of you can become a member of the family of God. If you are faithful here, when He shall come in the clouds of heaven, you will meet your father, and will be a united family.

In love,
Ellen G. White.

—Letter 165, 1905.